W ID

Using Experience
for Learning

Current titles include:

Using Experience for Learning

Edited by
David Boud, Ruth Cohen
and David Walker

The Society for Research into Higher Education
& Open University Press

Published by SRHE and
Open University Press
Celtic Court
22 Ballmoor
Buckingham
MK18 1XW

email: enquiries@openup.co.uk
world wide web: http://www.openup.co.uk

and
325 Chestnut Street
Philadelphia, PA 19106, USA

First Published 1993
Reprinted 1994, 1996, 1997, 2000, 2002

A catalogue record of this book is available from the British Library

ISBN 0 335 19095 2 (pb)   0 335 19096 0 (hb)

Library of Congress Cataloging-in-Publication Data
Using experience for learning / David Boud, Ruth Cohen and David
  Walker, editors.
      p.   cm.
  Includes bibliographical references (p.) and index.
  ISBN 0–335–19096–0. — ISBN 0–335–19095–2 (pbk.)
  1. Active learning. 2. Experiential learning. I. Boud, David.
II. Cohen, Ruth. III. Walker, David, 1938–
LB1027.23.U85   1993
370.15′23—dc20
                                                            92–47423
                                                                CIP

Typeset by Graphicraft Ltd, Hong Kong
Printed in Great Britain by St Edmundsbury Press Ltd,
Bury St Edmunds, Suffolk

Contents

List of Contributors

Lee Andresen, Professional Development Centre, University of New South Wales, Sydney.

David Boud, School of Adult and Language Education, University of Technology, Sydney.

Angela Brew, Educational Development Unit, University of Portsmouth.

Stephen Brookfield, Graduate School of Education, University of St Thomas, St Paul, Minnesota.

Ruth Cohen, School of Adult and Language Education, University of Technology, Sydney.

Costas Criticos, Media Resource Centre, University of Natal, South Africa.

Kathleen Dechant, Department of Management, School of Business Administration, University of Connecticut.

Elizabeth Kasl, Department of Higher and Adult Education, Teachers College, Columbia University, New York.

Victoria Marsick, Department of Higher and Adult Education, Teachers College, Columbia University, New York.

John Mason, Centre for Mathematics Education, The Open University, Milton Keynes.

Nod Miller, School of Education, University of Manchester.

John Mulligan, Human Potential Resource Group, Department of Educational Studies, University of Surrey.

Denis Postle, The Wentworth Institute, London.

Mary Thorpe, Institute of Educational Technology, The Open University, Milton Keynes.

Robin Usher, School of Education, University of Southampton.

David Walker, The Educational Centre, Randwick, Australia.

Introduction: Understanding Learning from Experience

David Boud, Ruth Cohen and David Walker

The idea for the book

This book is about the struggle to make sense of learning from experience. Although we spend most of our time learning from experience, this aspect of learning is greatly neglected in comparison with that which takes place in the formal classroom. However, the world of learning is rapidly changing. There is an increased interest in such things as recognizing informal learning for course credit, new forms of learning in the workplace and, in general, acknowledging the autonomous learning which takes place outside educational institutions.

There is also a dearth of consideration of personal experience and the context of adult learning in current educational writing. Most of what is written about learning is from the perspective of teachers or researchers who assume that there is a body of knowledge to be taught and learned. What is missing is recognition of the role and relevance of learning from experience no matter where it occurs. Learning involves much more than an interaction with an extant body of knowledge; learning is all around us, it shapes and helps create our lives – who we are, what we do. It involves dealing with complex and intractable problems, it requires personal commitment, it utilizes interaction with others, it engages our emotions and feelings, all of which are inseparable from the influence of context and culture.

The three of us who have brought this book together use experiential or experience-based learning with people in various situations to help them learn from experience. In our work, we sometimes design specific events to create new experiences for participants; at other times, we work with their past and present experience, helping them draw learning from it. In doing this, our awareness of the potential for such learning has been heightened.

The book has emerged from our personal and collective interest in how we and others learn from experience. Between the three of us we have many educational qualifications, but we are nevertheless conscious that very little of our present learning has been prompted by any of our formal studies. We have learned more things from more sources of influence than we could ever identify. Most of what is written about learning makes us uneasy, as it neither reflects our felt experience as learners nor the issues that we have come increasingly to see as important in our lives and work. We have come to recognize that ideas are not separate from experience, learning is not unrelated to relationships and personal interests, and emotions and feelings have a vital role to play in what we may later come to identify as intellectual learning.

The presentation of a book on the theme of learning from experience might suggest that experience is all that is required for learning. However, this is far from the case. Learning requires interaction, either directly or symbolically, with elements outside the learner, as Robin Usher points out (Chapter 12). It is only by counterposing experience with something which is external to the learner that meaning can be created.

The intention and process

Before introducing some of our themes and key ideas, it may be helpful to describe how this book arose and how it was written, as the process of creating the book has influenced our ideas about learning and experience. We have worked as colleagues in the Australian Consortium of Experiential Education and were members of the coordinating committee for the Second International Conference on Experiential Learning held in Sydney in 1989. In workshops and planning meetings, we have frequently discussed what we regard as important in experience-based learning.

The first idea for a book was prompted by our different experiences of the conference, which included both successes and disappointments. We had been excited about the diversity and richness of activity in the field and the pervasiveness of experiential learning across many settings and in many countries, but we were left with a sense that much was missing from the discussions and activities at the conference. There was a relative absence of debate about theories and concepts and an acceptance of ideas which, to our minds at least, had not been subject to critical analysis. What were the key ideas that underpin learning from experience? How do we learn from our experience? How can we best help others to learn from their experience? How does context and purpose influence learning? These became our starting point. We did not believe that the collected papers from the conference would address these questions and, rather than attempt to contrive a book from the conference, we decided to start from scratch and move in the direction of our concerns.

Part of our desire to produce this book was reinforced by our dismay that experience-based learning was in danger of being highjacked by professionals who were taking an excessively instrumental approach to learning, limited to exercise or technique-driven strategies. We saw at the major conference on experiential learning at the University of Surrey in 1991, that the field is becoming increasingly populated by practitioners who wish to use experiential learning in an instrumental way as 'an object of institutional policy and professional good practice' (Griffin 1992: 31). While we are not averse to such pragmatic approaches where necessary – indeed, we use them from time to time in our own teaching – we wished to draw attention to the much wider domain of learning from experience, of which these ideas are merely a small part. Experience-based learning is far more diverse and pervasive than most professional educators conceive.

Our original intention was to identify significant practitioners in the field and bring together a range of views and conceptual frameworks, some of which had not yet found expression in the literature, to illuminate issues of learning from experience. These ideas would be illustrated by personal examples and thus a framework for such learning would be established. Little did we realize that the task was not so simple and that we would have to take quite a different approach. We did identify significant practitioners, but in briefing them we became increasingly aware that we were in danger of portraying ideas in isolation from the experiences which had helped foster them, so giving the false impression that ideas develop independently of the experience of their authors. In writing about learning from experience, we saw the need for authors to acknowledge significant experiences which had led them to their present position. Thus we invited them to 'write themselves into their chapters' and to give an autobiographical account of what had led them to their present views.

When we saw the first drafts of chapters, we realized how difficult it was for many of them to respond to this request. We were also struck by the different impact the chapters made on us. When the experience of the author was vividly portrayed, the issues and ideas came to life and the concepts discussed took on a personal meaning and could be seen in context. We resolved then to strengthen our injunction and encourage the authors to make their chapters much more autobiographical. From tentative and cautious beginnings, rather formal expression became real life. Different authors accepted this challenge in different ways. Some presented their personal history, some pointed to significant events, some illustrated their ideas with anecdotes from their learning journey, and yet others wrote of the personal exploration involved in writing their chapter. We recognized that this did not cover all of the models described in the literature, but we decided that it was important to base the book on the actual experience of the contributors, rather than have them theorize on perspectives that might not have touched them personally.

Our learning

In parallel with the writing of draft chapters and getting feedback on them from other contributors, we were engaged in our own discussions to provide a framework for the whole enterprise. The process we adopted was to think aloud and talk at length about the issues until patterns in our thinking emerged. We brainstormed and associated ideas and used an electronic whiteboard to capture a record of our discussions. Ideas about learning and experience were identified, refined, moulded, unpacked as we reshaped our views. We were continually making assertions and testing propositions at a number of levels, relating both to our own learning and what we suspected for others. As we worked through the ideas, what became obvious was the critical role our different backgrounds and our own experience played in how we named the issues.

At one stage, we wrote short autobiographical statements, in an attempt to discern how important our past is to us in present learning. It was very exciting to play with these ideas, and we convinced ourselves that important learning was emerging. The meetings about the book allowed us to share our own learning histories and reflect together on how they have been shaped by personal experience. What often arose in our discussions was what we had left out of our stories, and now saw as relevant. They emphasized for us the importance of working with experience and returning to it again and again.

We were surprised that what seemed straightforward for us proved so unexpectedly tough for our contributors. Why was it so difficult? We realize now that we were asking a great deal in having them conform to our demands, not least of which was to accept our perspective without being party to the discussions which led to our decision. However, there were other challenges to meet. The culture of academic and professional writing has always insisted that single and personal examples are not appropriate. Somehow, personal experience has been devalued in the quest for objectivity and generality. How is Ruth's migrant background linked to her current interests in equity issues in the recognition of prior learning and women's education? What is the significance now of David B's early academic studies in which he became frustrated with formal teaching for his current leadership role in a formal learning institution? How does David W's study of the religious experience of a fourth-century monk link with his interest in experience and learning today? We sought explanations.

Whenever we addressed the learning issues from our own perspectives, we were drawn to focus on the importance of the personal in how people interpret their experience. Nod Miller gives a good example of this when she refers (Chapter 9) to her time as a student of sociology and the frustration she felt by the tendency of lecturers to dismiss personal experience as 'anecdotal', as if issues such as 'social class' were detached from the lives of the sociology students. We believe that processing and reflecting on the personal experience is clearly a major factor for developing higher-level learning.

Although we recognized that there is much more potential for capturing learning from experience than we had previously recognized, we also became aware of the difficulties that becoming too self-conscious about it can

generate. We do not go through life consciously seeking out every opportunity for learning where it might occur; none of us are fully rational, goal-
driven beings. If we turn the whole of life into a learning experience and
regard ourselves and others as learners first and foremost, we gain in some
ways, but we devalue other important aspects of our lives. This criticism can
be made of some parts of this book, but the tendency here is a necessary
one – it highlights the fact that we often fail to recognize the learning
which is present in all situations. Stephen Brookfield (Chapter 1), for example, discusses how learning to swim as an adult gave him insights into the
learning process and how he now incorporates these personal insights into
his learning in working with adult students.

Focusing on basic ideas

Wrestling with these difficulties and further contact with the writing of the
other contributors led us to what we regarded as central ideas about learning
from experience. We formulated these as a series of propositions, some
more universal than others in their scope. At one point, we had over thirty
'key' propositions which we felt contained the essence of our thinking.
Over the weeks, we reduced them to first-, second- and third-order propositions and then decided to use only those of the first order, which subsumed
the rest. We became aware of the baldness of some of our statements, how
contextually they are framed, how they (often unconsciously) incorporate
our values, the role and impact of other people, limitations in practice, and
the importance of self-reflection in learning from experience. And we were
dismayed when issues we thought we had concluded were raised again in
other contexts, and clearly were not resolved. ('In what way is an event
distinguished from an experience?' is a favourite. Oh, not again! Ruth
would sigh as the two Davids yet again dissected the elements of an event.)
Our consideration of these somewhat tortuous ideas were continually being
reshaped as we considered them more deeply.

The basic ideas and propositions which follow are designed to focus
attention on important issues in learning from experience. While they are
relevant to all modes of learning, emphasis has been placed on those items
which are particularly significant in experience-based learning, rather than
those more centrally related to learning with regard to formal bodies of
knowledge. Many of them resonate with ideas from learning theory, phenomenology or social psychology, and such ideas have certainly influenced
some of the contributors. They are expressed here as practical issues which
need to be brought into considerations of learning from experience.

A digression on the nature of experience

Before plunging into discussion of the propositions, we wish to make a brief
aside about language. In writing about learning from experience, we have

been mindful of the difficulty of writing about 'experience'. It is a term which has preoccupied philosophers and which many have tried to avoid. It contains many ambiguities, it acts sometimes as a noun, at others as a verb, and it is almost impossible to establish a definitive view with which to work.

The Macquarie Dictionary (1991) captures a variety of aspects of it in its explanation of the word 'experience'. Considered as a verb, it suggests it is either a particular instance or a process of observing, undergoing or encountering. As a noun, it is all that is known, the knowledge or practical wisdom gained from the observing, undergoing or encountering. These definitions give rise to a number of issues. 'Observing' suggests a somewhat detached role, 'undergoing' a passive role and 'encountering' a more interactive one. While all of these may be part of experience, it raises the question of how experience is to be seen as a whole.

While not subscribing generally to his philosophical views, we found Oakeshott's analysis on this matter helpful. He defines experience as standing for the concrete whole which analysis divides into 'experiencing' and 'what is experienced': '. . . [T]hese two abstractions stand to one another in the most complete interdependence; they compose a single whole' (Oakeshott 1933: 9). Experiencing cannot be severed from what is experienced and what is experienced cannot be severed from experiencing. He points out that while we can analyse experience, to distinguish it for example from sensation, or even reflection, volition, feeling and intuition, we cannot regard these as activities which are different in principle and can be readily separated from one another.

We, like Oakeshott, reject limiting experience to sensation. That is, 'direct experience, immediate, unmodified, complete and neither pointing to, nor involving any experience beyond itself'. In our view, the idea of experience has within it judgement, thought and connectedness with other experience – it is not isolated sensing. Even in its most elementary form, it involves perception and it implies consciousness; it always comes with meaning: 'Nothing, in short, can maintain its claim to be in experience which presents itself in utter isolation, alone, without world, generation or relevance. Experience is always and everywhere significant' (Oakeshott 1933: 14).

A similar point is captured by the concept of experience in Dewey's work, which includes at least both 'having' and 'knowing' (Duff 1990: 465). For Dewey, 'having' points to the immediacy of contact with the events of life; 'knowing' to the interpretation of the event. Experience is not simply an event which happens, it is an event with meaning. 'Events are present and operative *anyway*; what concerns us is their meanings' (Dewey 1925: 244). We consider meaning to be an essential part of experience.

This suggests that experience is a meaningful encounter. It is not just an observation, a passive undergoing of something, but an active engagement with the environment, of which the learner is an important part. 'Each learner forms part of the milieu, enriching it with his or her personal contribution and creating an interaction which becomes the individual as well as the shared learning experience' (Boud and Walker 1991: 18). This continuing, complex and meaningful interaction is central to our understanding of experience.

For the sake of simplicity in discussing learning from experience, experience is sometimes referred to as if it were singular and unlimited by time or place. Much experience, however, is multifaceted, multi-layered and so inextricably connected with other experiences, that it is impossible to locate temporally or spatially. It almost defies analysis as the act of analysis inevitably alters the experience and the learning which flows from it. The authors in this collection illustrate these complexities from their personal experience. The intensity and personal relevance of the learning is counterposed against the theoretical frameworks which they have come to adopt.

This book is not a treatise on experience. It is about using experience in learning and for the most part the contributors have adopted what may be to them a 'commonsense' view about the term experience. In so doing, they are moving our conceptions of learning away from matters which relate to externally defined curricula and syllabuses and towards those which have personal meaning to those involved. When we are dealing with learning associated with intimate matters – personal relationships, how we define ourselves – this is not particularly surprising. However, when we are dealing with learning in the context of formal courses, as many of our contributors are doing, then taking a view of learning as learning from experience is a significant challenge to the *status quo*. What we and they are saying is that even in the context of externally defined knowledge, we must take account of, and build on, the unique perceptions and experiences of those involved, for without this we are dealing with only the most superficial aspects of learning.

While the book portrays many useful ways of thinking about learning from experience and how these have been put into practice in both formal and informal settings, it is not a how-to-do-it book. It does not offer simple strategies which 'work' or which can be applied in many different situations. There are many books which describe a range of experiential techniques. Most of the contributors here would regard such recipes sceptically and urge instead a careful appreciation of the experience and the intentions of the learner before any particular strategy is even contemplated. A rich array of ideas and practices is provided here from which readers can draw. Nevertheless, if the readers' intention is to solve a specific problem, they may pick up something in passing, but the book is not for them and they will probably find it frustratingly elusive. However, if they are concerned with gaining some ideas about how they and those whom they assist can think about the messy, inconvenient, adventitious, but ultimately profound learning from experience which is available to them at many times and in many places, this book provides a ready entry point to the challenge.

Some propositions about learning from experience

Returning, then, from our consideration of experience, we outline below the propositions about learning from experience which we have identified. In discussing each one, we start by elaborating on the statement and follow this with reference to some of its implications, linking these to particular chapters which follow. The propositions are not of equal status; we have chosen them to highlight what we regard as the most significant points.

Proposition 1: Experience is the foundation of, and the stimulus for, learning

We found it to be meaningless to talk about learning in isolation from experience. Experience cannot be bypassed; it is the central consideration of all learning. Learning builds on and flows from experience: no matter what external prompts to learning there might be – teachers, materials, interesting opportunities – learning can only occur if the experience of the learner is engaged, at least at some level. These external influences can act only by transforming the experience of the learner.

Our assumption, and that of the book, is that every experience is potentially an opportunity for learning. While we often choose not to focus on the learning possibilities of events in daily life, any one of them could lead us into many different domains of human enquiry – personal or interpersonal, formal or informal, systematic or unstructured. The initiation of learning in this view is the act of framing some aspect of experience as something from which we can learn. This may take place explicitly when we identify a learning need and pursue it ('I need a new car, I must find out about possible choices') or implicitly when we find ourselves drawn to particular activities – in listening to music we discover ourselves learning a lot about the works of a composer we enjoy.

Learning always relates, in one way or another, to what has gone before. There is never a clean slate on which to begin; unless new ideas and new experience link to previous experience, they exist as abstractions, isolated and without meaning. The effects of experience influence all learning. What we are attracted towards, what we avoid and how we go about the task, is dependent on how we have responded in the past. Earlier experiences which had positive or negative affect stimulate or suppress new learning. They encourage us to take risks and enter into new territory for exploration or, alternatively, they may inhibit our range of operation or ability to respond to opportunities.

The challenge of new experiences acting to stimulate learning may be juxtaposed with the other challenge which has already been addressed – the seeking of new meanings in old experience. The experiences which influence our learning may be those occurring concurrently, from the recent past or coming from anything in our history. We bring the whole of

our life to every learning event and any aspect of our past may be brought
into play. In starting a new class or meeting new people, for example, we
bring with us memories and feelings of other similar events from our past.
Our personal history affects the way in which we experience and what we ⸵
acknowledge as experience. We do not simply see a new situation afresh –
what is before us – but in terms of how we relate to it, how it resonates with
what past experience has made us.

While we commonly assume that teaching leads to learning, it is the
experiences which teaching helps create that prompt learning, not primarily
the acts of the teacher. We have all had the experience of being exposed
to countless hours of teaching which had no discernible effect on us, but
from time to time we are engaged by something which the teacher says or
does which touches our experience, has meaning for us and moves us on
to further work. The teacher creates an event which the learner experiences
and may learn from. In fact, the event is an important learning experience
for the teacher as well. As Lee Andresen puts it (Chapter 4), 'to teach is to
learn twice, to experience a double delight'.

While experience may be the foundation of learning, it does not necessarily
lead to it: there needs to be active engagement with it. Working with our
experience is one of the keys to learning; it is an activity which we may do
alone or with others, it does not normally involve any intervention by
someone in a teaching role. The ways in which we can do this are limited
only by the range of examples available to us and to our imagination.
Learning does not emerge simply from experience even, when we work
actively with it. 'Experience has to be arrested, examined, analysed, considered and negated to shift it to knowledge' (Costas Criticos, Chapter 11).

For learning to take place, the experience does not have to be recent.
Learning occurs over time and meaning may take many years to become
apparent. The experience itself may not change, but the learning from it
can grow, the meaning of it can be transformed, and the effects of it can
be altered. The linking of new experiences with those of the past can
provide new meanings and stimulate us to explore again those parts of our
world which we have avoided. When we wrote and recounted parts of our
autobiographies to each other, we could find new meanings in themes from
our earlier lives and they helped us make sense of some of our present
preoccupations. For example, the current focus of one of us on writing and
publishing could be linked to negative experiences of learning English in
school. Both Andresen and John Mulligan (Chapter 3) show how they have
revisited formative experiences in their lives to shed new light on their
present understanding and development.

Such reflection plays a special role in drawing meaning from experience.
Reflection consists of those processes in which learners engage to recapture,
notice and re-evaluate their experience, to work with their experience to
turn it into learning. Two of us (David Boud and David Walker, Chapter 5)
have examined the role of reflection in learning in previous publications
and we reflect on the experience of applying our model of the process. Our

chapter suggests that it is through entering into a dialogue with our experience that we can turn experiential knowledge, which may not be readily
accessible to us, into propositional knowledge which can be shared and
interrogated. Mary Thorpe (Chapter 7) also uses this process in distance
education.

Reflection is not just an individual activity; engaging in the process with
another person or with a group can change the meanings we draw from
experience. When a group participates in a common event, each person
will experience it in a particular way and will have an interpretation of
aspects of that event which may differ from that of others. The recounting
of commonalities and differences can enable participants to reflect on how
their experience has been influenced by their unique history and perceptions
and can highlight the importance of not assuming that we all experience
events in the same manner. Formulating and articulating experience
transforms it in ways that can allow us to see it anew. In our case, the
reactions of the others to our autobiographies made us reassess what we
had written: 'Was it really as I described it?' 'Why was Ruth so surprised?'
'Can I continue to accept the interpretations I have always made about the
difficulties I had at school?'

In working together on this book, we spent many hours alone and together
identifying aspects of our own experience, unpacking it, trying to listen to
what it might be telling us, contrasting it with that of others and trying to
distil what we regarded as important from it. We have been reinforced in
our view of learning as an active process in which the learner needs to work
with experience again and again to appreciate the meanings associated with
it. An important lesson we have learned with John Mason (Chapter 8) and
others is to resist premature interpretation of experience. The more we can
enter vividly into the experience, the more we can draw on what it offers.

Proposition 2: Learners actively construct their experience

Each experience is influenced by the unique past of the learner. We are
attuned to some aspects of the world and not to others. This orientation
influences what we focus on and what we respond to. In the process, we
take cues from our environment and from our internal states to interpret
what is happening in the light of what has gone before. Our construction
takes all aspects of the experience into account – feelings as well as thinking
– and makes it our own. While much of this process occurs without us being
aware of it, it is nevertheless an active one which is always available for
reinterpretation and change in the light of new information or reflection
on the old.

We attach our own meaning to events. While others may attempt to
impose their meanings on us, we ultimately define our own experience;
others simply do not have access to our sensations and perceptions. We may
use language and ideas to express meaning, and in the process use externally

defined objects, but only the person who experiences can ultimately give meaning to the experience. In working with others, we attempt to share meaning and we can reach commonly accepted interpretations of the world which operate within that context, but these can never fully define the experience of the participants.

The meaning of experience is not a given, it is subject to interpretation. It may not be what at first sight it appears to be. When different learners are involved in the same event, their experience of it will vary and they will construct (and reconstruct) it differently. One person's stimulating explanation will be another's dreary lecture. What learners bring to an event – their expectations, knowledge, attitudes and emotions – will influence their interpretation of it and their own construction of what they experience. In general, if an event is not related in some fashion to what the learner brings to it, whether or not they are conscious of what this is, then it is not likely to be a productive opportunity. Much of what we label as 'poor motivation' is a mismatch between students' construction of the event, and our own as teachers.

Experience is created in the transaction between the learner and the milieu in which he or she operates – it is relational. An event can influence the learner, but only if the learner is predisposed to being influenced. Similarly, the learner can create a fruitful experience from a limited event, but only if there is something with which they can work. Teachers and facilitators need to acknowledge the agency of the learner and the importance of the learner's construction of the learning activities which they make available for them. The meaning attributed to an event by a learner may have little to do with external measures of achievement as Brookfield illustrates. The construction of experience by learners needs to be taken into account in judging the worth of an activity.

Perhaps the major influence on how learners construct their experience is what Boud and Walker (1990) term the learner's personal foundation of experience. This is a shorthand for the cumulative effect of learners' personal and cultural history: the influences of the events in their lives which have helped form the way they are now and their responses to the world. We are all predisposed to learn in particular ways or in response to particular situations. Some authors have referred to this as learning styles and attempted to classify them. While this may be convenient at times, more is often lost than is gained by ignoring the uniqueness of each person's history and ways of experiencing the world. Elizabeth Kasl, Kathleen Dechant and Victoria Marsick (Chapter 10) point out that assumptions about purpose can be more important than style.

Knowledge of one's personal foundation of experience may be well guarded; it is certainly not readily accessible to the learner or to others. Part of this foundation is revealed through the learners' intent. Learners approach each event with a set of expectations which attune them to some outcomes and be less sensitive to others. This intent may have little or nothing to do with the expectations of the planner of the event. Intent can be declared

in circumstances in which the learner is willing to explore their expectations and predispositions. For example, we will usually give a reason for our
participation in a course or workshop and, as we become more confident
and comfortable with what is happening, we may become willing to share
more about what led us to take part.

There are many devices to help learners in constructing and reconstructing their experience. These are referred to throughout the book. Thorpe
discusses forms of writing, and the ways intents can be explored through
different ways of reflecting using various forms of writing, and Kasl, Dechant
and Marsick write of the need for personalizing information to aid association
with ideas and events. In preparing the book, we worked collectively with
our experience in many modes: in writing mini-biographies, in discussing
events between us, in other writing tasks and in trying to reinterpret our
experience in the light of the many prompts which the chapters had provided
for us. Although there are many other modes to be considered, it is important
to note that the act of working with the experience provides a further
experience which may or may not be helpful in constructing the former.
Construction of experience is never ending.

Proposition 3: Learning is a holistic process

Learning is normally experienced as a seamless whole; there is a large
degree of continuity between all our experiences even while we label them
as different. Much writing about learning has treated it as if it existed
in different domains which are separated from each other. A common
division is between the cognitive (concerned with thinking), the affective
(concerned with values and feelings) and the conative or psychomotor
(concerned with action and doing). Although it can at times be useful to
think of these different aspects of learning, no one aspect is discrete and
independent of the rest and no one aspect should generally be privileged
over the rest.

The balance between aspects may vary across contexts, purposes and
time; none can ever be ignored. It is impossible to dissociate the learner
from his or her context, from the processes in which they are involved or
from their past experience. Learning is situated and contextualized and
claims to universal knowledge need to be treated with caution. While some
disciplines such as physics aspire to such knowledge, even there the process
whereby learners acquire such knowledge is being seen increasingly as
dependent on early experience and the context of learning.

In contemporary English-speaking society, there is a cultural bias towards
the cognitive and conative aspects of learning. The development of the
affect is inhibited and instrumental thinking is highly valued in education
and work. Clearly, in some situations, these aspects will dominate, but even
there it is not meaningful to exclude the rest from consideration: anything
and everything may be important. Within educational institutions, particularly

in higher education, the systematic bias towards the intellect and to the analytical is most pronounced and the influence of learning in these institutions has spread widely, leading to a lack of emphasis on people as whole persons and on problems which are taken out of context.

One feature of learning may be prominent at any particular time, but all learning involves the feelings and emotions (affective), the intellectual and cerebral (cognitive) and action (conative). These features interact in complex ways which are not possible to predict. While it is convenient to pretend that only one of these aspects is in play, this is one of the greatest errors in considering learning from experience. It is one we often make as teachers when we are unable to identify fully with the experience of our students. In recalling almost any experience, different features appear connected; to learners it is experienced as a whole.

Learning is not readily constrained by time or place. All of our experience, past and present, is potentially relevant to any given learning task. The bringing to bear of appropriate experience is one of the great challenges of learning. The fragmentation of experience in this process, while it may be useful for an immediate task, can also be restrictive. Both Angela Brew (Chapter 6) and Denis Postle (Chapter 2) stress the importance of attending to the whole of experience and of resisting the temptation to limit it. Openness to the possibility of learning from any event facilitates learning.

Proposition 4: Learning is socially and culturally constructed

While learners construct their own experience, they do so in the context of a particular social setting and range of cultural values; learners do not exist independently of their environment. This both limits learning and provides forms of expression for the learner. There are many examples in history of famous figures being persecuted or their work attacked when they pressed beyond the limits of the world their society had created. On a much smaller scale, there are many ways in which learning outside conventional bounds is circumscribed.

It is not possible to step beyond the influence of context and culture. However, their influence can be recognized, if learners' experience is then subjected to critical reflection (including that of their own and other contexts and cultures) aimed at exposing taken-for-granted assumptions. The need for this is especially important at times when societal values are themselves changing. Socialization is one of the processes through which we are socially and culturally constructed. We can never undo what has happened to us; the most that is possible is to find ways to reinterpret these events in the light of new knowledge and ways of thinking.

Learning does not occur in isolation from social and cultural norms and values. It is through these that we interpret experience and set our learning against that of others. Learning in groups, which is discussed by Miller, is a good example of a situation in which the influence of others is obviously present, but we cannot escape from external norms and values as they are embedded in the language we use and the concepts which we have developed to make meaning of experience. Social and political influence is easy for the outsider to see, for example, in Criticos's discussion of post-apartheid South Africa, but it often is present in our taken-for-granted assumptions which render invisible some of the factors which most influence us. We can also find examples of taken-for-granted assumptions in our own cultural experience. The pervasive influence of male pronouns and male examples in textbooks continue old agendas of expectation and organization, and perpetuate oppressive practices.

Critical reflection is required to examine the influences of our values and culture. We cannot easily transcend our taken-for-granted assumptions and see the conceptual baggage which we carry with us. The making problematic of the familiar is an important strategy in moving beyond the mental bonds which constrain us. We can only do this with great commitment and the desire to investigate what has made us who we are. This can take us inwards on the journey of self-exploration to our past and outwards towards engaging with powerful material and social forces of oppression. Our own autobiographies vividly demonstrate to us the pervasive influence of social class, gender and ethnic background on our own learning from an early age.

The most powerful influence of the social and cultural context on our learning is that which occurs through language. We have words and concepts in our language for some experiences, but not others. We have an extraordinarily well-developed set of concepts for technical and scientific phenomena, but our language for personal and emotional experience has hardly changed in modern times. John Mulligan's focus on the emotional aspects of learning identifies seven categories of internal processes including reasoning, feeling, imaging and intuiting, and he illustrates these from his personal experience. Naming them is important for their being. We give prominence to that which we can name and accord it a special place; the naming of experience provides a means for exploring and appropriating it. Usher points out that by creating a field for exploration labelled experiential learning, we are separating this from the everyday world of learning from experience and are in the process changing the events we are dealing with. Mason illustrates that it is not only our written or spoken tongue which creates the world, but also the language of mathematics. In this case, it is clearer to observe the limitations which facility with language places on us.

Proposition 5: Learning is influenced by the socio-emotional context in which it occurs

Of all the features that we have mentioned, emotions and feelings are the ones which are most neglected in our society: there is almost a taboo about them intruding into our educational institutions, particularly at higher levels. Postle refers to the cultural bias in favour of the intellectual and practical. Emotions and feelings are key pointers to both possibilities for, and barriers to, learning. Acknowledging them can enable us to significantly redirect our attention towards matters which we have neglected. Denial of feelings is denial of learning.

Brookfield also highlights the impact that visceral experiences have on us: we cannot separate out the powerful feelings that learning to swim generates from the psychomotor act of swimming. He suggests that the acceptance of our feelings can help us reframe our actions to make them more congruent with what we are attempting to do. The power of feelings and emotions in learning is emphasized by both Postle, who points out that '[e]ngaging fully the affective elements can lead to anxiety, pain and discomfort', and Criticos, who cautions us that much valuable learning occurs in circumstances which we would never choose if we knew what we might need to experience to reach that endpoint.

There are two key sources of influence: past experience and the role of others in the present as supportive or otherwise. The past creates expectations which influence the present and learners carry with them their own socio-emotional context which is their set of expectations about what can and cannot be done. The present context can act to reinforce or counterbalance this. Positive qualities of the present manifest through others such as their support, trust and confidence in the learner can help overcome negative influences and allow the person to act and think differently from the past. Similarly, conditions of threat or lack of confidence in the learner are usually antithetical to new initiatives and have a tendency to reinforce negative images of the learner. Thus, different kinds of learning occur depending on whether the context is perceived as positive or negative.

It is difficult to grapple with this alone. As with many issues which we have identified as influencing learning from experience, one of the most powerful is that of confidence and self-esteem; unless learners believe themselves capable, they will be continually handicapped in what they do. Engagement with learning tasks is related to belief in success. The extent to which we can change is often a function of the supportiveness of the environment we can create for ourselves. We need, as learners, appropriate support, trust and challenge from others. This can enable us to continue our tasks when they seem too much for us or when we get blocked (emotional support), to do things in more productive ways (practical support) or to challenge the assumptions of others (political support). We also need to be challenged so that we do not fool ourselves with our own distorted assumptions or fail to consider new information which is outside our present range of experience. At times we need self-chosen groups of people similar to ourselves to support and challenge us, for example those composed only of women. But in other circumstances, as Miller illustrates, diversity and difference of experience is necessary to move beyond what we take as given.

The way in which we interpret experience is intimately connected with how we view ourselves. Developing confidence and building self-esteem both flow from, and are necessary for, learning from experience. If we do not respect our perceptions and have confidence in what we see and feel, then we cannot make use of the information which we garner from the world. A belief in our ability to act and learn is a prerequisite for learning; without this we are passive participants in the constructs of others.

Bringing it all together

Having identified these propositions as ideas which underpin the book, we were faced with arranging the chapters in an appropriate order. The tidy order we had conceived of at the start proved no longer workable. The task was a difficult one, created by the approach we have adopted. We had selected authors whom we felt could reflect on their learning, reveal the experiences from which it had come and who could identify ideas which they now saw as informing their work. As our emphasis was to draw on the experience of the writer rather than on the conceptual framework they had come to adopt, the idea of sections with coherent and strongly related ideas had to be rejected.

The learning which has been recorded is unique and often disparate and does not pretend to cover the vast territory of learning from experience. It provides glimpses of a mosaic of ideas which suggests a pattern, but does not attempt to portray the whole. Readers can pursue their own themes as they appear in different chapters. They are arranged in three sub-books, in each of which appear illustrations of the propositions. Chapters which relate closely to each other are adjacent, as are those which deal with similar content areas. However, in each group there is a spectrum of issues to suggest the holistic nature of the ideas with which we are dealing.

While we have tried to summarize some of the recurring themes of the book here (and there are many others to be found), it is important also to point out the limitations of conceptualizing learning from experience. Our authors emphasize that learning can never be linear or neat and that lived experience can never be transmitted to another and meet with the same response. In the final chapter, Usher reminds us of something which is quite fundamental: experience always says less than it wishes to say, there are many readings of it, it is never exhausted and total clarity may never be reached. Nevertheless, we hope that this book will provide a range of perspectives to provide some clarity to help make sense of the most basic but elusive aspect of learning.

References

Boud, D. and Walker, D. (1990) Making the most of experience. *Studies in Continuing Education*, 12(2): 61–80.
Boud, D. and Walker, D. (1991) *Experience and Learning: Reflection at Work.* Geelong: Deakin University Press.

Dewey, J. (1925) Experience and nature. In Boydson, J.A. (ed.) (1981) *John Dewey, The Later Works, 1925–1953, Vol. 1: 1925.* Carbondale: Southern Illinois University Press.

Duff, B.E. (1990) 'Event' in Dewey's philosophy. *Educational Theory,* 40(4): 463–70.

Griffin, C. (1992) Absorbing experiential learning. In Mulligan, J. and Griffin, C. (eds) *Empowerment through Experiential Learning,* pp. 31–6. London: Kogan Page.

Oakeshott, M. (1933) *Experience and its Modes.* Cambridge: Cambridge University Press.

The Macquarie Dictionary (1991) Second edn. Macquarie University, Sydney: The Macquarie Library.

Part 1

Introduction

The basic assumption of this book is explored in this section: experience is the foundation and source of learning. Significant personal learning experiences are a powerful force in learning; to enter into dialogue with our own autobiography as learners is a helpful means to reflect on and reframe our practice as teachers and as learners. The authors illustrate from their own lives how their learning has been essentially linked to their personal experience. These chapters reveal the complexity of experience and learning and offer ways to approach it. They warn of the danger of not working with the whole experience, and in particular, the risk of neglecting the affective dimensions of experience.

The opening chapter by Brookfield, through focusing so clearly on the relevance of personal experience, helps underline the importance of learning from experience. He starts with the most basic experience of all – the visceral – and links this with the reframing of educational practice. By raising the issues of credibility, authenticity and critical reflection, he enables us to view our practice as teachers and learners from a number of perspectives and introduces many of the themes which are developed in later chapters. In the following chapter, Postle focuses on the affective aspects of experience and learning. Brookfield had already raised this issue, but Postle takes it up in detail. He explores the concept of 'emotional competence': capability in addressing emotion and feeling that actively supports facilitators' and learners' ways of learning from experience. He suggests specific criteria to assess the presence of emotional competence. Both Brookfield and Postle emphasize that creating artificial boundaries around experience limits the learning that lows from it.

Mulligan's contribution relates to the issues raised by Postle through his focus on internal processes associated with learning from experience. He stresses the importance of taking into account the internal as well as the external world, and is convinced that by helping learners discriminate between these internal processes he is helping them with the learning process itself. To achieve this, he outlines seven internal processes: reasoning, sensing, intuiting, remembering, imagining and willing. He illustrates each of these with events from his own childhood and points to means to explore them further. Andresen's chapter, in common with Mulligan's, takes up significant experiences from his past life to show how they reflect his present learning. Through the use of the metaphors of the mirror and the hall of mirrors, he revisits events scattered over fifty years of learning, teaching, learning about teaching, teaching about teaching, learning about learning, and teaching about learning, and shares the images that they reflect.

1

Through the Lens of Learning: How the Visceral Experience of Learning Reframes Teaching

Stephen Brookfield

This chapter outlines an approach to helping teachers reframe their practice by encouraging them to analyse their visceral experiences as learners. Interpreting practice as a consequence of experiencing learning is probably done anecdotally by many educators when they draw upon memories of their own student experiences and determine that they will never perpetuate the outrages that were visited on them by teachers. In this chapter, I make the case that our experiences as learners provide us with a powerful lens through which we can view our own practices as educators in a more formalized and purposeful way. In particular, I argue that regularly experiencing what it feels like to learn something unfamiliar and difficult is the best way to help teachers empathize with the emotions and feelings of their own learners as they begin to traverse new intellectual terrains.

How I learned to stop worrying and trust my experience: Notes for a screenplay

Opening Scene: Teachers College Swimming Pool, New York, November 1983

Spluttering, coughing out what seems like pure chlorine, I raise my head out of the water to see where I am. I know where I am in a larger sense – I'm in an Adult Swimming Class – but where am I in the pool? I also know that I've hit tiling (again) and that must mean that I've veered across the lanes and swum a width rather than a length of the pool. When I open my eyes, remove the chlorine solution and see that I'm at the other end of the pool from where I started a few minutes ago – that I've swum a length – I feel a startling jolt of pride, an unalloyed rush of pure happiness. I can't believe it – I've actually swum a length of a swimming pool! Me, who thought that practically all aspects of the physical, athletic world were closed to me. Me, who thinks of myself as a psychomotor dolt, someone whose limbs seem never to respond properly to signals from the brain. At some level, I believed I could never do this, never make it down from one end of a swimming pool to another.

Insight: The phenomenological meaning of a learning event can have little to do with supposedly objective measures of accomplishment. On almost any measurement scale available for assessing progress as a swimmer, my performance in swimming the length is pretty pitiful, not to say pathetic. People forty years my senior are zooming past me in the water as I splutter painfully down the designated slow lane in the pool. But that doesn't matter, or even register with me; my feeling of pride is so overwhelming as to make this first ever swimming of a length a critical high point in the phenomenological terrain of my experiences as a learner in the last ten years.

Cut to . . .

Scene Two: A rainy, foggy night on an Italian auto-route, November 1989

As a sabbatical project I have decided, at the age of forty, to learn to drive a car. Initially, at the end of a five-month stay in Provence, my goal was to be able to negotiate the road from the farmhouse where we are living into the local town three miles away. However, six weeks after starting to learn under my wife's instruction (despite the marital risks this entails), I feel so confident of my newly developed skill that I take the wheel for large chunks of our journey to Bologna where we are going to spend a long weekend. Ignoring my wife's warnings that driving on a foggy, rainy night is stressful enough for experienced drivers on quiet back roads, let alone on an Italian auto-route, I insist that 'the only way to learn something is to do it'. Eventually, after several 'white knuckle' experiences (a nicely descriptive phrase referring to passengers gripping the dashboard in anticipation of their imminent demise), I accept that I'm placing the lives of our family in real danger by persisting any longer in driving. I let my wife take the wheel and I sink into a near catatonic state, a state I imagine resembles the falsely comforting enervation travellers trapped in snow drifts feel just before they slip into their last sleep.

Insight: Under the adrenalin rush induced by making much quicker progress than they had anticipated in a learning project, it is easy for learners to develop a vastly inflated and (sometimes literally) dangerously unrealistic notion of their capacities. This is the dark side of self-actualization, the often unacknowledged contradiction at the heart of much rhetoric about self-direction. After emerging from my catatonia, I am reminded of how important (and how difficult) it is for me as a teacher to balance a healthy and necessary emphasis on nurturing learners' tentatively emerging belief that they can accomplish something they had previously considered beyond their reach, with an attention to the dangers entailed by espousing the rhetoric of empowerment and letting them think they have the ability immediately to do anything to which they set their minds.

The point of these opening two scenes is also the point of this chapter; as a teacher, one of the most useful, and most ignored, sources of insight into your own practice is your own autobiography as a learner. Most importantly, perhaps, is the visceral nature of the experiences your autobiography represents. Any number of texts emphasize the importance of reflecting critically on the assumptions underlying practice and there is plenty of advice on methods that can be used to this end (Brookfield 1987; Schön 1987; Mezirow and Associates 1990). But the stream of writing on reflective practice tends to appeal at a cerebral, rather than visceral level. Much staff and faculty development which is geared towards developing critical reflection does this through exposing educators to writings on critical pedagogy (Livingstone 1987), to descriptions of Freire's work (Shor and Freire 1987; Shor 1987) and to Schön's (1983) *The Reflective Practitioner*. These are valuable writings which I have used myself, but I feel there is a real possibility that they are often considered at a cognitive, intellectual level, without having the influence on practice that the emotionality of direct experience provides. For example, reading these works can fire us with radical zeal without giving us a sense of how that zeal can change our daily practices. We can readily agree with any number of exhortatory, prescriptive injunctions concerning the need for critical reflection, and profess that we exemplify this process, without changing any aspect of our practice. It is easy to read an inspirational text such as Collins' (1991) critique of mainstream adult educational practice, and then to vow to reappraise one's practice in terms of its hidden paternalism, relativistic naivety, masked technicism and repressive tolerance. Such resolutions are important and can have a marked effect, but they can also easily become sincerely espoused principles which somehow never quite manage to manifest themselves in markedly changed actions.

Letting go: Using the visceral experience of learning to challenge espoused orthodoxy in adult education

In this section, I would like to draw explicitly on two experiential themes in my own autobiography as a learner that have influenced my practice as a teacher. The experiences described are visceral rather than cognitive and both of them contradict some aspect of the espoused orthodoxy of adult educational theory and practice into which I had been initiated (and which I had accepted uncritically) during my postgraduate study. I will describe general features of these experiences and then try to show how my reflections on them caused me to question and reframe some part of my practice as an adult educator.

Screaming for attention: Participating in discussions

One of the most cherished tenets of adult educational practice is that discussion is an educational method that exemplifies the participatory, democratic spirit central to the field. In American adult education, I would argue that Lindeman's belief that discussion was the adult educational method *par excellence* (Lindeman 1987) continues to this day. More recently, this belief that participating in discussion represents the quintessential adult educational experience has been strengthened by the critical and theoretical edge evident in writings by Freire (1970), Mezirow (1991) and Collins (1991), all of whom draw on the Frankfurt school of critical social theory in arguing (convincingly, in my view) that adult education's task is to create conditions in which authentic dialogue and communicative discourse can occur. At almost all stages of my own career, I have used discussion as my preferred method, viewing alternative approaches as supplements of essentially inferior status. As an educator, I am very comfortable leading discussions and this method is still one on which I rely greatly. As a learner, however, my visceral experience is very different.

The defining feature of my experience as a participant in discussion is that I feel a constant and overwhelming compulsion to perform; in other words, I feel impelled to make what I believe others would regard as a series of startlingly profound contributions. I see discussion groups as emotional battlegrounds with members vying for recognition and affirmation from each other and from the discussion leader. As a participant, my energy becomes focused on listening for someone else in the group to make a comment to which I can make some kind of reasonable response. In doing this, I tend not to listen for the merits of different arguments. I am concentrating so hard on finding a conversational opening, a place where I can make some relevant interjection, that any kind of reflective analysis of the accuracy of other members' contributions becomes almost impossible. So, in my case, one of the chief arguments that I would cite as an educator for using discussion – that it opens learners to considering carefully alternative perspectives and interpretations – is invalidated by my own behaviour as a learner. When I listen to a spread of opinion voiced within a group, I am not considering seriously the merits or accuracy of alternative viewpoints, so much as seeking an entry point where my voice might be heard.

The reason why I participate in discussions this way is because I have accepted the assumption that successful discussion participation should be equated with the number of verbal contributions one makes. Anyone who speaks a lot, so I reason, must be a good participant; and anyone who is silent must, by definition, be mentally inert. As an undergraduate and then graduate student, I learned early on that discussion groups quickly establish a pecking order of communication. The longer one stays silent, the harder it is to make that first contribution. With my own personal mixture of arrogance and introversion, I never contributed to discussions unless I was fairly sure that what I was going to say would be universally admired. So,

once I found the conversational connection I was looking for, and I felt
that I had thought enough about that point of connection to be able to
make some contribution, I would spend minutes silently rehearsing my
remarks. After deciding that my putative contribution was word perfect, I
would summon up my courage and, with my palms sweating and my heart
cannoning inside my chest, I would stammer out my rehearsed contribution, often only to find that during the time I was rehearsing my comments
the discussion had moved on and what I was saying was now pretty irrelevant.

Over the years, the contradictions between my espoused theory of discussion and my experiences as a discussion participant have become more and
more glaring. They have prompted me to change significantly aspects of my
pedagogic practice. I now think much more carefully about why and when
to use discussion, I make much more of an effort to evolve ground rules to
guide discussion participation, and I am very careful to make explicit my
ideas concerning what good discussion participation looks like. As a direct
result of my own experiences as a learner in this format I am especially
concerned, as a teacher, to make it clear to members that it is as important
to listen carefully and critically to others' contributions as it is to make
them oneself. I broaden the definition of participation to include not only
the act of speaking, but also more silent contributions such as being a
group recorder or summarizer, bringing a salient piece of research or
polemic to the session for the group's attention, calling for periods of silent
reflective analysis in the midst of heated debate, and xeroxing insights
about the nature of previous discussion sessions that were contained in a
participant's learning journal. Also, I'll try to remember to begin a discussion session with a new group by telling them that they don't need to speak
frequently as a way of signalling their diligence, and that I don't equate
active listening or silent reflective analysis with mental inertia.

Overall, my repeated experiences as a discussion participant have alerted
me to the fact that participating in authentic dialogue, or meeting the
minimum conditions of communicative discourse, is not something which
comes easily to adults. As described by Collins (1991: 12), this kind of
discourse is 'a kind of on-going, thoughtful conversation' in which 'all
participants anticipate that their individual contributions will receive serious consideration from others. At the same time they remain open to
changing or reconstructing their own stance on the problem under consideration in the light of what others have to say and on the weight of all
relevantly identified information.' Since many group contexts of adult life
are infused with considerations of power and status – we learn that success,
conventionally defined, is often attained by flattering or mimicking those in
power – it is naive for a discussion leader to imagine that adults can sign
up for a course and engage immediately in democratic, critical, authentic,
reciprocal, respectful discussion. Yet, as I reflect on my practice as an educator, I am embarrassed to realize just how much I have assumed that this
capacity is innate, or easily awakened, and have missed entirely the dynamics and tensions of power differences, and the need learners feel to please

the leader by mimicry, that have been such a feature of my experiences with this method as a learner.

Practising what you preach: The importance of credibility and authenticity

Allied to adult education's traditional reverence for the use of the discussion method is the emphasis placed in the field on small group exercises. Most variants of small group exercises ask participants to offer some part of their experiences for analysis by other group members. When people hear the term 'andragogy', they probably equate this with some form of small group exercise, and, in the USA at least, a regular reliance on the small group method is generally taken as evidence of adult education's admirable learner-centred, democratic, collegial character. In my own practice, I have often moved to some kind of small group task as early as possible in the belief that doing so sends a strong symbolic message that my ideas and experiences are not the most important resources in the learning group. Indeed, I have often opened the first meeting of a course by telling participants that as adults they probably have the skills and knowledge they've come to learn, it's just that they're not aware that they already possess these. My task, I continue, is to help them realize that they already know much more than they think they do, and I urge that they look to their own experiences, rather than to my supposed expertise, as they negotiate this course. As I make this speech, I have often taken a quiet pride in the fact that such acknowledgments of the value of learners' experiences show me off to good personal advantage; as a self-deprecating, collegial, down-to-earth sort who has no time for academic pomposity.

During my years of behaving this way as an educator, I was also witnessing this kind of interaction from a participant's view, without ever connecting the two in my mind. I would often show up at professional gatherings, academic conferences and in-service workshops eager to learn something from the person or persons advertised as leading a particular session. What caused me to choose one session or workshop over another was the fact that leading the event would be a particular individual, whose word-of-mouth reputation, published work or conference biography promised that my time would be well spent. Yet, when this same person, citing 'principles of good adult educational practice', came into the session and announced that we, as participants, already knew what we thought we had come to learn, and that we were going to form small groups and spend the first portion of the event taking an inventory of all the valuable experiences we had accumulated, my first reactions were to feel annoyed and cheated. I had come primed to learn from this person, and I would say 'how dare he or she put the emphasis right back on me'.

This question would quickly be followed by a rueful admission to myself that I was falling into the same teacher-dependent, passive modes of learning which I was trying to avoid perpetuating in my own students. So, for quite a few years I would say to myself, 'alright, so I'm temporarily feeling cheated by this person's throwing the emphasis for my own learning back on to my shoulders, but this only goes to show just how deeply those despicable other-directed, dependent ways of learning are internalized, even in supposedly progressive educators!' But the feeling of being cheated never really went away and, as a result, a new interpretation began to emerge; one which is, incidentally, confirmed in many adult learners' critical incident reports, interviews and learning journals (Brookfield 1990a). This interpretation runs as follows.

Before educators can ask groups of strangers to turn to each other, form small groups and reveal something about their own experiences, those educators must somehow model the process themselves. They must take the initiative, through their actions, of setting an emotional tone for small group work. Teachers must earn the right to ask people to reveal aspects of themselves to strangers, by first doing this publicly in front of their learners. Teachers' actions, whether they like this or not (and most adult educators I know detest this idea) are granted enormous symbolic significance by learners. So for an adult educator to walk into a room full of strangers and to ask them to 'share their insights and experiences' with each other in small groups, without first having done this himself or herself in front of the whole group, is to miss entirely a crucial moment in terms of creating the right emotional tone under which authentic discourse can occur. I realize now that I, and others, are sometimes right to feel cheated when the first thing that happens is that we are put into small groups. It is as if the leader has asked us to be open about some aspects of our lives, but has personally refused to do this. There is often a consequent sense that the leader sees herself or himself as somehow above the fray, as possessing a superiority of insight, a private analytical line on truth. There is also the suspicion that the leader has some kind of hidden agenda that will be revealed at a later point, by which time we will have spoken things that, in terms of this agenda, make us look stupid.

As I think about learning episodes in my life that have held, or do hold, enormous terror for me, I realize that one of the most important factors which pulls me through these activities intact is my trusting in the educator's credibility and authenticity. When I feel that someone has some valuable skill, knowledge, experience and insight, and when I know that he or she is being open and honest with me, I am much more willing to try to do something which holds great threat for me, and to risk failure in the attempt. I have, for example, resisted for many years trying white water rafting; but if I am ever cajoled into taking a white water rafting trip, the last thing I want is to be on the river bank one morning with the distant sound of churning rapids pounding in my ears listening to the instructor tell me that I already know how to do this, that the instructor will learn as much from me as I will from him or her, and that the other fear-stricken novices in the group are as valuable a resource as the leader's experiences. What I need to hear is that the leader has navigated this stretch of river, or others like it, a thousand times, and that if I just learn some basic rules of survival I'll stand a much better chance of making it through this experience physically and psychologically intact.

One of the experiences which perhaps parallels the terror that would be induced by learning how to participate in white water rafting is learning how to take someone through childbirth. Anyone who has gone through the experience of watching someone they love give birth to a child knows the terror this prospect can induce. Our daughter had been born by a Caesarean section operation after an excruciating forty-six hour labour and one part of me hoped that if ever we were going to have another child the doctors would insist on rescheduling this operation. When we learned my wife was pregnant with our second child, and that a natural birth was possible, I experienced a cowardly craving for some honourable way to avoid being a 'coach'. I secretly longed for an earlier era when all I would have been required to do was hang around in the waiting room and give out cigars when the good news came through. All the pain, blood and suffering of a natural childbirth (there didn't seem to be much that was natural about it to me) was something I would have been glad to avoid, if there had been a suitable available excuse for someone who, like me, professed feminist ideas. However, no politically correct exit with honour was possible, so in 1990 I became a member of a refresher course on preparation for childbirth. I learned how to shout out instructions to my wife about breathing through the contractions of childbirth, and how to tell her when, and for how long, to push out our son. As I tried out these skills, and learned to recognize the cues for different breathing techniques and patterns, I needed our childbirth instructor to show me explicitly and exactly how she would do these things and to give me a solid grounding in timing contractions, changing breathing patterns and yelling out instructions for pushing.

In this situation – faced with the fact that I now had to live up to my espoused values – the last thing I wanted to hear from my instructor was that I already knew how to do this, it was just that I didn't realize I had this knowledge and skill dormant within me. I knew, at a deeply internalized level, that that was total rubbish. And if the first thing that had happened in the class was that we were put into small groups to discuss how our past experiences had helped us develop these skills without our knowing it, I would have left. As soon as I had learned the basic techniques under expert instruction, however, I was then quite ready to participate in small group discussions with other 'coaches' about the fears we were suffering regarding our abilities to be of any use to the mother in the delivery room. I was also ready to hear from others who had been through the experience before, and to review events in my own life to see if there were, indeed, times when I had been required to act in ways that weren't so different from what I was going to have to do in the delivery room.

Insight: What I have drawn from this and other similar experiences as a learner is that small group work can be enormously beneficial when the leader of the activity models the qualities of openness and honesty he or she hopes will characterize the small group interactions. Small group work has to be timed carefully, and progressively minded adult educators like myself have to resist the temptation of hurtling precipitously and mindlessly into such exercises. I have also come to realize that when an educator gives participants (particularly those who are terrified at the prospect of doing something they would much rather avoid) the sense that they are in the hands of someone whose experience in this area is of considerable breadth, depth and intensity, the level of anxiety surrounding the new learning is considerably reduced (though never entirely eliminated). These insights have directly influenced how I approach teaching critical thinking (Brookfield 1987, 1990b).

My approach to teaching critical thinking is one which emphasizes participants' exploring their own autobiographies, using their experiences as the raw material for critical analysis. I rely a great deal on small group exercises, conducted in triads, through which participants are asked to choose critical incidents which illustrate the kinds of assumptions that have framed their actions, and which they have accepted uncritically. One of my own framing assumptions regarding how critical thinking can be developed, is that since it is enormously difficult to stand outside of one's own interpretive frameworks through an act of one's own mental volition, this activity is usually best conducted in small group formats. In earlier years, I would move as quickly as possible to small group exercises in which participants told stories about high and low points in their experiences, and then invited other triad members to tell them what assumptions they thought were embedded in those stories.

Reflecting on my own insights as a workshop participant in small group exercises, I began to realize that I was missing an important step. Now, before asking groups to engage in any analysis of critical events in their own lives, I am careful to undertake this activity in front of them. I try to earn the right to ask them to think critically about their own experiences by first inviting their critical analysis of my own actions. I speak, as honestly and descriptively as I can, about a high or low point in my life as an educator and then invite participants to give me their best insights about the uncritically accepted assumptions they see informing my choice of that particular event as good or bad, and about the assumptions they see embedded in the specific actions I describe. Very frequently I discover a dark side to the 'high' events I choose as learners make interpretations and detect assumptions which cast my conduct in much murkier light than I would wish. Since making this key change in my practice, I have often had people come up to me and tell me that seeing me first take the risk of inviting critical analysis of my own hidden, taken-for-granted assumptions encouraged them to be more honest in their subsequent small group exercises than would normally have been the case.

In an interesting commentary on the reluctance of adult educators to see their practice as teacher-centred as well as learner-centred, Collins (1991) argues that 'it is more efficacious to think in terms of engaging thoughtfully with theory and, then, putting ourselves into practice rather than putting theory into practice' (p. 47). This is a nice turn of phrase which is full of rich implications for the development of educators. It means that we must take seriously the consequences that our own actions have within a group and that we should stop pretending that how we behave has no symbolic or political significance. As someone who is asked quite frequently to advise on faculty development and in-service education, I believe that the best use of often limited time is for teachers to find ways of studying how their actions are perceived by learners. Realizing how crucial it is for me as a learner to trust an educator's basic credibility and authenticity – in particular, for me to feel that the actions and words are consistent – has made me much more attuned to making sure that I don't espouse one way of working and then behave in a way which contradicts my avowed beliefs. Better to make no promises at all than to commit to some way of working and then fail to follow through. I am now painfully aware that the extent to which I model the application of critical analysis to my own beliefs and actions is sometimes directly connected to learners' willingness to behave in the same way.

Scrutinizing our biographies: Critical checks on generalizing from experience

The kinds of subjective, idiosyncratic experiences outlined in this chapter cannot, of course, be considered as the only basis for developing a practical theory of teaching. Indeed, there are very real dangers in relying on one's autobiography as a guide to action. So much of our experience is irredeemably context-bound; what are thought to be well-grounded insights culled from reflective analysis of experiences in one context can be rendered wholly invalid in another context. As Usher and Bryant (1989) point out in their analysis of the processes of practical theory development, experience without critical analysis can be little more than anecdotal reminiscence; interesting, but unconnected, experiential travellers' tales from the front lines of practice. Simon (1988: 3) also recognizes the conservatism inherent in much rhetoric on experiential learning and asks 'how can one avoid simply celebrating personal experience and confirming that which people already know?' If experiences like the ones I have described are going to have a serious, continuing influence on practice, they need to be submitted to two different forms of critical review.

First, formal theory has an important contribution to make in helping to convert situationally specific, informal hunches into well-framed theories of practice. Collins (1991: 51), for example, writes that 'serious commitment to adult education as vocation implies that its practitioners as intellectuals should be prepared to read and engage with theoretical texts as they begin to theorize their own practice' and argues that 'serious engagement with theoretical models improves our potential as reflective practitioners, which in turn manifests itself in actual performance' (p. 47). To Usher (1989), formal theory serves as 'a kind of resource and "sounding board" for the development and refinement of informal theory – a way of bringing critical analysis to bear on the latter' (p. 88). In the process of practical theory development, the inductively derived, situational insights regarding practice which are embedded in particular contexts and experiences can be reviewed through the more universalistic lens provided by formal theoretical perspectives. Hence, it is important that these formal perspectives be developed as carefully as possible.

Secondly, assumptions derived from experience that frame practice can be submitted to a form of collaborative scrutiny; that is to say, educators working in similar and allied contexts can compare their hunches, instincts and intuitions. In this way, educators can gradually become more sophisticated at recognizing contextual cues – events and features that signal those times when certain assumptions should be held in check and those times when they can confidently be used as provisional guidelines for action. In my own in-service and faculty development workshops with teachers, I have experimented with the critical incident technique as a means of helping them uncover the assumptions that undergird their habitual ways of acting and reasoning about their practice (Brookfield 1992). After assumptions have been identified through a process of small group analysis, I ask group members to pick out those assumptions on which there exists the greatest amount of agreement. When these assumptions have been identified, group members are asked to take each assumption in turn and to draw on their experiences to find three invalidating circumstances (the number is arbitrary); that is, to find three factors, events or variables that, if they existed, would make following these commonly held assumptions a risky prospect. For example, one common assumption that surfaces with teachers can be stated as follows: 'praising learners for work well done strengthens learners' desire to engage in further learning'. When teachers have examined their own experiences of giving praise, they have identified various invalidating circumstances that, if they are in place, would call this assumption into question. The three most frequently mentioned invalidating circumstances are:

1. When the praise is given so fulsomely that learners infer that they are so expert at the task or subject matter involved that there is no more learning that needs to be done.
2. When the method of giving praise is so laconic and understated (perhaps the praiser equates giving praise with not publicly tearing another's efforts to shreds) that it is not explicitly recognized by the learner as praise and therefore has no encouraging effect.
3. When there is something in the cultural background of the learners that makes the public receiving of praise an uncomfortable experience for them.

Through exercises such as those described, practitioners can serve as reflective mirrors for each other's informal theories, helping to focus attention on those parts which have the greatest validity across contexts, and on those parts which are unique to a specific setting.

References

Brookfield, S.D. (1987) *Developing Critical Thinkers.* San Francisco, CA: Jossey-Bass.
Brookfield, S.D. (1990a) *The Skillful Teacher.* San Francisco, CA: Jossey-Bass.
Brookfield, S.D. (1990b) Using critical incidents to analyse learners' assumptions. In Mezirow, J. and Associates, *Fostering Critical Reflection in Adulthood.* San Francisco, CA: Jossey-Bass.
Brookfield, S.D. (1992) Uncovering assumptions: The key to reflective practice. *Adult Learning,* 3(4): 13–14, 18.
Collins, M. (1991) *Adult Education as Vocation.* London: Routledge.
Freire, P. (1970) *Pedagogy of the Oppressed.* New York: Continuum.
Lindeman, E.C.L. (1987) The place of discussion in the learning process. In Brookfield, S.D. (ed.) *Learning Democracy: Eduard Lindeman on Adult Education and Social Change.* London: Routledge.
Livingstone, D.W. (ed.) (1987) *Critical Pedagogy and Cultural Power.* South Hadley, MA: Bergin and Garvey.
Mezirow, J. (1991) *Transformative Dimensions of Adult Learning.* San Francisco, CA: Jossey-Bass.
Mezirow, J. and Associates (1990) *Fostering Critical Reflection in Adulthood.* San Francisco, CA: Jossey-Bass.
Schön, D.A. (1983) *The Reflective Practitioner.* New York: Basic Books.
Schön, D.A. (1987) *Educating the Reflective Practitioner.* San Francisco, CA: Jossey-Bass.
Shor, I. (ed.) (1987) *Freire for the Classroom: A Sourcebook for Liberatory Teaching.* Portsmouth, NH: Boynton/Cook.
Shor, I. and Freire, P. (1987) *A Pedagogy for Liberation.* South Hadley, MA: Bergin and Garvey.
Simon, R. (1988) For a pedagogy of possibility. *Critical Pedagogy Networker,* 1(1): 1–4.
Usher, R.S. (1989) Locating adult education in the practical. In Bright, B. (ed.) *Theory and Practice in the Study of Adult Education: The Epistemological Debate,* pp. 65–93. London: Routledge.
Usher, R.S. and Bryant, I. (1989) *Adult Education as Theory, Practice and Research: The Captive Triangle.* London: Routledge.

2

Putting the Heart Back into Learning

Denis Postle

Learning from experience generates knowledge. Attending to the whole of experience appears to lead to the generation of realistic, useful and relevant knowledge directly supportive of human flourishing. So far as I edit, limit, deny or ignore areas of my experience, this appears to narrow what I learn from it. This restriction may aid my short-term survival, but at the cost of some detachment from reality. In this chapter, I begin by inviting you to look at the range of possibilities for learning from experience. I then go on to outline a model of how as adults we might not be able, or not wish, to attend to the whole of our experience. Finally, I outline some behavioural criteria that show how the heart can be put back into learning.

John Heron has put forward a scheme, 'multi-modal learning' (Heron 1990, 1991, 1992), about what may be going on in the human psyche when we are learning from experience. I find it very useful for helping to ensure that my learning from experience remains comprehensively carnal, zesty and fruitful. Heron points to the existence of four modes of learning from experience, each dependent on the other and arranged in what he calls an 'up hierarchy' (see Fig. 2.1). The first of the four modes, at the top of the pyramid, is a *practical* mode of learning from experience. This refers to 'learning through doing', expressed through the competent practice of skills. Adjacent to this lies a *conceptual* mode of learning from experience. This refers to the use of language in some form, whether spoken, mathematical or symbolic. It features learning 'about' a subject, making statements and propositions. It embraces analysis, logic, proof, argument and debate. A third, *imaginal* mode of learning, refers to learning through the use of imagination. It finds expression through envisioning and devising possible futures but, most fundamentally, through the intuitive grasp of sequences, processes and situations as a whole. A fourth, *affective* mode of learning, refers to learning by encounter, by direct experience. It finds expression through 'being there', through immersion in an experience.

Heron contends that the focus, range and relevance of the practical mode of learning, has its roots in the strength and clarity of the conceptual

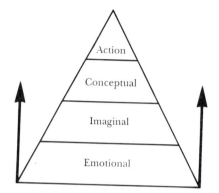

Figure 2.1   Multi-modal learning.

mode. These in turn are rooted in and nourished by the imaginal mode of learning, both in the sense of using the imagination, of being aware of its pervasive contribution to all our perceptions, and of seeing things as a whole. All three of these modes of learning grow out of and depend in turn for their nourishment on the affective mode, the capacity to learn at an emotional level.

The 'upward hierarchy' emphasizes that each succeeding layer relies on that below it. It also underlines the vital importance of the affective, emotional mode of learning. It forms the base, the foundation on which the others rest. Heron asserts that 'Valid knowledge – knowledge that is well grounded – depends upon its emergence out of openness to feeling'. In support of this, he quotes Langer (1967): 'the entire psychological field, including conception, responsible action, rationality and knowledge is a vast and branching development of feeling'. Elsewhere he points out that 'It is not a matter of control and rulership of the higher by the lower, but of the higher branching and flowering out of the lower' (Heron 1990).

I like this scheme; it clarifies some of the sequencing of how I learned how to learn. Life at home always had a strong vein of practicality. Later, an art school education added a broad layer of the imaginal. This was followed by a struggle in my thirties to contradict my grammar school experience and build a capacity for conceptual learning. And much later, through a sequence of life crises, I discovered how restricted affective learning shaped all these capacities.

Clients in psychotherapy and counselling, students in facilitation training and group work training provide most of my work these days. In all of it identifying and remedying under- and over-functioning in these four modes of learning from experience form a common thread. I use the perspective of Heron's multi-modal learning model explicitly, often putting it forward for clients, students and group participants as a map of the territory we are exploring together.

What stops free and equal access to all four modes? I see two main reasons why access to one or more of the four modes of learning from experience is often restricted, or even absent while others are over-worked. The first is that a key element of our white, western, mindset is the over-valuation of the practical and conceptual modes of learning:

> ... there is no place in the curriculum for the cultivation of emotional and interpersonal competence, of decision-making (including political competence). It is assumed that if the student becomes intellectually proficient through the formal curriculum, they will learn privately to introduce rational control into the management of their feelings and conduct. If they fail to do this to a degree that is socially incapacitating, the concept of mental disorder or illness is invoked and the psychiatrist or psychotherapist is called in.
>
> (Heron 1982)

This idealization of intellect and action often seems to be in the very 'grain' of us as persons and because of this I have certainly been in danger of seeing it as given, as part of nature.

But no longer. The spell has been broken. The Cartesian, western intellectual tradition of the last 500 years has been exposed (Griffin 1978; Daly 1979; Easlea 1983; Abram 1988) as a collusive conspiracy. Defending and sustaining patriarchal power and dominance comes higher on its agenda than deepening learning and scholarship. At the very heart of the conspiracy and driving it, the technocracy of intellect keeps in place the fiction that as a healthy, 'normal' person, I should attend to the emotional content of my experience only so as to keep me feeling comfortable.

Emotion and feeling then become associated with 'weakness', 'loss of control' and 'neurosis'.

> "Do you cry often?" is a question designed to measure neurosis on many psychological tests. Most people do not cry often. The norm is therefore "no". But suppose one discovers, as we have, that normal people do have easy access to their tears, and it is the culture that has established a behaviour of holding back which is, in reality, not normal.
>
> (Janov 1990)

I believe that this cultural bias in favour of the supremacy of intellect, coupled with the idealization of practicality, too often acts to lock out from the generation of knowledge, the riches of the universe of feeling.

Secondly, as I see it, we often cling, with the intensity of addiction, to the comfort that comes from staying with our preferred mode and keeping away from the other modes. I remain convinced that this is usually because at some point in our history, one or another – or all – of the four modes

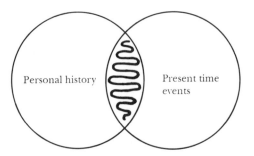

Figure 2.2 Interaction of past and present.

of learning may have become debilitated or ruined. If this debilitation or damage was severe, either locally or generally, then staying with the preferred mode may also successfully defend us against the feelings associated with that early hurt. If so, then our interest in action, or dreaming up futures, or caring, or arguing, whichever most keeps quiet our painful history, can indeed come to have the intensity of addiction.

Either of these sources of bias can, and I believe often do, extinguish a big portion of our capacity to learn from experience. Taken together, they amount to a potentially disastrous distortion of the human potential for survival and flourishing both socially and personally. Taking steps to locally remedy, and so far as possible structurally correct, the imbalance in favour of the conceptual and practical modes of learning seems an obvious response.

For both the above reasons, installing affective learning as the foundation for the other learning modes, tends to meet with resistance. It's easy to see why. Government, industry, business, the professions and not least education cling to the pre-eminence of intellect and action. They unawarely equate feeling and emotion with weakness and irrationality and try to exclude them from decision making. Similarly, individuals seeking comfort and ease who buy into this mindset, which is most of us at some time, understandably come to associate feeling and emotion with a Pandora's Box of threat, danger, 'mental illness' and the Unknown.

To meet this resistance and do business with it, I have found it useful to have a model that can show how, for individuals, the use of the learning modes that Heron has described may become distorted, stalled or ruined. My scheme (see Fig. 2.2 and below) draws attention to the contribution that personal history makes to the outcomes of my encounters with present time events and processes. It begins with the proposition that, wherever I am, whatever I am doing, however I am attempting to learn from experience – alongside the *existential*, present time elements of the experience – broken traffic lights, too much coffee, too little food, not enough sleep and so on, there lies an *archaic*, historical dimension too. In any situation, I encounter people and events bearing my personal history. I see it through the eyes, feel it through the skin, hear it through the ears, of my history.

This history includes early learning that supports my flourishing as an adult: 'It's your choice and either way you can count on my support . . .', i.e. realistic, reliable, relations with myself and others, qualities that together support good health and survival in home, street and work life. These very likely include learning from experience across all four modes. I have in mind practical skills such as driving, the ability to think things through, accuracy of perception and intuition, rapport and emotional bonding with partners, friends, relatives and colleagues. All this favourable learning probably has threaded through it veins of early learning that limit or undermine my flourishing as an adult: 'If you really loved your mummy you wouldn't do things that make me cry like this . . .'.

I find it useful to distinguish three different kinds or flavours of these. Each has an effect on how we learn from experience. First we have *omitted learning*. This refers to learning which could be expected to have taken place in childhood but didn't. Unearthing omitted learning can prove difficult. How do I look for what I don't have? What was omitted for me was love. As a young child I was always fed and clothed. There were no catastrophes, no divorces, no deaths. And there was little or no love either. Holes like this in our learning, particularly around core needs or commonsense skills or knowledge, can be as important for later behaviour as what we do learn. I have often struggled as an adult to contain a layer of hostility that I now recognize as the likely, even commonplace, adult outcome of omitted learning around how to love and be loved.

A second vein or layer of unfavourable early experience is *distorted learning*. Here we have learning in which those close to us when we are young feed us a distorted or inaccurate picture of reality, or of our ability to learn from it. Distorted learning arises from being told we are stupid, thick, clumsy, slow, 'the runt of the litter', hopeless, 'bad', brilliant, talented, lovely, pretty, etc., when this generalizes isolated incidents, or reflects what the speaker wants us to be, or is simply untrue. An example of distorted learning from my own life arose from the commonplace statement in the community of steelworkers in which I grew up, that 'you can't do what you like in this life, you have to do what you are told'. Distortions such as these usually serve someone else's needs rather than our own. I still have occasional tension around 'doing what I like and liking what I do'.

Thirdly, there is *distressed learning*. This refers to learning reinforced by distress, in the form of hurt or pain due to actual or imagined punishment. Examples of distressed learning include being beaten, smacked, humiliated, deprived of food or affection by someone who intends to enforce compliance with their demands. Distressed learning includes anything that puts the nervous system into overload, so that survival requires that the pain be shut off from consciousness (Janov 1990). Other sources of distressed learning include traumatic events such as birth, accidents or sexual abuse. My own distressed learning includes a forceps-delivery birth and starvation as a baby through not being able to feed. The distressed early learning of birth set up a deep and global expectation in me that 'life is a struggle'. The starvation distress still drives some weird food likes and dislikes but, more importantly, an expectation 'that I will not get from others what I need'.

Distorted, omitted and distressed learning have vast power. They can drive us on and out into the most bizarre forms of 'I have to' or 'I can't' behaviour. They compel us to devise and instal incredible institutions both of personal and social behaviour with the purpose of keeping us safely in our familiar 'comfort zone'. We then may go too often to the same parts of life's landscape and rarely or never to other districts. We may end up learning from experience in narrow, congested or overheated ways. Either way, our intelligence is denied access to much of reality. Such learning also leads to the accumulation of a lot of body memories in the form of distressing, painful or uncomfortable emotional material. These in turn are likely to drive equally distressing or uncomfortable imaginal output in the form of dreams, nightmares or paranoid fantasies. Thinking, argument, logic and language become biased towards 'either/or' logic, abusive labelling and the use of words as defence against feeling. Finally, all three contribute to compulsive or inhibited action poorly attuned to present time needs.

Taken together, this contributes to a substantial structural bias in how we learn from experience. Engaging fully in the imaginal and affective modes will, from time to time, almost inevitably take us into anxiety, pain and discomfort. This may be enough to push any of us into the practical and conceptual modes of learning from experience as a way of recovering our 'comfort zone'.

So does all this mean that our unworked distressed, distorted or omitted learning occupies the driver's seat in our lives, inflating our learning from experience in some ways and eliminating it in others? I would argue that if you don't know what, where or how your learning from experience is restricted by unfinished business in your personal history, then the answer is probably yes.

If you can accept the picture I have outlined of both a potential for multi-modal learning and the parallel likelihood that some or much of this capacity will be disabled, what would count as an intelligent and effective response to it? What would be a level of competency around emotion and feeling that would actively support our own and our clients' or students' or colleagues' ability to learn from experience. How might it be defined?

In answer to these questions, I want to offer a set of ten criteria, primarily for emotional competence, though they also reach into the imaginal mode too. I intend them to provide a guide to what being competent in the affective mode of learning would look, sound and feel like. The criteria that follow (Postle 1992) outline a strong version of emotional competence. Each of the criteria I identify may correspond to a range of ability depending on the training or experience we've had, and also time and circumstances. Everyone will be more competent at some times, and in some situations, than others. I have attempted to restrict the criteria to those that, if they are in place, will most enable the other three learning modes to flourish freely.

The criteria are not very sharply differentiated, they overlap here and there. Some might be considered more essential than others. The value of criteria such as these emerges most strongly when individuals breathe life into them, when they adopt them and make them their own. Nor are the criteria necessarily comprehensive. For example, 'congruence' between verbal and non-verbal behaviour might have been included, as might the capacity for taking responsibility for the consequences of our action/inaction.

Criteria for assessing emotional competence

1. *An emotionally competent person has ready access to their emotions and feelings.* This is another way of saying that I am in touch with what is going on in my body. It means, for example, that if I have to make a decision, or reach out to someone, or deny a request, what I feel in my body (my 'gut feeling') will be accessible to me and thus be a source of intelligence. By contributing relevance and value, access to feelings can improve the quality of my decisions and extend the range of my choices:

   . . . every emotion has a signal function. Not every emotion signals danger. But every emotion does signal the "me" I put into seeing "you". It signals the often unconscious perspective we apply when we go about seeing. Feeling signals that inner perspective.

   (Hochschild 1983)

2. *An emotionally competent person (a) can express feelings freely, where and when appropriate; (b) can hold on to feelings for later expression; and (c) can tolerate the expression of feelings, including distress, in other people.* This means a capacity for allowing myself to feel, without guilt or blame, delighted, joyful and zestful, or sad, angry, anxious or frightened, and where appropriate, to laugh, cry, or cry out, to resist physically, or complain angrily. It especially means a capacity for remaining intelligent from within whatever feelings or emotions are running. Secondly, it means being able to choose to hold on to any of these feelings if expressing them will be inappropriate, unhelpful or damaging. Lastly, it means that I can tolerate the expression of feelings, including distress in other people, without having to move in to try to rescue them or put a stop to their feelings.

3. *An emotionally competent person has discovered the main elements of their traumatic early experience and appreciates how they influence adult behaviour.* This means that I have adequately enquired into, discovered and explored the most formative items of my personal history. Also, that if I become aware of any manifestations of them in present time, I have an adequately developed capacity to choose to acknowledge, interrupt and deal with it.

4. *An emotionally competent person actively seeks to identify and own projection and displacement, transference and counter-transference.* This is a competence which overlaps with the imaginal mode of learning. A lot of early learning is likely to predispose us to see some people as 'Prince Charmings' and 'Fairy Godmothers' and others as poisonous or dangerous. So far as I have no competence to recognize, and own, these 'projections' onto others, or when they are taken into myself, 'introjections', I will have little idea of where I stop and other people begin and life may often become extremely complicated:

> When we find in another person, an institution or an object some echo of a part of ourselves that we lack, hate or refuse to accept, we escape the inner discomfort by attaching our disowned faults or qualities to them. We can then convince ourselves that they don't belong to us. If we feel bad we may believe that other people are bad; if we lack good feelings, we may think others are wonderful.
>
> (Postle 1989)

5. *An emotionally competent person will have an adequate appreciation of the contribution of oppression both covert and overt to feelings and emotions.* This means being aware of the personal in the political and vice versa. So that in supporting other people I take care to check out the extent to which any difficulties they are experiencing come not from their personal histories but from present-time oppression, i.e. sexist, racist, ageist attitudes, or actual or implied threats or violence. In other words, taking care not to ascribe the origins of all present-time feelings and emotions to personal history. Conversely, it implies taking care not to ascribe all difficult feelings to some political origin.

6. *An emotionally competent person can supportively confront unaware behaviour in others.* Supportive confrontation implies that when I draw your attention to some behaviour of which you appear unaware, while doing so I am able to maintain a loving, caring, supportive relationship with you as a person.

7. *An emotionally competent person can cathartically release strong emotions.* This means that I can, given the occasion and a safe environment, allow myself to fully connect with whatever strong emotion may be seeking to come into consciousness. 'Fully connect' here means catharsis, not 'abreaction' or 'acting out'. Catharsis is recognizable as a behavioural sequence where bodily arousal in sympathetic mode first increases to high levels, as this arousal peaks there is an abrupt collapse into parasympathetic mode, usually with crying or laughter.

7a. *An emotionally competent person can transmute tense emotion through choosing to make a shift in consciousness.* Transmutation of tense emotion refers to a process, complementary to catharsis, through which 'the distinctly agitated, hurting energy of the distress is changed and refined into the calming, peaceful energy of a positive emotional state' (Heron 1989).

It may involve revaluing my attitude to painful feelings so as to remember not to deprecate and cast out what I feel ashamed of in myself, but to see that my shadow side can also be an asset, a compost to be positively accepted as a nutritious source of growth. For example, realizing that the pain of working through a specially hurtful history of say, oppression, may eventually mean that I will be specially qualified to help others escape and survive similar oppression.

8. *An emotionally competent person takes responsibility for commitment to developing and sustaining their emotional competence.* This seems self-explanatory. I would like to see the task of developing and maintaining emotional competence recognized as a fundamental attribute of an educated person and also as a primary professional obligation. It might need to be supported by external resources such as in-service training, or by supervision arrangements, but should not be driven significantly by them.

9. *An emotionally competent person will have an adequate repertoire of skills for dealing with feelings and emotions arising from a need for cooperation or negotiation.* This seems an obvious requirement for anyone who works with people in groups or teams, but it has relevance also for people who work one to one. It implies a capacity for assertiveness and the absence of aggressive, submissive or manipulative communication, coupled with the abilities in criteria 1, 2 and 6.

10. *An emotionally competent person has a self-reflexive approach to monitoring the quality of their attention, relations with others and general health.* This means that they will always have a bit of their attention open to what their bodily environment or the world around them might be trying to tell them. Examples would include paying attention to dreams, accidents, coincidences, 'Freudian slips', sleep disturbance, lapses of attention, loss of appetite (or over-eating) as signals that merit attention. By self-reflexive, I mean that this monitoring does not significantly depend on input from other people, that is to say it's proactive, voluntary, my preference. I don't only do it because I have to.

These criteria form practical working rules of thumb for estimating whether someone, in learning from experience, has adequate and competent access to the emotional and, to an extent, the imaginal modes of learning from experience. Try them for yourself. How do they sit with you?

Developing the 'strong' version of this competence involves commitment over several years at both a group and individual level. However, development of a 'weak' version, with some competencies in place and others beginning to move from awareness to practice doesn't take long, and (Postle 1989) can beneficially transform relationships and cooperation in groups. Let's take an example from life. It gives a glimpse of how, through helping keep open all four modes of learning from experience, being emotionally competent might affect the outcome of a challenging life situation.

Alice discovers that her partner Roland has started a relationship with another woman. He says he wishes to continue with it yet insists that he remains fully committed to Alice. Even though they have many interlocking family and work commitments, Roland believes that they can still have a future together combining the old and new relationships. Alice still loves Roland but finds his proposition of a three-way relationship lacking in credibility. It doesn't seem practical to her.

Emotionally, Alice feels very upset indeed by the news of the affair. She feels devalued. She feels that the new relationship defiles their previously delightful and flourishing life together. As she struggles to decide how to respond to Roland's proposal, she becomes very agitated. Initially, she stays away from work because she feels constantly on the edge of tears.

Alice has an intensive need to learn from experience across all four modes of learning. Luckily she has a considerable level of emotional competence. Let's see how it helps her. At the practical level she has a need for action. How can she continue to relate to Roland? Does she sleep with him or make love with him? Does she seek support or advice? How can she test Roland's assertions about the future? How well can she listen to him?

The multi-modal learning model suggests that the strength and realism of Alice's actions will greatly depend on the words that she uses to describe her rights and needs, to argue her case and to set the boundaries on what she will and will not tolerate. Similarly, the quality and effectiveness of the action she takes depends on the conceptual maps she can draw on to make sense of what is happening, to gain perspective and to have some sense of what might be the consequences of her actions.

The words she uses in turn depend on what her imagination throws up and how she manages it. A shower of imaginings around her partner and his lover seem probable. What are they doing and when? And how often? And why does he prefer this other woman? Also, at least to begin with, a twenty-four hour parade of 'what will happen if?' scenarios seems inevitable. In the absence of information, her imagination will rush in to fill out the picture.

To summarize so far, the practical decisions that Alice may need to reach rest on the words and arguments she uses to frame them. Both of these rest on the images which her imagination cannot help but provide and, at an even more fundamental level, these in turn grow out of the emotions evoked by her situation.

It's no surprise that Alice will find herself fully engaged with the affective mode of learning. A rich mix of feeling and emotion seem inevitable. Betrayal, jealousy, grief due to the loss of love; anger because she's been deprived of choice; fear of what will happen now; and just plain agonizing hurt. Also, she's sleeping poorly, and finds great difficulty in concentrating.

Now if we look, albeit briefly, at Alice's situation in the light of the emotional competence criteria what can we see? How does being emotionally competent help her? As an emotionally competent woman, Alice will be able (criteria 1) to express her feelings through crying and angry storming, and may learn from their intensity how much value she places on the relationship and what priorities she has for resolving the crisis. Similarly if, from time to time (criteria 2), Alice can hold on to her feelings and tolerate anger and exasperation from her partner and not dump them on him or act them out in damage or punishment, the chances increase of hearing what her partner says and digesting it intelligently. When she does manage this, she immediately notices that some of his criticism of her and his irritability sound like guilt in disguise.

Alice had a hugely catastrophic early reaction to the crisis. She felt completely devastated. Later, she realized (criteria 3) that Roland's actions echoed some aspect of her early traumatic experience. When she could separate the archaic reaction from the present stimulus, and see how much she clung to his coat-tails, how she uncritically bought into his reality, she felt shocked to see how much she had contributed to Roland's move away to another woman. Parallel with this, Alice is active (criteria 4) in checking out, as far as she can, the extent to which her projections and fantasies match the facts of the crisis.

Roland has imposed oppressive, peremptory, unilateral decision-making on Alice. A good sense (criteria 5) of how much this contributes to feeling and emotion can become an essential ingredient in resolving a crisis such as this. How much of Alice's hurt and pain is existential distress due to Roland's abuse of her trust? How much does she bring to it from her history? Alice will (criteria 6) unavoidably need to confront Roland about the hurt and agony he has precipitated. If while doing this she can maintain a clear, direct and assertive communication, she has a better chance of standing up for herself and negotiating a satisfactory outcome for herself.

The hurt incurred by a loss of love on this scale can be enormous. Because Alice knows (criteria 7) how to release cathartically this distress from time to time, she gradually emerges from feeling inundated by the weight of emotion. Because she can allow, trust and even encourage the catharsis, she begins to discover some pearls of insight on the other side of the tears and anger.

Holding on to much of the above, while in a maelstrom of hurt and upset, requires (criteria 8) that Alice's capacity for self-direction holds steady enough to enable her to reach out to seek help and support and keep perspective. As it happened, Alice had some journal-keeping skills, and she also sought out some counselling too. Her self-directing capacity also enabled her to see that she could come out of the crisis strengthened rather than wrecked.

For obvious reasons (criteria 9), Alice's repertoire of skills for dealing with the feelings that arise over tense or distressing negotiations prove essential in asserting and defending her rights and needs. Lastly, but most essentially, Alice keeps track (criteria 10) of her health and attention and vigilantly checks for untoward body signals or ailments that might indicate that the limits of her coping had been reached and that she needed to take action to avoid becoming ill.

An impossible ideal? I believe not. Alice is not an idealized heroine, she exists. These criteria for emotional competence and the multi-modal learning model form a substantial part of the core learning objectives in the two-year Diploma in Humanistic Psychology courses that I co-facilitate with my partner Jill Anderson at the University of Surrey. They feature implicitly in all of the thirty similar courses validated by the Institute for the Development of Human Potential, London (Postle 1990), that have been held in the UK over the last twelve years.

I intend these criteria for emotional competence as a support for the generation of knowledge that is useful, empowering, accessible and relevant, i.e. based awarely on the inclusion of feeling and imagination in all learning from experience. Acquiring emotional competence does not require an MA, a PhD or even a first degree. A diligent utilization of co-counselling (Heron 1979; Rowan & Dryden 1990), for example, is enough to instal most of these competencies at a viable level.

A final word on assessing emotional competence. As educational theory and provision evolves, one of the emerging tendencies looks like a trend towards devising sets of sub-categories of competencies or modules that can be individually tested and later pasted together to make a 'qualification'. I cannot stress too strongly that the foregoing emotional competence criteria lie outside this trend. On the page they may look like an isolated set of 'measurable' skills. The missing context, both in terms of meeting the criteria and developing the competence in the first place, features both a strong self-directed commitment to learning from experience and a professional or personal need to learn in this way. Alongside this must run continuous self and peer assessment and, if necessary, self and peer accreditation.

In the long run, a key criterion that could be held to override all of the others is, 'Do I know when I am, or am not fulfilling the criteria for emotional competence?' 'Am I comprehensively emotionally competent?' may be a less relevant question than 'Am I aware of the circumstances and situations in which my emotional competence is limited or absent?' If my answer to the second question is 'don't know', can I really count myself as an educated person?

Acknowledgements

In putting this piece together, I am indebted first to John Heron for continued support both on this topic and elsewhere; to Jill Anderson for dialogue, testing and review of these ideas and practices; and to all the learning communities which have so boldly taken risks with themselves, these ideas and me.

References

Abram, D. (1988) *In Gaia: The Thesis, the Mechanisms and the Implications.* Wadebridge: Wadebridge Ecological Centre.

Daly, M. (1979) *Gyn/Ecology.* London: Women's Press.

Easlea, B. (1983) *Fathering the Unthinkable.* London: Pluto Press.

Griffin, S. (1978) *Woman and Nature.* New York: Harper and Row.

Heron, J. (1979) *Co-counselling.* Guildford: Human Potential Resource Group, University of Surrey.

Heron, J. (1982) *Education of the Affect.* London: British Postgraduate Medical Federation University of London.

Heron, J. (1989) *The Facilitator's Handbook.* London: Kogan Page.

Heron, J. (1990) *Helping the Client.* London: Sage.

Heron, J. (1991) *Multi-modal Learning.* Unpublished lecture notes.

Heron, J. (1992) *Feeling and Personhood: Psychology in Another Key.* London: Sage.

Hochschild, A.R. (1983) *The Managed Heart: Commercialisation of Human Feeling.* Berkeley, CA: University of California Press.

Janov, A. (1990) *The New Primal Scream.* Wilmington: Enterprise Publishing.

Langer, K. (1967) *Mind: An Essay on Human Feeling.* Baltimore, MD: Johns Hopkins University Press.

Postle, D. (1989a) *Synergy: Creativity in Interpersonal Relations.* London: Wentworth Institute.

Postle, D. (1989b) *The Mind Gymnasium.* London: Macmillan.

Postle, D. (1991) What is the Institute for the Development of Human Potential? *Self and Society, European Journal of Humanistic Psychology,* XVIX(4): 14–16.

Postle, D. (1992) *Emotional Competence: A Luxury or a Professional Obligation?* London: Wentworth Institute.

Rowan, J. and Dryden, W. (1990) *Innovative Therapy in Britain.* Milton Keynes: Open University Press.

3

Activating Internal Processes in Experiential Learning

John Mulligan

In this chapter, I will try to give the reader some sense of my personal learning journey which led to the development of a model of internal processes or skills that can be used to improve the way people learn from experience. I will first give a rationale and overview of the model, then give some personal background to the formation of the model and later expand on the categories which comprise the model.

The model offers a way of categorizing internal actions, required to learn effectively from experience. Each category can then be subdivided into separate processes or skills. The assumption and rationale for the model is that different kinds of learning tasks require different types and sequences of learning process. As processes, they are often undifferentiated or under-developed in the immature learner. Helping learners to discriminate between the different processes will make them more accessible to intentional use and easier to communicate to learners who may not have such processes in their repertoire or be aware of their benefits and purpose. By placing greater emphasis on teaching such learning processes, rather than content, we could enable learners to become more autonomous and perhaps improve their intelligence also.

The seven categories – reasoning, feeling, sensing, intuiting, remembering, imagining and willing – are presented in their dynamic form to emphasize their existence as processes and are further expanded later in the chapter. The categories are presented as a model to highlight their inter-relatedness. Reasoning requires a rational, objective framework and feeling requires a subjective, emotion-based response and are therefore set as polar opposites in the model. Likewise, sensing and intuiting are a polarity in their manner of functioning, the former gathering information by way of the overt and empirical, the latter by way of the undercurrent and covert. Both imagining and remembering depend on sensing, intuiting, reasoning and feeling to function effectively, but are placed opposite each other to reflect their temporal orientations towards what has been and what has yet to come into being. Willing is necessary to organize the functioning of the

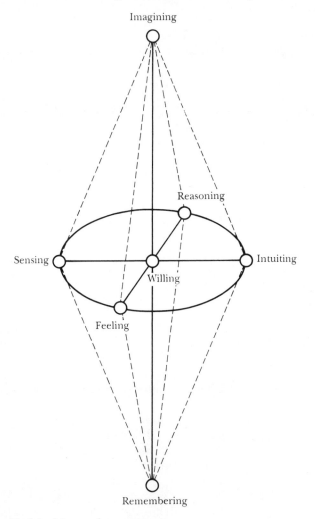

Figure 3.1 Model of internal processes.

other six towards specific learning tasks, which is why it has a central position in the model.

Personal reflections

The personal development journey which has informed the model in its present form has been slow and meandering, and though easy to trace in retrospect it was not intentional. It is a difficult journey to portray meaningfully, so I have selected some personally significant experiences which I hope will give the flavour of the journey and have included references to the work of others used to elaborate the model. A great variety of influences contributed to my appreciation of the need for and significance of my discoveries, though not all of them were experiential or my own and only some are described here.

I find some reassurance for the task in Polanyi's (1966) words 'We know more than we can tell', so I will begin with a description of some of my early background and experiences and hope they will show the beginnings of what was later to become the model of internal processes. The model continues to develop and I welcome comment and suggestions.

Insights and experiences from childhood

I was brought up in a family that lived on a small farm, though both my parents also worked in nursing and welfare. Little attention was paid to our inner world. Even less guidance was provided about what went on there and how I should conduct affairs in this territory. Life for me was lived in terms of events in the external world of empirical realities, on the farm, in school and in church. Value, as I remember it, was placed on what you knew about the world and what you could or did do. I assumed that what was inside related to what was outside and therefore for the most part people knew what was in there, though admittedly there were certain details that one was expected to declare to the priest in the confessional if those in authority did not get it out of you first. As a result, I grew up with a minimal sense of differentiation between inner and outer worlds and a moral 'downer' on what was inside, since it was usually the place where I concealed lies and the knowledge that I really did not know things which I pretended to know as a way of making up for my perceived shortcomings.

This undervaluing of my inner world was compounded by my being often told from an early age that I had a great *imagination*. For example, I once told neighbours that a cock had laid an egg and persisted in my assertion of its truth despite gales of laughter from my listeners, two farming women. Imagination became synonymous with lies and untruth and was to be avoided as morally suspect. However, like all healthy children, I continued to play with my toy soldiers in the sand pit and played cowboys and indians with other children – all out there in the external world and 'only' play. Nevertheless, play often seemed to come to an abrupt and embarrassed halt under the detached gaze of the adult onlooker. The world of imagination often collapsed in confrontation with the 'real world' and play never did seem to carry the same adult and parental approval or interest as work. I became an excellent worker and learned to tell the truth.

Later in childhood and into my teens, this lack of an inner world troubled me in many ways. For example, mathematics for me became a frightening and often meaningless quagmire of formulae and applied sequences of computation. I had little appreciation of what they represented and I was often dumbfounded and mentally paralysed when confronted by the exasperated exhortations of my teachers to 'think, man think!' in response to supposedly obvious errors. Unaware of what 'thinking' (or *reasoning* as I label it above) entailed, I became an excellent guesser not knowing what other magical act was being demanded of me. But alas my guesses were too often off the mark leaving me with the belief that I had a Winnie-the-Pooh brain.

In my teens, imagination for me took the form of boasting, another unhappy habit to which I was prone and which often got me in trouble with my peers, especially when I failed to live up to my claims. In retrospect, I now understand that the hoped for acclaim and appreciation which I desired and which motivated such boasting did not always materialize. But in one case it did and this was to bring about a remarkable change in my self-esteem and greatly reduced my compulsion for boasting.

Towards the end of my first year in secondary school, I saw another boy from my year doing a pole-vault jump at about seven and a half feet. I must have been in need of some ego boosting on that day and true to my usual self-help methods I proceeded to be critical of the boy's performance, saying that it was not very good and that I could do much better. I was challenged to do it by my mocking peers. I duly tried but while coming very close I was unable to equal the other boy's achievement. I felt sorely stung by the ridicule which followed, especially since I had almost achieved what I had said I would. I quietly resolved to prove myself right, I would show them what I could do and felt such desire and strength of *will* to relieve my hurt feelings and gain their respect that in the following year I far outstripped my fellow pole-vaulters and gained the admiration of not only my peers but of my superiors. I did not have a reputation for concentration or strong willpower, so this achievement was all the more significant for me and is one of my earliest memories of the connection between wish, motivation and willpower, though I did not appreciate the connection at the time.

Not only did I experience delight in my achievement and willpower – I did it and nobody else – but I had in the process spontaneously begun to practise my pole-vaulting in my imagination, often getting myself into a lather of sweat in the process before going to sleep at night or upon waking in the morning. I kept very quiet about this *sensing* that I might receive yet further reward for having a 'great imagination'. However, by using this method, I was able to coach myself and correct many of the faults standing in the way of improved performance. Little did I know at the time that I was becoming quite skilled at what was later to become known to me as kinaesthetic *imagining*, a powerful learning tool currently used to accelerate learning.

Regrettably, my superior performance on the athletics track was not matched by similar achievements in the classroom and the examination hall. Looking back with my years of teaching experience, it was my relatively undeveloped *memory* skills which accounted for much of my poor performance rather than my Pooh-sized brain. If I'm honest, not much of what I was learning appealed a great deal to my brain in any case, so it is not surprising that it did not retain it very well. Or, when it did, as a result of that force-feeding technique appropriately called cramming, it relieved itself shortly afterwards in disinterested forgetfulness. Clearly, my teachers had little appreciation of the interdependence of will, emotion and memory. Nor did it occur to me at the time that I did not remember things because I had little interest in them. The obvious explanation which seemed to be reinforced by my teachers and examiners at the time was that I simply was not endowed with a superfluity of intelligence by whoever dealt out those particular cards. Begrudgingly, I was forced to accept this view, though I never totally believed it was true as is evidenced by the fact that I now work as a university educator and am writing about learning.

I had other talents though which received little recognition within the school curriculum. I seemed to have an uncanny ability to 'read people's minds' so to speak. I was tuned in to what people wanted, often recognizing it before they had articulated it themselves. I got appreciation from adults as a helpful boy, but this same ability to sense what was going on in people could also be used hurtfully and spitefully and often resulted, together with some of my other less charming attributes, in my being excluded from childhood gangs. A cousin later told me that they used to have kangaroo courts in the gang to find out who was telling me of their plans, I had such an ability to anticipate what they were going to do or where they were going to go. That basic ability, under the now more credible title of *intuiting*, still serves me well today when I facilitate groups of experiential learners and in my role as counsellor, though I hope my use of it is more subtle and constructive.

Another asset, though one which in my teens I came to regard as a liability, was my *feeling* nature. I wore my heart on my sleeve and remember clearly my tearful disappointment when I failed to win the All-Ireland Junior Pole-vault Championship at 13 years of age. I also felt ashamed in front of my peers as 'big boys don't cry'. It was one of the last times I was to cry for very many years. It was also one of the last times that I allowed myself to want or long for something so much. After that, life became somewhat more provisional. I stopped reaching for the stars, gradually demanded or expected less of life and myself, I could not bear the disappointment of not getting it. Better to give up wishing so hard or committing oneself so deeply, better not put all one's eggs in one basket! This inability to handle the emotional impact of my experiences often lead to poor life and relationship choices, to not going after what I really wanted and often therefore to limited levels of satisfaction with what I did choose.

Having my feelings so close to the surface also meant that they got hurt easily, and in my early teens I often responded the only way I knew how – with my fists – which meant finding myself in many fights, not one of my strong points either since it was more often guided by seething emotion than good fighting strategy or technique. I began to suppress and lose touch with my emotions, a process I later had painfully to reverse.

I was very observant (*sensing*) and could pick up practical skills very quickly, often after seeing something just once or even on television. My pole-vaulting experience was evidence of this ability, as were the many practical skills which I learned on the farm, though there was little outlet for these skills in the classroom. I seemed to be good at paying attention to details when interested, and successfully stripped and rebuilt my motorcycle in my late teens, when it needed a new big end, without having done anything like that previously. My brother suggested that I would make a successful career as a mechanic but, while I had an interest in what went on under the bonnet of a car, I found people much more interesting. A great deal of my time since then has been occupied in one way or another in the observation and understanding of what goes on under my own and other people's bonnets.

Within these experiences, the reader may recognize the seven processes outlined in the model below, albeit in a crude or primitive form. These experiences also give some insight into my motivation for wanting to de-mystify intelligence and to extend the normally accepted understanding of the concept, thus making it more accessible to many who are excluded from the club from an early age and with such dire consequences. My later teaching efforts have been focused on the potential of such people and I have grown alongside them in insight, both into my own and their difficul-ties in learning and living. It was through my acknowledged success as well as encountering my own limitations in helping socially deprived young people in my twenties that I began to consciously explore what was 'wrong with them'. Little did I know that it would take me into an exploration of what was wrong with me and what was happening in my internal world.

A growing space between worlds

Since the focus of the chapter is on internal processes, I will briefly mention the need for a concept of reality which includes an internal world to be experienced as well as an external world. It seems to me to be important not to reduce our inner world of experience to a mere processing unit for experience of the external world lest we discount untold riches and personal potential therein. No such reduction is implied here, although the inten-tion is to focus on internal processes as different categories of functioning which can be utilized to transform events into learning and store it. My more recent experience over the past ten years or so gives some idea of the evolution of the model in my own thinking and the emergence of my consciousness of my own inner world. Such consciousness now seems cru-cial to its emergence.

It may seem surprising to many that I did not begin to entertain the concept of an inner world until I was in my late twenties. Despite having engaged in fantasy play, progressed through tertiary education which made considerable intellectual demands, and being a teacher of emotionally and socially deprived children, I had not even begun to consciously formulate maps or models of my own or others' internal worlds as ways of processing information, much less as a world to be experienced in itself. It was as if inner and outer worlds were fused together in a symbiotic union which defied reflection on itself.

Separation of the two was gained painfully through the increasing tension which arose between what I was and what the world appeared to demand of me. It was as if a space began to emerge created by these two different forces drawing farther apart. As this space between the worlds slowly began to grow, I gained a greater perspective on what was on either side of it, past and future, inner and outer. In my life up to that time, there seemed to be little space for my imagination and reflection to operate independently of my emotions and instincts or of my actions in the external world. The emergence of this in-between world has been of enormous value to me. I experience it as a place where I neither am nor am not, a place of becoming, of potential, a place of freedom from which I can witness in a detached way, look backwards or forwards, observe inwards or outwards and make choices.

As the separation of inner and outer worlds progressed, the separation of different internal processes from one another also started to occur. First was the ungluing of my thoughts and feelings which began to happen when I began co-counselling (Heron 1979). This is a personal development method which involves regressing to earlier periods of one's life through memory techniques, re-experiencing and releasing blocked emotion, and allowing insight to emerge in the quiet aftermath of the release. Following this re-evaluation of life decisions, beliefs or scripts associated with the original event in terms of their impact on one's current life can occur. Many repetitions of this process helped me appreciate the way in which earlier events and experiences had formed my belief systems and the concepts and attitudes with which I approached my world. It demonstrated for me the way in which clogged-up emotions limited insight and distorted my thinking and ability to relate. It showed me new ways to help me remember, to feel emotions and how to distil the beliefs or scripts which had been until then inextricably entangled together. Most of all, it showed me that things could change, the god-given and the lurking Winnie-the-Pooh self-concept which resulted from them were no longer god-given, I could take charge of my own life! This was indeed liberation, and all apparently from a few simple techniques.

Gestalt growth groups provided a wonderful opportunity to develop my capacities for sensory and intuitive awareness, particularly sensory. Many of the exercises were directed towards various areas from which we draw our awareness – internally from our bodies, mentally from our memories and imagination, or externally from our environment. Through these exercises, I developed abilities to use attention intentionally, focusing, concentrating, indwelling, selecting, avoiding and so on. Through the use of these skills of attention, I learned to discriminate between the many subtleties of feeling, attitude, assumption, interpretation, projection and observation, in short how to unpack my experience and sharpen my perception by what at the time felt like quantum leaps.

The memory techniques I encountered through co-counselling reversed my usual practice of drawing the past into the present and instead had me return to and re-experience the past. I was no longer the distant onlooker but an active participant in my past experience. These techniques were in stark contrast to my teacher training, where not even the memory techniques which Buzan (1984) was popularizing, such as the use of association, humour, rhyme, location and so on, were taught. But useful as they were, Buzan's techniques seemed instrumental, dry and unattractive and little of them were utilized by students or teachers. Perhaps this was not surprising given the content focus of most curricula in mainstream education. However, the demands of experiential learning in the facilitator training courses which I attended in the early 1980s highlighted the need for a broader range of memory skills than those required for text or content-based education. Memory techniques such as those described in co-counselling and others used by various therapies strengthened and vitalized my remembering.

I was unable to remember a great deal of my childhood. Besides those sources mentioned above, Neuro Linguistic Programming (NLP), a therapeutic and learning system developed by Bandler and Grinder (1979), enabled me to make a major advance in my own ability to remember through the use of representational modes and accessing systems. For example, when I was asked to remember something that I had learned I would invariably access verbal or auditory memory and often come up with a blank. NLP helped me realize that there were other storage systems besides auditory and that in fact my strongest and most accessible mode was kinaesthetic. Also, by using the visual accessing method, I could remember pre-verbal childhood memories which are more difficult to access through my auditory verbal mode because language is undeveloped at that time of life. These insights and techniques have also proved invaluable in helping learners with process review and other memory problems.

Many similar stories relate to other categories. Neuro Linguistic Programming and transpersonal psychology continue to be a very rich resource of concepts and processes for developing and using will and imagination in learning. Despite considerable work with images over the past ten years or so, I feel that I am only beginning to appreciate fully the possibilities which internal image work opens up in terms of learning and change and in particular of that 'inner world to be experienced' which I mentioned earlier.

More important for the reader who may be interested in using the model in their teaching, however, is the implicit message here about the need to develop one's own repertoire and ability to use these processes. While I was aware of the value of imaging in learning (Bruner 1966), it was not until I had time to develop my own capacity to use images that I mustered the commitment to integrate these processes into my practice as a learner. Only in this way did I expand their use in my educator role. This has also been true for my development within each of the categories and in order to acquire such competence I have often had to go outside the field of education.

A new synthesis

I have tried to give the reader a sense of what life and learning was like for me prior to having a concept of 'inner world', and also a sense of how my inner world and a range of processes which formed the early elements of the model evolved in my own consciousness. The model has since been developed and refined through my own experience and that of others and expanded using the work of various authors who have written about one or other of the categories (see, for example, Jung 1977; Myers-Briggs 1980; Kolb 1984).

The model poses a challenge to educators to demystify intelligence and the range of learning processes which give rise to it. It offers educators and learners alike a way of abstracting and labelling the internal processes or skills which are often implicit in the way different subject disciplines are taught, but which need to be made more explicit if they are to be more widely and intentionally used. In short, the model is a means of helping learners learn how to learn by making them aware of the great range of internal processes which can be used to bring it about.

Bringing these different processes together from their diverse sources and their identification as learning processes may be new, but the processes themselves are not. Further exploration of the interrelationship between these processes and extension of the range of options within each category is needed. A fuller delineation of the range of processes in each category is beyond the scope of this chapter, but a brief outline of the scope of each category and some further examples of the different processes within each is offered to help readers increase their understanding of the model.

Willing

Willing is perhaps the most important processor in that it is the one which integrates and harmonizes the use of all the others (Assagioli 1974). It is the means of self-direction, choice and commitment. It is through willing that our wishes are converted into reality (May 1972). When performing its proper function, willing governs both our attention and mediates our intention (Wood 1949). It enables the individual's centre of consciousness to deliberate what is a worthwhile or realistic learning goal by drawing on the contributions of the other functions. It is the function through which choice is mediated, decided and acted upon. It can be likened to the conductor of an orchestra and, like the conductor, willing can only perform its function if cooperation of the other players, i.e. the other internal processes and sub-personalities, is forthcoming (Assagioli 1975). It is not just the Victorian imposition of the will/discipline which is being advocated here, but a harmonious orchestration of all aspects of personality and internal processes, both conscious and unconscious.

Remembering

The memory of a computer is a useful analogy. Information has to be entered in a certain way using an access code which will later help retrieve the information. Fail on either requirement and one will be unable to find the information intentionally. Like many of our memories, recovery will probably be unpredictable and will diminish our learning capacity. Another, though less used analogy for the memory is that of a mountain with its humps and hollows, darkened caves and outstanding crags and peaks. The memory, no less, has its clarity and blanks, hidden recesses and readily accessible recordings.

Effective remembering is a far cry from the rote learning with which it has become associated; it requires the skill to input and search both the logical structures and mountain-like terrain of the memory (for further reading, see Baddeley 1976; Bandler and Grinder 1979; Houston 1982; Buzan 1984; Rose 1985).

Imagining

Imagining is related to our ability to create images; but not just visual images, for like the memory, imagination also uses sensory-based auditory, kinaesthetic, olfactory and gustatory images as well (Richardson 1969). Imagining enables us to transcend existing reality (Gawain 1978), to create images which reflect new perspectives, which may draw us forward into the future or even keep us locked in the past. Thus imagination is the art of the possible, the beginnings of our giving form to the possible, and to latent potential. If we can imagine something, we stand a greater chance of achieving it. Imagination can play a central role in learning but is underutilized (Houston 1982).

Acts of imagination can help generate possible choices as in brainstorming. They are the basis of pretending, which allows us to act 'as if', role play or rehearse behaviours which lead to the acquisition of skills and understanding. Perhaps more potent still is the relatively unexplored facility it provides for internal rehearsal (Gallwey 1982). The image also helps us to bridge the gap between our experience and conceptual theories and models (Bruner 1966; Salmon 1988), often by formulating analogies or metaphors which, though imprecise, embody the essence of the concepts we are trying to formulate, thus allowing us to play with it mentally to further refine them.

Sensing

Good sensory contact enables us to gather less distorted data about the externally observable world and become able to distinguish between such data and the products of our internal world (Stevens 1971). For example, being taught to 'see' in life drawing or sculpting training has the effect of successive layers of cataract being shed from one's eyes uncovering a vividness and detail one would never have thought possible. This detailed attention to observable data lies at the heart of the developed sensation function and we may be unaware that our sensory contact is limited (Houston 1979). Good contact requires training of the attention (an aspect of will), the clearing of the perceptual 'noise', clarifying of personal constructs, beliefs and expectations which so often result in us seeing what we expect or want to see rather than what is actually there. Being able to gather undistorted sensory data, or at least being aware of one's bias, is one of the cornerstones of learning and scientific knowledge.

Feeling

Feeling is one of the two major ways in which we make judgements about the world. It underlies our preferences and our values and emphasizes what is subjectively important to us. It is a judgement based on emotion and is therefore an extension of the pleasure/pain response. It tells us if our needs are being fulfilled or not. It is subjective in the sense that it is self-centred, referring to what I like or what I dislike. When working well, our emotions ebb and flow in response to internal and external events. They can warn us when we are in danger, impede us when we are anxious or get us ready to attack when we are under threat, and so have a very noticeable impact on learning, especially in group or social situations (Jersild 1955). Emotions also arise when our expectations are – or indeed, are not – met and therefore fine discrimination and judgement is required to know when to control, redirect, express or transmute the emotion being experienced (cf. Ellis and Grieger 1977; Heron 1983).

Reasoning

Reasoning is the second form of judgement function, perhaps more usually called thinking. De Bono (1988), for example, uses the word 'thinking' to apply to reasoning but also to imagination, intuition and emotion as well. In order to reason, we must call upon a range of theories, constructs, concepts and beliefs which may be used to understand and make sense of our experience. Reasoning at its best tends to be logical and objective in so far as it is based on abstract frameworks, theories or concepts rather than personal like or dislike. Our reasoning skills can help us refine our constructs and theories. These constructs and theories in turn enables us to describe, explain and predict phenomena and outcomes in the world, a much desired learning goal which enables us to transfer our learning from one situation to another (Kelly 1955; Bruner 1966; Hudson 1968; Piaget 1970). At the simplest level, such rational constructs help us categorize and order our experience; at worst they can become the basis of stereotyping and prejudice.

Intuiting

Like sensing, intuiting is also a perceptual function but is perhaps the least mapped and understood, though one which is beginning to attract considerable attention from managers and educators in particular (Ornstein 1977; Vaughan 1979; Goldberg 1983; Agor 1984). This function has been described as a way of direct knowing, not dependent on sensory data, which requires standing back from or de-focusing on the object or situation. It is often used to get a 'sense' of what is unstated, hidden, covert or undercurrent (Gendlin 1980). It is a 'seeing' in terms of wholes, often detecting underlying patterns, potential or possibility which is not, or has not yet become, accessible in terms of sensory data.

The developed intuitive function has the capacity to pick out the essence of a situation or what is most important in a communication. It can often identify what is missing or needed in a situation. Its language is usually that of image, symbol, metaphor or analogy and can be vague and somewhat imprecise in its articulation. Guesses, hunch and hypothesis are often reflections of the intuition at work and often point to the answers or indicate the direction in which the answer can be found. Unlike sensation, intuition requires a more passive, receptive stance.

Conclusion

Clearly, there may be other, perhaps even better, ways of categorizing such processes but had I, or more realistically, had my parents and teachers had some way of mapping and explaining such a concept and been able to make and communicate discriminations between different categories and sorts of internal action which were open to and often demanded of me, I believe that much of the suffering and self-doubt which I endured would have been unnecessary. More importantly, my ability to engage efficiently and fruitfully in the learning process would have been greatly enhanced. If my struggles to cope with life and learning are typical of many, and my experience in secondary and tertiary education assures me that it is, then this collective experience amounts to a massive waste of human effort and potential and needless personal suffering. The model of the seven internal processes which I propose could go a long way towards alleviating the problem.

References

Agor, W.H. (1984) *Intuitive Management.* New York: Prentice-Hall.
Assagioli, R. (1974) *The Act of Will.* Wellingborough: Turnstone Press.
Assagioli, R. (1975) *Psychosynthesis.* Wellingborough: Turnstone Press.
Baddeley, A. (1976) *The Psychology of Memory.* New York: Harper and Row.

Bandler, R. and Grinder, J. (1979) *Frogs into Princes*. Moab, Utah: Real People Press.

Bruner, J. (1966) *Towards a Theory of Instruction*. New York: W.W. Norton.

Buzan, T. (1984) *Your Perfect Memory*. New York: E.P. Dutton.

De Bono, E. (1988) *Six Thinking Hats*. Harmondsworth: Penguin.

Ellis, A. and Grieger, R. (1977) *Handbook of Rational-Emotive Therapy*. New York: Springer.

Gallwey, T. (1982) *The Inner Game of Tennis*. London: Bantam.

Gawain, S. (1978) *Creative Visualization*. New York: Berkley Books.

Gendlin, E. (1980) *Focusing*. New York: Bantam.

Goldberg, P. (1983) *The Intuitive Edge*. Los Angeles, CA: Jeremy Tarcher.

Heron, J. (1979) *Co-counselling*. Guildford: Human Potential Research Project, University of Surrey.

Heron, J. (1983) *Educating the Affect*. Guildford: Human Potential Research Group, University of Surrey.

Houston, J. (1979) *Listening to Your Body*. New York: Delta.

Houston, J. (1982) *The Possible Human*. Los Angeles, CA: Jeremy Tarcher.

Hudson, L. (1968) *Frames of Mind*. Harmondsworth: Penguin.

Jersild, A. (1955) *When Teachers Face Themselves*. New York: Teachers College Press.

Jung, C. (1977) Psychological types. In *Collected Works, Vol. 6. Bollingen Series XX*. Princeton, NJ: Princeton University Press.

Kelly, G. (1955) *The Psychology of Personal Constructs*, Vols 1 and 2. New York: W.W. Norton.

Kolb, D. (1984) *Experiential Learning*. Englewood Cliffs, NJ: Prentice Hall.

May, R. (1972) *Love and Will*. New York: Fontana.

Myers-Briggs, I. (1980) *Gifts Differing*. Palo Alto, CA: Consulting Psychologists Press.

Ornstein, R. (1977) *The Psychology of Consciousness*. New York: Harcourt Brace Jovanovich.

Piaget, J. (1970) *Genetic Epistemology*. New York: Columbia University Press.

Polanyi, M. (1966) *The Tacit Dimension*. New York: Doubleday.

Richardson, A. (1969) *Mental Imagery*. London: Routledge and Kegan Paul.

Rose, C. (1985) *Accelerated Learning*. Missenden, Bucks: Topaz.

Salmon, P. (1988) *Psychology for Teachers: An Alternative Approach*. London: Hutchinson Education.

Stevens, J.O. (1971) *Awareness*. Moab, Utah: Real People Press.

Vaughan, F.E. (1979) *Awakening Intuition*. New York: Anchor Books.

Wood, E. (1949) *Concentration*. Wheaton, IL: Theosophical Publishing.

4

On Becoming a Maker of Teachers: Journey Down a Long Hall of Mirrors

Lee Andresen

Revisiting life-experience and being part of all one has met

In my frequent consultings with academics who complain of difficulty 'getting through' to students, I have wondered whether their problem may have its roots in a kind of forgetting. One plausible interpretation of this failure *as teacher* may be that one forgets what it was like to be ignorant and one is now unwilling – unable? – to revisit the experience of not knowing those things at which one is now expert.

In my own failure to substantially influence their teaching, I suspect I may have been guilty of finding it inconceivable that anyone could (apparently) not understand the 'obvious': that in teaching one needs somehow to make that uncomfortable journey back to ignorance. These are all matters of concern to me as an academic staff developer. They are also the central themes of this chapter.

I currently teach graduate classes for university lecturers who want to improve their teaching. Several subjects begin with the students writing autobiographical reflections on being first a learner, then a teacher. It pleased me when after one course some students wrote illuminating – and unsolicited – remarks about the autobiographical process itself. About their astonishment and unexpected delight in revisiting formative life-experiences where they had either learned or taught. They told of having forgotten, or failed to attach value to, events crucial to their becoming the people they presently are; events whose meanings are keys to understanding the professionals they now are.

Anticipating later discussion of that graduate programme, two observations are pertinent now. First, the experience of designing and teaching that programme may have led me to plan to adopt the explicitly autobiographical style of this chapter. Secondly, its design and implementation probably have been strongly influenced by the personal reflections on life-experiences I now recount in it.

Autobiography remains, in much conventional academic discourse, a disputed, even a suspect, element. Its particularity, its (purportedly) unrepresentative and ungeneralizable nature as data, the temptation it offers for narcissistic indulgence or fantasy reconstructions, are all familiar pitfalls. Brookfield argues persuasively in its favour, however, claiming that 'aspects of generic processes are evident in single acts'; how 'the phenomenological truth of an insight does not depend on the number of people who report its occurrence'; how 'aspects of many teachers' experiences can be embedded in one teacher's actions'; and how 'One person's formulation of a problem, or exploration of a dilemma, may contain many points of connection to others' experiences' (Brookfield 1990: 39).

I certainly hope that out of what I have written the reader may learn something more than merely 'this is what happened to a particular teacher', but if I were to be totally honest I would admit at this point that the exercise seems more than mildly presumptuous. Faced with this risk, I take heart and proceed.

On language, metaphor and a debt to Donald Schön

I shall use the 'mirror' metaphor extensively. It came from Donald Schön's *Educating the Reflective Practitioner,* as did also the 'hall of mirrors'. Schön uses these mainly in analysing coaching within a reflective practicum (Schön 1990: 253). I use them differently, for processes that link one teacher, his work, and his reflections upon that work, over a lifetime. But I think I use the metaphor in a way Schön might recognize and understand. I hope so, because I owe him a considerable debt for providing it.

I call an event a 'mirror' to declare that a subject can recognize within it an image of some other event(s). Experiences that, phenomenologically, 'mirror' one another are connected in a particular way. Images of experience associated with one event can be found within reflections upon experiences associated with the other. In a 'hall of mirrors', we observe images of, and connections between, multiple events. In a hall that contains many, one mirror might catch images multiply reflected from others. So within any particular event in which we learn through experience, we might see reflected some of the qualities of any other event through which we may have similarly learned. There may be one mirror in which we can see *all* the others if we try.

More than merely metaphors, these mirrors have heuristic power (a fact well known since Plato's day) which this chapter attempts to demonstrate. Examining our lives by invoking the Schönian 'mirror' notion, we can be prompted to search for repeated patterns in our personal history of making sense of experiences. We are, consequently, apt to learn things about ourselves of which we were ignorant, even unsuspecting. Moreover, the 'mirror' metaphor flags the possibility of using experiential pattern-repetition in designing learning experiences for others. Sometimes, I take a sizeable mirror with me to presentations about teaching and learning. At one point I hold it up, challenging the audience to search for earlier events of which some present event in my presentation is a kind of image. The exercise sharpens interest in asking the question 'of what kind?' and stimulates a concern for looking below the surface of events.

One teaching career: Through a (Schönian) glass, darkly

I will trace the experiential origins of views I currently hold on how to 'make' university teachers (or, for that matter, any other kind). I intend to revisit multiple-related experiences in a Schönian hall of mirrors: events scattered across fifty years of learning, teaching, learning about teaching, learning about learning, teaching about teaching, and teaching about learning. I invite readers to enter my personal hall of mirrors, and to reflect upon their own.

I found myself, in childhood, becoming a teacher concurrently with my earliest self-conscious experiences of becoming a learner. I have never been able to untie the knot between these two events. Not until recently, however, searching for a philosophical base on which to construct a graduate teaching programme for academics, did I trace the origins of virtually all I presently understand about teaching and learning to those childhood events. Those events, their associated desires, needs and long-term impact are what I must now tell.

I describe each in terms of a mirror. There will be five in all, though more may exist of which I cannot yet talk. Stand by me at one end of a long hall, mirrors facing on either side, while a child emerges through the farthest door. We shall view events in the child's life, then the adult's, directly as they happen. We shall also see the events reflected in our mirrors. The reflections are not so much the events *as such* but, in an ancient sense, their essence.

Mirror One: The recapturing of joy

A child aged seven or eight, I would stand behind a low table on the verandah overlooking my parents' garden. In a makeshift open-air classroom, my audience – a handful of neighbourhood kids – would sit on boxes. For a period, I taught them daily my most precious understandings, discoveries I was privately making through my own kitchen science experiments. Each smell, explosion, colour-transformation I proudly demonstrated had been my prior, private discovery. That I could then teach it to others became a second discovery, with lasting impact on my whole life. Through my own volition and my playmates' collusion, I set out, innocently, on a lifetime career of preparing designs for others to learn by. I now realize the first mirror was being put in place in my spontaneous discovery that to teach is to learn twice, to experience double delight.

What stimulated my fascination with natural science had almost certainly been a turn-of-the-century hand-me-down textbook an uncle used at school thirty years before. Everything important in it I first tested, appropriating it through first-hand experience, then shared it with my 'students'. Their delight at watching science 'happening' in front of them was nothing short of palpable. Mine was even more.

Watching these kids gasp delightedly at the magic of my chemical tricks became another way of experiencing the magic myself. I could recapture the joy of my own first discovery. I also discovered through teaching a different satisfaction: that there is delight in making sense of the diversity of ways in which it is possible to teach others. I became interested in getting them to understand, each in their own ways, what I had already understood in my way. And sometimes I delighted to understand it differently, even better, through teaching it.

The postulate of a primary phenomenological reality

Dare I now extrapolate these reflections on my own beginnings as a teacher? Might there be a generic process, some of whose aspects are present in these 'single acts'? Let me try. Readers who are also teachers will judge the closeness of fit between my interpretation of my private experience and their interpretation of their's.

Let me postulate, for perhaps *any* teacher, some primary reality. Probably residing in long-forgotten childhood events, a reality possessing an image able to be recaptured virtually every time one teaches. I have personally come to believe that the reality in question is – for me – the childhood discovery of joy in learning. That discovery of joy presumably comprises all those first, barely conscious but exquisite experiences of satisfying my native childhood curiosity: of making the transition from not knowing to knowing (through effort and intention or luck and circumstance); first catching a glimpse of a likely meaning in things; sensing the possibility of design in the world; ideas going 'click' and fitting together; responding with a Koestlerian 'Aha!' when confronted with the unanticipated connection.

In teaching, the original experience of joy can be not only relived, but a substantial satisfaction awaits within its recapture. My own way of now understanding the appeal of each successive career development within teaching is to view it as a search, a pilgrimage, towards recapturing that primary joy. In the stage I have presently reached in my reading/living of a teacher's life, I incline to regard this as probably the primary stuff – rock-bottom, foundational, essential experience.

I cannot recall actually speaking about this, but after observing many good teachers engaging in their craft I speculate that it may be a common satisfaction. More confidence comes as I currently observe how, in my graduate courses, using this idea as a primary thread in weaving the tapestry of a design for academics to learn teaching by, the effect is to raise the sense of relevance and immediate meaningfulness of any course. The graduate programme of which I spoke earlier is based on the precept of grounding teaching in understanding student learning; in much the same way as I now describe interpreting my teaching through understanding my own learning.

As a postscript, since first writing these paragraphs, I encountered Hans Furth's book *Knowledge as Desire: An Essay on Freud and Piaget* (1987). Furth's thesis concerns the development of higher cognitive powers simultaneously with the resolution of the child's primary emotional/libidinal conflicts. It was instantly recognizable as being a psychologist's analytical account of the phenomenon I, as Teacher, already understand through reflection on life-experiences. I recommend it.

Mirror Two falls to earth unexpectedly

Mirrors can grow dull; there comes a limit to learning more about something every time one teaches it. When I cease learning more each time I teach, I am in danger of tiring of teaching itself. The quality of teaching diminishes, becomes less convincing, less vital. One can easily burn out. To forestall imminent danger, I left home to teach on another continent, to students of another culture, another race. While there, my pedagogic 'territory' (the world of school science teaching) burst into an exciting new era. A rocket called *Sputnik* spawned in the West a host of curriculum development projects. These soon transformed not merely the way some students were taught but the way many teachers *thought about teaching*. Finding myself in a project selecting and adapting the best of western science teaching for use in a developing country, the second Schönian mirror appeared within my hall.

If the name of Mirror One had been joy, this mirror's name has to be design. I discovered how to reflect on both my own teaching designs and those of a host of talented and ingenious other teachers who became my unknown yet ever-present colleagues. Out of their shared designs for learning, I could develop design options for teacher-clients who came to me to learn to teach science better. In Mirror Two, design for teaching becomes a thing in its own right. The design of a lesson can be extracted from the particular events of teaching it, reified into a manageable pursuit which – like teaching itself but at one level removed – has its own artistry, craft and technology.

Design had (and has) its own particular satisfactions. While in one sense unique, these are rooted in the primary satisfactions of teaching; therefore, ultimately, in the joy of learning. In Mirror Two, I see the child in the make-believe backyard classroom clearly reflected. In both mirrors, I see the reflection of the child discovering science, doing it himself.

Curriculum projects such as Nuffield, Harvard Project Physics and PSCS/ BSCS were transforming; full of possibilities unrealized and unexpected – ripple tanks, oil-drops, frictionless pucks. These all formed bases for stunningly elegant design to teach concepts that had often seemed unteachable. Simply doing them was a joy, even to a teacher who already knew the theoretical outcomes. The delight of seeing familiar concepts demonstrated and explained with brilliant clarity was surpassed only by the joy of watching students fall under their spell. These ingenious designs for teaching put students in touch with science, and put me in touch with my original joy of discovery in learning. The mirror of design became a magic glass for many years of benefit, long after the curriculum projects had come and gone. Mirror Two showed that one could capture, within a design for learning, something of one's own – and one's colleagues' – teaching genius, to then be shared with others. I could do the same with my designs. I could examine the very best of my own teaching and ask 'what makes it good?'; holding up a mirror to my own teaching, catching whatever there was of genius or inventiveness in it, then communicating it to other teachers.

Much later I have come to see, in my own curriculum designs, eventual reflections of my own discovery of joy in learning. Prefiguring this I saw, and instantly identified with, the pleasure of teacher-trainees as they used my designs and found them to work. Better still, I saw them studying mine and inventing their own – which generally worked even better. The beneficiaries of this process of sharing designs for learning extended beyond the teacher-trainees who learned directly from them. These new teachers taught more intelligently, hence added to the benefit of their own students who, in part by virtue of good teaching design, discovered for themselves the enjoyment of learning some subject or other well.

Mirror Three and the importance of being there

Following hard on my encounter with Mirror Two, and enlivening my subsequent career, Mirror Three has given a quantum leap to the number of reflections and connections possible. I see into Mirror Three on each privileged occasion I observe anyone teaching. I began observing student-teachers; but today, as consultant to already practising teachers, the subjects of my observations often include colleagues, friends and professional clients, and of course my present 'students', themselves university lecturers. This mirror – observation – is a wide and spacious glass. As observer I can critically reflect upon how another teaches, discover designs in their teaching (designs they are often unaware of) and evoke real and hypothetical design possibilities in my own teaching by imagining how I might have taught each lesson.

One outcome is wonderment at how there seems no end to the variety of successful designs by which to teach any conceivable lesson. A more durable reward is continual replenishment of my stores of original joy in learning. In observing, I learn how another designs and implements a teaching episode; how students respond to it; how I respond to it as student; how I might have taught it (had it been my own lesson). I visualize designs different from this teacher's and perhaps in some ways better still; I imagine some hypothetical students responding with excited pleasure to these 'super-lessons'. Each mirror in turn dutifully reflects images of images of images. Somewhere in the distance, through Mirror Three, then Mirror Two, then Mirror One, is a child bursting with delight at discovering he can do Science by himself.

The observer role is not all delight; one also re-lives the frustrations of teaching. My teachers stumble, falter, forget, encounter hostility and apathy. They deal with all this alone; I cannot do it for them. My position of privilege permits reflection upon all this in a way impossible for the observed teacher. Afterwards, however, my teacher and I may return to the original experience and jointly reflect-after-action.

But if my teacher, immersed in the experience of problem-solving, was – as Schön suggests – reflecting-in-action, my operation as observer must be reflection-at-a-distance, or reflection-once-removed. Which is why I call the teaching-observer's role a privileged one. There is further privilege in visiting the private professional space of another teacher. And again in being able to enjoy the freedom of these reflections-at-a-distance within an existential space in which one bears minimal personal responsibility for immediate outcomes (though considerable responsibility for eventual ones).

Out of double privilege comes a different responsibility. Each observed lesson can become not merely an experience to be savoured but a phenomenon to be documented, studied, researched, for understandings that (however interim) deserve eventually sharing with the teacher whose work it all is. I find operating in this manner consistent with much of what Elliott Eisner (1985), in his inspired *The Art of Educational Evaluation*, calls 'educational connoisseurship'.

Responsibility is particularly substantial when the teacher observed is one's own student. A pleasant challenge in designing graduate programmes for lecturers has been exploiting the potential of letting teachers observe one another: within the metaphor, introducing them to multiple mirrors. I have been struck (so have my colleagues who have tried it elsewhere) by the reluctance (is it resistance?) with which many lecturer-students approach the notion of seeing their own work reflected – whether in my teaching or in one another's.

Some need to be led by the hand and told how to look, where to look and what to look for before they 'see' what seems so obvious to me. But this facilitation comprises merely one more design task for myself as teacher. That, on my beginning analysis, means I must myself find ways of returning to a place where I also was unaware and ignorant of the mirrors.

Mirror Four: A conversation piece

Four is the mirror of reflective consultancy, only a short step beyond Mirror Three. From observing and assessing student-teachers on practicum, appraising and supporting university teachers, or researching classroom events as unobtrusive observer, it is a simple but significant step to becoming consultant to teachers.

The essence of Mirror Four is the power of reflective conversation with a teacher, often after a lesson observation. Joint reflection on a shared teaching event fits perfectly into Schön's model of coaching within the reflective practicum. If it works, there is *sympatico*, and language and empathy suffice, it can become at best a joint search among the fascinating worlds of design possibilities. Together, without intimidation, we can relish the good bits, savour the successes, recognize the bad bits, be frank about failures, and share in the enlightening search for reasons. The relationship must be symmetrical: we are not judge and miscreant, only two teachers talking about the work we love.

Such joint reflection, a conversational search, contains the latent possibility of Schönian multiple layers of reflection. As needed we can move up and down the reflective ladder, now sharing responses to the raw data of the lesson, now rising above that and posing hypotheticals of what might or could have been 'if only', now asking what our present relationship has to say about possible teacher–student relationships, now standing aside wondering what it means to be talking about a lesson in this manner, now asking what teaching is all about anyway.

For the consultant, Mirror Four provides a further opportunity. It is that of discovering a design, or possible designs, for conducting the consultancy process itself (viewed as a particular, specialized kind of teaching). There should exist ways of engagement that elicit critical judgement but avoid judgementalism, that invite viewing a lesson as a student might have, holding up a mirror to the lesson – both threatening *and* fascinating. And surely irresistible for any teacher who genuinely wants to know. A good consultancy experience contains the possibility of personally re-experiencing that primary joy of which I wrote. It arises out of becoming aware that a teacher is beginning to see, within some private mirror, their own primary experience of joy in learning. It allows both consultant and client (separately or together) to intuit fresh designs for learning that may potentially provide quality learning experiences for students.

Facing Mirror Four I am reminded of the most salient dilemma facing me as teacher of my graduate classes. Mirrors, as the ancients well knew, are magic and cunning devices. They extend vision and multiply available images, but they also have the disarming effect of multiplying both *me* and *them*. Who am I? Who are my students? We each are many. These many roles the mirrors give us are easy to confuse, and often hard to distinguish. The teachers I teach are my students. They are also teachers – to their students. They are students of their students' learning, as I am student of their learning. They and I are also colleagues, fellow academics. Together we are consultant and client. We move between these roles as we work; sometimes awkwardly, sometimes unconsciously easy. Some of the worst times come when we engage in assessment within subjects they are studying. Things generally improve when we talk about our assessing them as a reflection of them assessing their students. It helps to remember which mirror one is looking into and why.

Mirror Five: The making of teachers

This is where I think I am today. I find challenge and satisfaction working on the design and implementation of an innovative postgraduate programme on teaching and learning for academics. To achieve both an appropriate curriculum and an apt methodology, I look into a mirror that seems like the widest of all. Carefully viewed, it can catch the reflected images of each of the previous four, and all of everything they caught.

The goal is a curriculum to introduce university teachers to reflective practice in teaching as a lifelong professional stance. That deserves to be achieved through a unique pedagogy, and my decision has been to construct it around reflective practice. The process will mirror the content and the goals. I am within my own hall of mirrors but also within reach of the halls of my teacher-students. Reflection upon practice. Which practice? Which reflections?

First, the practice of my 'students' as they continue to teach, since they are required to be engaged in teaching while studying. Next, my practice as I engage with them, in a variety of roles, as teacher/facilitator, supervisor, consultant, assessor. Then our public 'classroom' practice as we engage in exercises and experiences within workshops. Then the practice of fellow teachers, observed in videos of model lectures. Then the practice of other teachers – colleagues and fellow participants – outside the classroom, observed in real teaching situations within a peer-support relationship.

My challenge is to prepare designs by means of which others may learn design. This means teaching others to teach. It involves my becoming a person who in the sense of the first mirror 'doesn't know how to teach' in order to find a design out of which my participants might learn how to teach. Programme design for reflective teaching means creating a milieu within which teachers can engage in their own course of discovery of what teaching is all about. It involves (though perhaps goes beyond) what Bowden, Marton and Ramsden (in Ramsden 1988: Part 4) have addressed as the imperative goal of university academic staff development – 'reconceptualizing' *both* learning and teaching.

Here I find that the return to primary, quintessential joy can often happen faster, presenting its images more vividly to consciousness, than my metaphor of many mirrors might suggest. When a graduate student makes the unsolicited comment, 'The trouble with this course is that it gives me so many sleepless nights – I don't think I've stopped thinking about teaching for five minutes since we started. I'd never felt like that about teaching before', I exult because the child teaching his playmates backyard science is not far away.

The mirrors can nevertheless be baffling, presenting me with sheer complexity, tantalizingly hard to unravel. In discussions with colleagues engaging in projects having similar goals to mine, I have tried to develop a graphic representation of some of this complexity. No matter how far we develop it, the picture always seems incomplete; maybe that's the way with mirrors and infinite regress. But we have found it a fruitful starting point for examining and comparing what we are each doing.

Looking back along the hall

Mirror Five reflects Mirror Four directly. Within the graduate programme, consultancy is reconceptualized as joint experimentation on possible designs for teaching. Events here occur mostly within peer-support group sessions; teachers offer problems they have met and we 'brainstorm' possibilities for solving them. Such sessions, and the structures of peer-support within which they operate, are a critical part of the programme's success.

There is plenty of one-to-one consultancy and supervision around individual action-research projects into which participants contract. A talented team of co-supervisors is needed to carry this out. The programme is built around such projects as its centrepost, and every subject is studied by undertaking such a project within students' own teaching commitments. Success means carrying the project through to its contracted end, and providing evidence of learning from experience and engaging in critical reflection upon practice while doing it.

Mirror Three, teaching observation, is met whenever we watch or hear tapes made by participants teaching their own classes. We revisit the land of discovering teachers' intended designs, comparing them with what we would have done, letting ourselves become their student. Does their teaching give me the 'Aha!' I would want if I were a student?

Mirror Two, curriculum design, is never absent from view. The programme requires drawing upon all my own experience of how to help to 'make' teachers, borrowing from others who have done the same, in order to produce programme designs that contain the best genius I can muster. An interesting part of this is collecting interactive workshop strategies that have proven power to stimulate movement along the direction of 'reconceptualizing both learning and teaching'. In adapting, for instance, a variety of widely used games and simulations, powerful introductions to the discussion of a range of issues have proved possible. I cannot escape images of earlier discoveries of ripple tanks and frictionless pucks as my high school students once discovered basic physics concepts and principles through inventive learning designs I had borrowed from other teachers.

Regular reflection upon my own learning designs for graduate students is, I believe, a necessary part of being true to a commitment to reflection upon practice. As often as possible I, and my team colleagues, try honestly to 'give reasons' for what we have decided to do in class. The premise is simple: as their teachers, we give them reasons about our designs; as student-teachers they give us reasons about their designs; they eventually may, as teachers, find it possible to give their students reasons about their designs; their future students may, in turn, give reasons about their own attempts at designs for problem-solving in the learning of academic and professional subjects.

To help achieve the dialogue necessary for stimulating and sustaining such a reciprocal reason-giving exercise, I find I must keep in touch with students between our scheduled fortnightly workshops. A newsletter despatched a week after each meeting lets me share my reflections upon the last meeting and assess our achievements in breaking out of the silent cocoons that entrap university teachers. In it I can give reasons for things done, or planned for, and maybe establish a lasting habit of public reason-giving about teaching and learning.

Mirror One, the experience of teaching itself, and recapturing the primary joy of learning, is never hard to discover at the end of the hall. I am privileged to share with a talented inter-university team the task of conducting both on-campus graduate classes and also developing open-learning packages for future off-campus participants. With this challenge of open learning, I find myself asking the same questions any teacher would ask when creating a design for learning: 'Could *I* learn well through this?' and 'If I didn't know it beforehand, *would I know it now*, after this class?'

Open learning seems to demand, in a particularly heightened and vivid manner, that the teacher be willing to occupy the role of the absent student. I am again in my childhood garden performing magic with chemicals to the attendant wonder of my playmates who are as curious to learn what I know as I am to tell what it is – and to keep discovering more about it. The difference now is, could I have taught them had they not been there in front of me?

After surviving two years of our graduate programme, I retain a firm belief that teacher-making should be constructed around the practicum. Teaching seems to be best 'learned' through the central experience of being with students and responsible for the conditions of their learning. The late Northrop Frye (1988), in a keen critique of the way we conventionally state educational goals, said 'There can really be no goal where taking the journey itself is the best thing to be done.' We learn to teach by taking the journey.

In the personal Hall of Mirrors through which we have now strolled together, every reasonably clear reflection makes contact with and perhaps recaptures the primary experience I described as the joy of discovering knowledge: making connections, and seeing something of the design of things. It is only honest to admit that it is not always easy to keep the mirrors clear, the images sharp, the reflections in focus. However, the nature of my current work has probably stimulated me to do so with a particular energy and commitment. And if there is any benefit now to readers who share these insights from my own experience and reflection, I am doubly delighted.

Doubtless the multiple reflections in one's personal hall of mirrors may sometimes dazzle the eyes; and over-much peering may prove counterproductive. At any rate, for each particular time, from each particular vantage-point, the eye will selectively perceive – something I will have done many times in this chapter. But there is never any doubt that the mirrors – and the connected images they transmit – are always there. And that by standing in the right place, and maybe squinting, one can see – pedagogically – forever.

References

Brookfield, S.D. (1990) *The Skillful Teacher: On Technique, Trust and Responsiveness in the Classroom.* San Francisco, CA: Jossey-Bass.

Eisner, E.W. (1985) *The Art of Educational Evaluation: A Personal View.* Lewes: Falmer Press.

Frye, N. (1988) *On Education.* Ann Arbor, MI: University of Michigan Press.

Furth, H. (1987) *Knowledge as Desire: An Essay on Freud and Piaget.* New York: Columbia University Press.

Ramsden, P. (ed.) (1988) *Improving Learning: New Perspectives.* London: Kogan Page.

Schön, D.A. (1990) *Educating the Reflective Practitioner: Towards a New Design for Teaching and Learning in the Professions.* San Francisco, CA: Jossey-Bass.

Part 2

Introduction

Reflection is a central focus in this section: how to approach it, foster it and work with whatever emerges from it. The reader is challenged to reflect on what learning is – not just as an accumulation of new facts, but a re-evaluation of experiences from the past and a transformation of our perception in the present. Why are learners sometimes unable to face up to certain issues? What prevents them from engaging with and learning from their experience? How can conventional learning inhibit the process of knowing ourselves? These are some of the questions addressed. The role of others in our learning, the importance of collaboration in our decision-making as educators, and the need for mutual cooperation and generosity to provide a creative learning milieu are other matters discussed in this section.

The section opens with the contribution of Boud and Walker. It is placed here because it embraces a wide range of issues, some of which are taken up by the other authors in this section. These two authors reflect on their experience of working together over a period of ten years, using the model that they have developed. They reveal the unpredictability of such reflection, and how difficult it can be to share one's experience with others. This chapter focuses on barriers to learning from experience, which emerged from the application of their reflection model to their shared experience.

Brew also focuses on working with past experiences. She shows how new learning can help unlearn what flowed from past experiences. She presents knowledge as a quality of perception, our way of making sense of phenomena. What we learn from experience does not simply add new information, but transforms our way of experiencing. It can challenge the basic framework of ideas, beliefs, attitudes and values which have been the foundation of our experience. Continuous reworking of experience is the way to appreciate who we are as learners, what has influenced our learning, and how our experience transforms our perception.

The relationship between learning, experience and reflection in distance programmes is treated in Thorpe's chapter, as she reflects on her own experience as a learner through the process of developing a specific distance learning course. This experience as a team member and writer focused her attention on the importance of providing time for reflective activities. The relevance of reflection and awareness of the legitimacy of the learner's perspective ultimately led to changing the course structure and content to accommodate these through such activities as the learning portfolio. Her approach gives greater autonomy to students to recognize and shape their own learning and analyse the role of the milieu in which the learning takes shape.

Mason leads us into his reflection through mathematics. He emphasizes the importance of an active presence within experience, and to experience. This can be achieved by developing one's ability to notice. What is being noticed is not only the elements of the experience, but also what is taking place in the learner as well. By relating current experience to past experience, the learner builds up a rich network of interconnected memories, which in turn can provide access to alternative behaviour in the future. This insight into one's own experience is a powerful influence in helping the teacher enter into the experience of others, while at the same time legitimizing the students' experience in a learning situation.

5

Barriers to Reflection on Experience

David Boud and David Walker

Having given quite explicit guidelines to our co-authors, we were confronted with the task of writing our chapter within the framework which we had provided. We had said to the others, 'write yourselves into your chapters, don't just treat experience as if it happened to other people. Tell the story of how you came to adopt your present perspective on learning from experience.'

Our plan was quite straightforward. We would use as our organizing theme an account of, and reflection on, our work together over the past decade. We decided to take our earlier model of reflection on learning (Boud *et al.* 1985) and work through it focusing on our collaborative activities. We would do this as a real exercise and we would follow wherever our reflections led us. This meant going back through our experience of collaboration, drawing out what we considered to be significant (*return to experience*); working with any feelings that had come out of it, that might help or hinder our reflection (*attending to feelings*); and then going on to reappraise the experience in the light of what had arisen (*re-evaluation*). This final stage involved singling out an aspect of the experience and relating it to previous experience and learning (*association*), integrating the new experience with previous learning (*integration*), testing its validity (*validation*) and making it our own (*appropriation*). We proceeded along these lines.

However, having done it, we were confronted with an unexpected experience in the light of the reactions of several colleagues to the draft that we had produced. They failed to see connections that were obvious to us. We reflected further. These reflections brought home to us the unpredictable nature of the process of learning from experience, led us to new ways of viewing our own experience, and clarified for us what was involved in using our model for reflection. We have incorporated this new learning into our chapter.

Return to experience

We met for the first time through being allocated to the same table in a workshop on self-directed learning which Malcolm Knowles conducted near Sydney in 1978. We had both heard of his work, had some sympathy for his outlook on learning and wanted to meet the famous man in person. Little of the workshop remains in mind, except for the tremendous impact of Knowles as workshop leader – he provided clear leadership, but essentially trusted us to look after our own learning. Perhaps it was this which prompted us into conversation, perhaps we would have talked about learning whatever the quality of the workshop. Regardless of causes, our continuing relationship emerged from our mutual interest in the role of experience in learning.

We visited each other's workplaces and discovered that our specific educational practices had more in common than we would ever have imagined; one of us was an academic with an interest in improving teaching in universities and the other was a priest who was committed to bringing spirituality into organized religion. Our involvement in the Australian Consortium on Experiential Education (ACEE) – a Sydney-based group of teachers and trainers involved in helping others learn through their experience – maintained our focus on the importance of experience, and developed our confidence in its central role in learning.

However, it was some time before we started to collaborate. The impetus was a move, within ACEE, to explore how experience leads to learning. Members of the organization conducted workshops in which were demonstrated various approaches to teaching and training. They provided a range of different experiences, techniques and strategies. However, organizing frameworks which transcended the particularities of any given method were absent and there was little explanation of how best to draw learning effectively from experience. While the workshops were highly stimulating, they ultimately left us feeling unsatisfied.

This dissatisfaction, together with our belief that we were engaged in very worthwhile activities, stimulated a group of us to undertake a more systematic study of factors which are important in facilitating learning from experience. The key factor which we identified for closer exploration was that of learners reflecting on their experience. Different descriptions were used for what we termed reflection: debriefing, processing, journal keeping, each with a characteristic flavour, but we took all to have a common core in which learners examined their experience and worked with it in some way leading to the possibility of new learning.

The outcome of the study was a book which described a variety of techniques relating to reflection. Together with our late colleague Rosemary Keogh, our role was to provide the conceptual glue which held the collection together. Little did we know at the beginning how difficult our task would be. None of the existing frameworks provided a satisfactory structure in which to place the rich and interesting techniques of experiential learning which were so ably described by others.

After many meetings in a smoke-filled corner of the government building in which Rosemary worked, and after many drafts and false starts, we finally arrived at a model with which we all felt comfortable. It didn't include everything which we had originally hoped for, but it did satisfy our basic criterion of simplicity and it did point to key ideas about which we were enthusiastic. In our efforts to understand experience further, we had moved from a focus on the experience itself, to working with that experience through systematic reflection.

While it took us twenty-three pages to describe (Boud *et al.* 1985), the essence of the model was that there were three key factors in reflecting on experience. The first was a return to the experience, in which the learner recalled the experience, in a descriptive way as it had apparently occurred, without judgement or evaluation. The second was to attend to feelings that arose out of the return to the experience. Obstructive feelings needed to be worked with so that reflection could take place constructively, and supportive feelings needed to be fostered to assist the process of reflection. The third factor was the re-evaluation of the experience, in which learners linked with this experience elements from their past experience (*association*), integrated this new experience with existing learning (*integration*), tested it in some way (*validation*) and made it their own (*appropriation*).

This model pointed to enough important features of reflection to enable us to help learners make a useful start on reflecting on their past experience. The framework was a generic one which could be readily translated into specific circumstances, e.g. in debriefing group activities, in keeping a learning journal or, as we are doing in this chapter, providing the structure for reviewing an entire sequence of activities. However, this did not seem enough. The model referred to a particular circumstance of reflection – what happens after the event – but what should occur at other times?

The stimulus and opportunity for the additional work needed to develop our ideas further came with the Second International Conference on Experiential Learning, held in Sydney in 1989. The ACEE was the joint sponsor and we became heavily involved in the organizing committee. Our work associated with the conference led us to focus again on the experience itself, to explore further the elements that were important within a learning event. We realized that we had not yet taken sufficient account of learners' prior experience, and their intent, on what and how they learn. These needed to be related to our reflection model. We saw, too, the need to focus on the opportunities which occur for reflection while the learner is still engaged in an activity. Our experience at the conference of trying to implement our views about experiential learning, alongside others which we felt to be incompatible, highlighted for us that reflection happens in the midst of action, not only in the calm light of recollection at leisure! We were also well aware of the fact that our model did not fully capture what we ourselves regarded as important in our own learning: the surprise of meeting the unexpected, the change of direction required as we confronted difficulties, and the importance of advance preparation to help address at least some of the challenges which may arise.

We devised a number of activities for conference participants to help them focus on their intents and their expectations of the conference. These included pre-conference correspondence, daily sheets of simple reflective exercises related to each stage of the conference (entering and departing from the experience, noticing and acting within it), a workshop which examined the framework we were using, and a final keynote workshop to help conference participants reflect on their learning from the week. These activities brought together our ideas and their personal experience of the conference. While we did not achieve all that we had hoped, we received enough encouragement from the participants who appreciated what we were doing to enable us to persist in the direction we were taking.

Following the conference, we entered a tortuous period in which we took some time to focus on the next stage of our research. In retrospect, we realize that we needed time to recover emotionally from the conference, but rather than fully debrief the experience we spent meeting after meeting with a whiteboard and pen trying to pick out ideas from among the feelings. At many points we felt that we had reached an understanding only to find that what seemed so clear when we talked, not surprisingly, did not translate into writing. While we were searching for expression of our thoughts, we received an invitation from Deakin University to write a monograph for a distance education course they were designing about adult learning in the workplace. We proposed that we would write about our current thinking and they accepted. As it turned out, we were not able to write a monograph for students without including other material, thus reducing the space for our new thinking. So we worked in parallel on the monograph (Boud and Walker 1991) and a paper (Boud and Walker 1990).

Our reflection in the midst of this action focused enough on our feelings from the conference for us to reach beyond them and begin building our thinking anew. We reminded ourselves that what had brought us together was an interest in the role of experience in learning. We had begun to collaborate around the issue of reflection after the experience, and this had led us back to explore further the nature of experience. We had begun with a model for reflection, but now we were being drawn into a model of experience which included much more than reflection after the event.

We took up again two important concepts: *personal foundation of experience* and *intent*. We singled out two further aspects of experience which we had begun to work with earlier, but which now became the focus of our attention: *noticing* and *intervening*. We saw these two activities as part of the dynamics of reflection-in-action, which led us to apply our previous research on 'reflection after the event' to 'reflection which takes place during the event', and which is an important constituent of it. We also became more aware at this time of the need to *prepare* for the experience. We summarized our work diagrammatically (see Fig. 5.1).

We have written thus far mostly about the development of our concepts

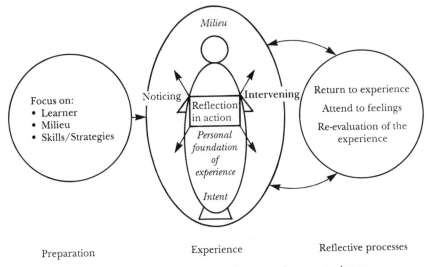

Figure 5.1 Model of reflection processes in learning from experience.

and the events which have been a catalyst to that development. However, there was also a very definite feeling dimension to this collaborative experience. It was a mixture of excitement and frustration, certainty and doubt, unity and discord. We experienced high excitement and certainty when we reached stages where we could look at what we had achieved and say, 'damn it, this really does make sense. It doesn't matter what anyone else thinks, what we have here is worthwhile just for us.' This often came after periods of doubt and what felt like wallowing in uncertainty. There was frustration as we tried to articulate our perceptions. Yet we had to make a statement and stick to it. We had to persist and not let our feelings of inadequacy hold us back. In our efforts, we were encouraged by feedback which made us feel at one with the on-going research being conducted by our colleagues. However, at times, there was a discordant note as comments and actions of colleagues made us feel somewhat apart from the mainstream.

As we looked back over our work together, we understood that we had tried to explore how to facilitate learning, and were offering our thoughts on how this could be done. However, there remained a discord. We recognized a tension between what we have understood and were satisfied with, and what is left out of our portrayal of the process of learning from experience.

In focusing on positive action around reflection, both after and in the midst of action, we had not explored sufficiently the many negative aspects which impede learning. It became glaringly obvious that we had not directly addressed the issues of barriers which inhibit working with experience. We had confronted our own barriers to learning as a result of our experience at the conference, but even then we had not been able to name them as barriers, even though we had experienced a strong sense of being blocked.

We knew that barriers are strong and that many are not easily susceptible to removal or being circumvented. Some have indeed served an important purpose in our lives, for example, in protecting us from the degree of pain we would have had to face if we not held back from jumping into a difficult situation from the deep end. It was this focus on barriers to learning, both conceptual and emotional, that emerged from our return to the experience of working together. However, before focusing on them further, we needed to proceed with the next stage of our model. These barriers became the focus of our further reflection.

Attending to feelings

The excitement and sense of achievement, which has been predominant, remains strong. We have fostered these supportive feelings by sharing our research with others, and attending to their feedback. Our mutual acknowledgment of the feeling provides further strength and helps the positive mutual interaction. Conversely, we have experienced a sense of frustration as to the adequacy of our expression. Are we presenting our ideas well and taking account of all the issues relevant to them? We sometimes doubt that we can do justice to our research within the space limitations of a chapter. There is the feeling, too, of academic caution, which sometimes can bring a paralysis that prevents publication. However, our challenge to – and support for – each other helps to overcome these obstructions, and the desire to go on being creative is an effective antidote to them.

Building on the positive is an important part of our dynamic. At times, there was a shared feeling of 'pumping up' the mental adrenalin to generate enough enthusiasm and achievement to carry us through the often tedious task of writing it down in a way which would made sense to ourselves and, hopefully, other readers. This building of momentum was only noticeable in retrospect, but always included a clear sensation of the need to get far enough in one of our meetings to carry us through to the next.

Re-evaluation of the experience

Association

After we reviewed our experience together and explored the feeling dimension, we moved into a new phase. We turned to the whiteboard and spent an absorbing few hours engaged in an exercise which we have often used in our workshops. In the centre of the blank space, we wrote 'BARRIERS TO WORKING WITH EXPERIENCE' and sat back and pondered on that theme. At times we wrote furiously, at others we waited for associations to strike us as we trawled our consciousness and waited for our intuition to provide inspiration. As we wrote, we thought and discussed and attempted

Table 5.1 Our brainstormed list of barriers to working with experience

---

- Presuppositions about what is and is not possible for us to do.
- Not being in touch with one's own assumptions and what one is able to do.
- Past negative experiences.
- Expectations of others: society, peer group, figures of authority, family.
- Threats to the self, one's world view, or to ways of behaving.
- Lack of self-awareness of one's place in the world.
- Inadequate preparation.
- Hostile or impoverished environments.
- Lack of opportunity to step aside from tasks.
- Lack of time.
- External pressures and demands.
- Lack of support from others.
- Lack of skills: in noticing, intervening.
- Intent which is unclear or unfocused.
- Established patterns of thought and behaviour.
- Inability to conceive of the possibility of learning from experience: 'this is not learning', 'this is not possible'.
- Stereotypes about how we learn.
- Obstructive feelings: lack of confidence or self-esteem, fear of failure or the response of others, unexpressed grief about lost opportunities.

---

to articulate to each other what we were trying to express. We made no attempt to fit the fragments together and find patterns, just to associate whatever was in our consciousness relating to barriers to working with experience.

At the end, the board was packed with words, phrases and fragments of ideas, too messy and dense to reproduce here. However, to give the flavour, we list in Table 5.1 some of the associations which emerged from our own experience, and that of others, about barriers to working with experience. Although we had not only been thinking of ourselves during the generation phase, as we transcribed them and read through them individually, we recalled examples of each of them in our own lives: 'you're not allowed do that' (translated as: someone from your class/with your accent must be excluded from these privileges); 'I'm not bright enough to go to university'; 'I'm too frightened to try that again', etc.

We were somewhat overwhelmed by the number and diversity of blocks to learning we had identified. Nevertheless, we were satisfied that we were beginning to come to grips with a very important issue to us and we pressed on to see if any *integration* of all this was possible.

Integration

In meetings following our session with the whiteboard, we played with the ideas generated and struggled to articulate some of the patterns which were emerging for us concerning barriers to learning. We returned again to some of our earlier thinking and came to a working definition: barriers are those factors which inhibit or block learners' preparedness for the experience, their active engagement in it, and their ability to reflect rationally on it with a view to learning from it. With this definition in mind, it was possible to bring together our ideas under a number of headings: understanding barriers to learning; their origins; their interaction with each other; how to deal with them; and how to work with them.

Understanding barriers to learning

Our working definition points to the fact that barriers can inhibit learning at each stage of our understanding of the learning process: the preparation, the experience itself and the reflection on it (Boud and Walker 1990). In preparation they can inhibit learning by reducing the learning potential of the experience, by limiting the learner's awareness of the learning environment, failing to focus existing knowledge and skills in relationship to it, and creating a vague or ill-defined intent for entering the experience. Within the experience, they can limit the essential processes of noticing and intervening, thereby having an adverse affect on the learner's engagement in it. They can paralyse the reflection processes within the experience, and after it, so that the experience becomes non-reflective and is robbed of much of its learning potential. After the experience, these barriers can raise emotional factors which made reflection impossible or limit it; they can isolate and impoverish the new experience by making it difficult to relate the new experience to past experience; they can make it difficult to integrate new learning with past knowledge, and to make judgements and draw conclusions from it. They can also make it difficult for the learner to appropriate the new learning.

Looking at the barriers in terms of their origins in relation to the learner, some barriers are external impositions while others stem from ourselves. External barriers can come from people, the learning environment, the larger personal situation and context of the learner, and social forces, such as stereotyping, cultural expectations, classism and so on. Internal barriers stem from the unique personal experience of the learner. They can include previous negative experiences, accepted presuppositions about what the learner can do or about what learning can take place, a lack of awareness of one's assumptions, the emotional state of the learner, established patterns of behaviour.

Classifying types of barriers in terms of whether they are external or internal to the learner raises the important point of the interaction between them. Many of the supposedly external barriers only begin to have real force when we take them on ourselves and think and act as if they were true. Often self-imposed censorship is more pernicious than anything imposed by others. The power that external forces have is in proportion to the degree to which we appropriate them. There is a strong dynamic whereby learners are tricked, or trick themselves, into thinking barriers are external when they are not – 'no-one from my background could possibly aspire to a job like that'.

A second realization was that personal distress mixed with the mostly unconscious oppressive behaviour of others underlies many of the barriers we identified. Although we experience barriers as internal – 'I can't possibly do that' or 'I don't want to do that' – they often arise from external influences which impacted on us at an earlier time and which left us feeling disempowered or de-skilled or inhibited. When we were treated as working-class boys who 'should' have low expectations of life, rather than as the particular individuals whom we were, we internalized the external oppression and censored our own aspirations.

Our own experience led us to the view that barriers to learning revolve around the individual learner, even when the key factors involved appear to be social or cultural. While some influences may impinge on many people, in the final instance, a barrier is only a barrier when a particular learner is impeded in learning. What may seem to be endemic, may not apply in a given case. This means that the real battleground for working with these barriers is the learner; the learner is the locus within which we need to situate barriers to learning. While it is in this individual context that barriers are revealed, and it is here that often one must address them, we cannot deny that social intervention on a broader front aimed at addressing endemic discriminatory practices is also necessary to achieve a learning society.

Discovering barriers to learning
We were not content to leave our considerations of barriers there. We wanted to make learning more effective, to change it, not just to understand it. We wanted to know how to help learners (ourselves included) work with the barriers and find ways of eliminating or circumventing them. Facilitation of learning is essentially about helping learners deal with their barriers to learning. Helping them to conceive of a barrier to learning as susceptible to influence rather than an inherent deficiency can be a personally empowering step. However, a key element in facilitation is raising awareness of the existence of barriers, and their origin and nature.

How does one notice a barrier? Comparing one's thoughts, feelings and behaviour with those of others can indicate that we are experiencing differently, which can prompt us to ask why. The feedback of others can also help us recognize inadequacies in our ability to work with experience, as can working through a common experience with a group. Exposure to others is one of the best ways of becoming aware of barriers to learning from experience. Hearing them tell their story, and telling our story to them, can help us to see ourselves and how we experience and learn.

Sometimes, it is necessary to cease being involved in a certain type of activity in order to become aware that it may not be fruitful in terms of learning. Action not only reinforces presuppositions, but sometimes obscures the assumptions from which it flows. Action of a different kind, exposure to new experiences, reaching beyond the confines of a limited set of experiences, can expose limitations, highlight barriers to learning, and give us a new appreciation of our learning capacities.

Our own personal awareness, our instinctive feelings, can also alert us to barriers. Heeding our own comfort level within a given situation can bring us to an awareness of our abilities, or lack of them, to work with experience as a source of learning. Being in touch with oneself within the experience is an important way to appreciate one's potential, or lack of it, to learn from the experience.

Working with barriers
Some barriers stem from the perception of the learner, and a transformation of that perception can lead to their diminishing or disappearing. Others, however, are more deep-seated. The barrier has been learned and the ability to respond has been impaired. Sometimes, this is an emotional impairment which has occluded the learner's capacity to learn anew. This can often require the learner to re-visit past experiences and examine them from their current, more powerful perspective. At times, more intensive therapeutic assistance may be required, which goes beyond the scope of the educational facilitator.

It is important to recognize whether the barriers can be altered or transformed with ease or with difficulty. Four useful steps emerged from our considerations on how to work with barriers. The first is to acknowledge that they may exist. An acceptance of their presence is the beginning of working with them. Secondly, having acknowledged them, they need to be named (Griffin 1987). The more clearly we understand them and can describe them, the more easily we will be able to work with them. This clarifying and naming can come from our own reflection and experience, or from the help and experience of others.

The third step is to identify how the barriers operate by examining their origins. A useful concept in this regard is that of critical reflection, which presupposes that our experience is substantially influenced by presuppositions we bring to it. These exist prior to experience as part of our personal foundation of experience. The forces that shape these presuppositions and fix us into certain patterns of behaviour, thought or feeling sometimes need to be recognized and challenged. Critical reflection is a useful instrument for recognizing these forces, both those which come from our own personal story and those which come from the social, cultural context in which we have developed. The enlightenment that comes through critical reflection helps us to understand the origins of barriers to learning from experience, and offers us new opportunities to overcome them, by clarifying how they operate and what needs to be done to counter them. As we reflected on this step, we became aware that the very model of reflection which is being illustrated in this chapter can have an important role to play in critical reflection.

The fourth step is to work with the barriers. Working with them can involve strategies which are confrontational or transformative. Re-examining past experiences from a current, more powerful situation, or reframing old experiences or concepts in the light of new understanding can lead to their transformation (Minsky 1982; Bolman and Deal 1991). The recognition of one's powerlessness or lack of awareness in past situations puts them in a new perspective and transforms our understanding and appropriation of them. Sometimes, confrontational strategies are appropriate. This involves taking a stance which contradicts the influence of the barrier in every respect. For example, a barrier which causes a learner to believe that they cannot do something, when there is no apparent external limitation present, can be contradicted by the learner acting as if they could undertake the task and dealing with the feelings that this stance provokes. One can find ways of contradicting former patterns of behaviour and substitute them for the former ways. One can enter into forbidding experiences with new awareness and knowledge and work through the issues as one is experiencing them.

Validation

Much needs to be done now to validate these ideas in terms of our own experience. To what extent does it help us make sense of our own experiences, the barriers we have encountered to learning and the way which we have been effective in dealing with these barriers in our own lives? We have done this implicitly to some extent in constructing the thinking we describe above, but we now need to extend this to other examples, ones we were not thinking of before. These thoughts also need to be checked against the experience of others. This occurred as others read this account in draft form and their comments helped to clarify and explicate our thinking about barriers.

One of the most significant points that emerged from our integration was the application of our reflection model to using critical reflection in dealing with barriers. It became the immediate focus of our research, and we set to working on a paper in which we relate our model of reflection to the exercise of critical reflection (Walker and Boud 1992).

Appropriation

We cannot tell in advance what knowledge we will make our own. Having a theoretical framework in itself does not remove the barriers. The next step is to accept the challenge which our reflection has posed for us. Explaining a problem does not mean that we have dealt with it. We feel that we have made some progress, but this needs to be consolidated and made our own. What we have appropriated about barriers to learning from experience we will only be able to be identify in retrospect.

Second thoughts

We had shown a draft of the preceding sections to two of our colleagues. To our surprise, they found a massive discontinuity between the experience of collaboration we had described and the reflections on barriers which followed. They saw a huge leap from the account of the experience to the later reflection, which seemed unconnected, both in style and content, to the recount of the experience which led to them. Our immediate reaction was to protest that this couldn't possibly be the case – our experience was seamless, we moved from one section to the other without being at all conscious that we were doing anything other than continuing the natural course of our reflection. Our considered response led us to reconsider what we believed about learning from experience.

Re-reading our text, it was clear that the reference to barriers had emerged rather abruptly and unexpectedly from what had gone before. Yet we knew that it had come directly from our experience. In describing our experience, we had not captured something important. How on earth did we get from the stage of feeling good about writing together to that of confronting major barriers to learning from experience? It clearly did not come directly from our experience as we described it. What had led us to move from the reflection on our collaborative experience to a focus on barriers? As we reflected further, several possibilities emerged.

Our work together had been an exploration of learning about learning from experience, and a focus on the essential elements of it which could be developed to enhance learning. In presenting those elements of learning from experience, we tended to emphasize their positive contribution to learning. However, what we had presented could also have implications for impediments to learning. The focus on barriers which emerged was simply a development of our original thoughts, a consideration of our key points from a different point of view, i.e. how learning can be impaired. We needed to develop this aspect of our thoughts to appreciate the full significance of the elements we had been emphasizing. As we reflected in this way, the movement from our previous work to a consideration of barriers did not seem quite so abrupt. However, it did not explain why we had made the transition from one to the other. We searched further for some explanation.

A possible explanation for this related to the work in which we were concurrently engaged on critical reflection. We had received an earlier response to our model which had questioned its application to critical reflection. This had led us to begin to explore this area and, while working on this chapter, we were simultaneously working on the paper on critical reflection for the Third International Conference on Experiential Learning held at Pondicherry in India (Walker and Boud 1992). It was an application of our model to critical reflection. We investigated the sources of the critical reflection movement, and found that they were very much concerned with the assumptions and presuppositions which limited the experiences of people and constrained their freedom. We could see how our current preoccupation with such limits and constraints could cause us to move from the positive aspects of the work we had been reflecting on for this chapter, to explore how learning from experience could be limited or impeded.

Two important realizations emerged from these reflections. The first was that our present preoccupations had deeply influenced our reflection on past experience. They had caused us to view our experience in a new light and open up areas that previously we had not noticed, or at least did not consider important enough to explore. This whole experience gave us another view about how our model for reflection could be used, and how, in using it, one needs to be aware of one's present situation and pre-occupations.

This experience also brought home to us that our lived experience can never be fully transmitted to another person, even when we go to great lengths to describe that experience. Sometimes, important dynamics operate which seem so commonplace to us that we do not include them in our descriptions. Indeed, we may not even be aware that they exist. There are many stories we can tell about our experience. All may be 'true' to the teller, but they each reflect some part of the whole. Some will resonate more with the reader than others as they touch their sensibilities and have meaning for them. The more the reader learns, the more they can build a fuller picture; but this picture is always partial, large chunks are obscured and many meanings can be drawn from it.

Conclusion

This reflection on our collaborative work in the light of our model has been a more enriching experience than we had anticipated. It has given new meaning to our past experience and aspects of it that we had hitherto overlooked. It has enabled us to apply the model we had developed, and given us new ways of seeing how it can be used. Above all, it has given us some fascinating insights into the ways in which we create our own version of experience.

We had thought that we could end this chapter by making some useful remarks about barriers to learning and the importance of reflection. But we can no longer do this in the way we had anticipated. What we can say is that learning from experience is far more indirect than we often pretend it to be. It can be prompted by systematic reflection, but it can also be power-fully prompted by discrepancies or dilemmas which we are 'forced' to confront. It can be helped by 'naming' the process and admitting that there is an event which is unresolved. Other people can provide an invaluable means of identifying the discrepancy or dilemma; they can often see what may be obvious, but which is too close for us to notice. By supportively drawing it to our attention, they can help us learn from experience, even when they do not see themselves in that role.

Much as it can be convenient to break up our experience, to name the parts and to work intensively on some aspects of it, we have come now to recognize the importance of what some of our colleagues elsewhere in this book are emphasizing. Whatever else we do, we must always consider the whole. We must treat the whole of our experience as relevant and not be too surprised when connections are made which, previously, we had been unable to see. Much as we may enjoy the intellectual chase, we cannot neglect our full experience in the process. To do so is to fool ourselves into treating learning from experience as a simple rational process.

References

Bolman, L. and Deal, T. (1991) *Reframing Organisations*. San Francisco, CA: Jossey-Bass.

Boud, D. and Walker, D. (1990) Making the most of experience. *Studies in Continuing Education*, 12(2): 61–80.

Boud, D. and Walker, D. (1991) *Experience and Learning: Reflection at Work*. Geelong, Victoria: Deakin University Press.

Boud, D., Keogh, R. and Walker, D. (1985) Promoting reflection in learning: A model. In Boud, D.J., Keogh, R. and Walker, D. (eds) *Reflection: Turning Experience into Learning*, pp. 18–40. London: Kogan Page.

Griffin, V. (1987) Naming the processes. In Boud, D.J. and Griffin, V. (eds) *Appreciating Adults Learning: From the Learners' Perspective*, pp. 209–221. London: Kogan Page.

Minsky, M. (1982) *The Society of Mind*. London: Picador.

Walker, D. and Boud, D. (1992) Facilitating critical reflection: Opportunities and issues for group learning. In *Proceedings of the Third International Conference on Experiential Learning*, pp. 43–57. Pondicherry, India: Union Territory Administration.

6

Unlearning Through Experience

Angela Brew

There is an interesting contradiction in a book about learning from experience. Reading an academic book is a special kind of experience. But books are based on a particular view of knowledge and of the learning process which stresses its cumulative nature. As we move from chapter to chapter, we build up a knowledge of the subject or extend our range of understandings of the ideas the author wants to convey. There is also the assumption that the logic of the argument or the potency of the ideas will persuade us; that the book has the power to convince. Moreover, there is an assumption that, as we progress through a series of academic books, our understanding develops. Learning is presumed to be cumulative and knowledge incremental.

There are two conceptions of knowledge contained here. One is the idea of knowing as a quantity. We get more ideas as we proceed. The other sees knowledge as a quality of perception or our way of making sense of phenomena. It is also useful to distinguish, as Heron (1981) does, between: *propositional* knowledge, which claims to be assertions of facts or truths which are added to the store of knowledge; *practical* knowledge, which broadly refers to skills and abilities; and *experiential* knowledge, which is knowing a person (which can be oneself), an event, place or thing in direct interaction.

I am focusing on the process of reading an academic book because that is the experience in which you, as reader, are currently engaged. But also because this process says quite a lot about the way in which our knowledge is presumed to develop in our culture. In microcosm, reading academic books and indeed, for that matter, writing them, embodies a whole range of views about how we learn, many of which are presumed to apply to the process of learning from experience as well. For, after all, as I have said, reading books is a special way of learning from experience.

What I want to share with you in this chapter is my view of a rather different model of learning and knowing. I want to look at how the process of learning from experience can destroy previous learnings. I am concerned with those cases where new experiences transform our learning into something else. The phenomenon I am talking about exists on a variety of different levels from the relatively trivial to the profound and life-shattering. My concern is how we can develop the capacity for transformation. For the paradox is, that out of such unlearning, real knowledge does develop and grow.

When I talk about unlearning, it must be clear that I am not talking about forgetting. Forgetting is like dropping a few stitches. Unlearning is like unravelling the whole and knitting it all up again. In this sense, forgetting is relatively trivial because we can relearn that which has been forgotten. Unlearning means that what we know changes our world view, or an aspect of it, and we cannot reconstitute it in its original form.

If we view cognitive knowledge as the building up of a set of interrelated conceptual structures, we can see how that knowledge develops through a series of re-evaluations of previously held models in the example provided by Kuhn (1977). He describes how a boy, going for a walk with his father, learns to distinguish geese, ducks and swans. The boy not only learns about ducks from statements about what is not a goose, etc., he also learns general principles such as the idea that species breed true. New knowledge adds to or disconfirms ideas held already. The former happens when the new idea fits in with the already existing conceptual framework. The latter happens when an anomaly is evident, causing the whole framework to be revised.

A similar mechanism operates on a global or cultural level when a set of anomalous ideas cannot be incorporated within a framework of understanding and a complete conceptual reordering takes place. This represents a paradigm shift where paradigm refers to a whole, more or less self-consistent, framework of ideas, beliefs, attitudes and values in a given community. This is the Kuhnian notion of a scientific revolution. A conceptual reordering takes place and old ideas and explanations undergo reassessment, often with painful consequences.

But these examples refer to cognitive knowledge, not to the experiential domain and as such are relatively trivial. I know the earth goes round the sun, but I see the sun going across the sky each day. The effect of the Copernican Revolution on my daily experience is relatively unimportant. But there are occasions when my experience takes on a transformative capacity; when unlearning is by no means trivial. Learning from experience has the capacity to transform even prior experience and to undo prior learning. The extreme state is a position of total ignorance; a situation in which what we know is only what we thought we knew as when, for example, a stable family life is rocked by one partner leaving. This is a personal Copernican Revolution. It can affect the whole edifice of our lives as our world view shatters. This process may involve the crumbling of dearly held views. A new world view is needed and we may have no idea how to even begin to get it.

I believe that it is important for us to come to understand the mechanisms of this process, because as soon as we begin to unravel some of the boundaries and constraints on our conventional views of knowledge and how we learn it, we begin to see the way in which traditional ways of learning and conventional views of knowledge can get in the way of our coming to know; can be a way, again paradoxically, of preventing us from knowing. In particular, can effectively prevent us from coming to know ourselves. In this sense, reading a book on learning from experience can be a way of avoiding really learning from experience!

Some time ago I set off on a research journey. The idea was to explore how we come to know and in what that knowing consisted. There are a number of rules which bound and guide what counts as knowledge in our culture. These have their expression in traditional academic inquiry. There are the rules of objectivity, of separation or detachment of the knower from the known. There are rules about what is relevant to inquiry, about the separation of different domains or topics of inquiry, and about the relationship of ideas to each other as expressed in logic or hierarchies, and about processes and products being kept separate, and so on. But what happens if you break these rules? My concern was to see if new ways of knowing or new forms of knowledge were possible and, if so, what they were like.

I registered for a PhD. I was engaging in a process of coming to know; a learning process. It was experiential in the sense that I chose to come to know, not simply by reading up the literature, but by reflecting on the process of experience itself, recording both the experiences and my reflections on those experiences. These reflections were informed by reading and further experiences in a cyclical process of deepening understanding (Brew 1988). That is, after all, what research is – a process of learning from particular kinds of experiences.

But there is an assumption here of accumulation: either a progressive discovery of more and more facts which perhaps shed light on a particular issue, or a growing and deepening of understanding of the issues. The assumption that you learn more and more as you proceed, which we saw held for the reading of academic books, also holds in the research process. Indeed, our Western education systems are premised on it. There is also the presumption that learning gets more and more difficult as you proceed.

I do not wish to deny that, in a broad, general sense, we do know more at the end of a research process or of our education than at the beginning. At the very least, we probably have a wider repertoire of cognitive skills and more, and perhaps more complex, ideas. However, to argue that this of itself makes us more knowledgeable, least of all wiser, is misleading because it does not take into account a range of experiential knowings, including our inner knowing.

Learning from experience is similarly often held to have a cumulative quality. We talk of learning from our experiences. Wisdom is thought to come from experience. The assumption is often that it is the accumulation of experiences which leads to or parallels the accumulation of knowledge.

So I set out on my research. I was looking at how knowledge develops.

What I found was that while there was an appearance of a progressive deepening of my understanding, and that this was fed by a strong desire to find out, to know, there was also, following me along, a strong desire not to know or to not know.

Gradually, it became clear that there were a number of issues which I did not want to think about, which I did not want to acknowledge. Indeed, I even did not want to know what these issues were. I not only feared to know what I didn't want to know, I also feared to know what it was I didn't want to know. You may protest that for you things are different, that you want to know everything, but what I found was that I have a whole repertoire of mechanisms and procedures for preventing me finding out what I didn't want to know. Some of these were particular to me and were derived from my own personal history. For example, I did not want to know that I couldn't spend the rest of my life in the house I adored. But some I found embedded in the culture of academic inquiry. For example, in its emphasis on detached, impersonal knowledge, traditional academic inquiry de-emphasizes the role and value of human subjective experience. Indeed, even within the human sciences such as sociology or psychology, the emphasis on objectivity means that self-knowledge is excluded. Indeed, it is possible to argue that if we wanted to invent a form of inquiry that prevented us from knowing those things which we fear to know and also prevented us from coming to know ourselves, we could do little better than our traditional scientific method.

Whether or not we are engaging in a research process, we are all products of our culture and this means we are products of an educational system which supports and sustains a range of acceptable knowings and excludes unacceptable ones. Yet when we look at what is excluded, we find a number of interesting areas. The criterion of demarcation between acceptable and unacceptable knowledge is determined, so Popper (1963) argues, by its falsifiability. Anything else is defined as meaningless or metaphysical. This puts, for example, alchemy and astrology outside the range of scientific knowings. This is unfortunate. Each of these is concerned with the relationship of the self to the world of which it is a part. For example, in alchemy, the concept of 'innerstanding' gives expression to the idea that we shall understand the world when we understand ourselves (Klossowski de Rola 1973). Scientific knowledge defines self-knowledge as outside its range.

The implications of this for learning from experience are rather worrying. What it suggests is that the learning we do can be a way of avoiding what we need to or should learn. It means that a whole lifetime of experience and the learning so derived can be a defence against knowing those things we least want to acknowledge. It means that we can build a whole edifice of false knowledge in order to avoid facing what we do not want to know. It also means that we may be using inadequate criteria for checking the accuracy of our knowledge.

Supposing that we decide, fairly and squarely, to face those things we do not want to know. What are the implications? In my own case, I discovered that there was not a whole list of things, issues, ideas I did not want to face, which by bringing to light I could carry on as before, as if nothing had happened. During my research, facing what I didn't want to know involved a conceptual reordering of whole areas of my existence. In turn, these had to be translated into action; action which fundamentally changed my life. For example, acknowledging in an instant that I was a stranger in my house and garden and that liking it masked a fundamental alienation to that part of the country, led some five years or so later to a change of job, house, location and lifestyle.

The conventional view of learning from experience which I have portrayed here suggests that it is always a little blind. In that experiences, and the learning derived from them, are thought to be more or less cumulative and consistent, this blindness is inevitable. But I do not think learning from experience is really like this. Our memory is a compilation of what happened to us, together with our interpretation of those events. Even the past changes when we revisit it imaginatively in the light of new interpretations. This process can be traumatic. It can also be transformative.

The question for us then is: how can we ensure that we do not simply pile up a set of erroneous interpretations one upon the other, in blind disregard for a set of alternative explanations? How can we ensure that our learning is not based on an avoidance of those things we do not want to acknowledge? This question is also about how we can ensure that learning from experience is truly effective. If learning from experience is truly effective, then we are open to the opportunities for unlearning which are presented to us. We are ready for complete or partial conceptual reordering. We are open to new realities.

As I have said, in my doctoral research, I was concerned to break the rules to see whether new forms of knowledge were possible. In many situations of life, we are accustomed to judging whether something is relevant to the issue under consideration without any evidence and prior to the investigation. In traditional inquiry and, indeed, in educational settings – even some experiential learning ones – topics are separated and relevance is pre-judged. On the level of academic disciplines, for example, historical issues and sociological issues are separated off; emotional considerations are left out of biology.

One of the rules I broke in my research was the requirement to specify a clearly defined topic area. I was concerned not to pre-judge the relevance of any ideas or events to the inquiry. This was not something I could do in an instant. My academic training had given me clear yet unarticulated criteria for judging relevance which could not easily be abandoned. It was something I had to learn how to do. However, I discovered that if you act on the assumption that everything is relevant, you find some astonishing connections. These assist the learning process because they draw attention to otherwise unrecognized phenomena. For example, for some weeks I was totally preoccupied with pruning the garden hedges. The job was getting in the way of my research. How could I be discovering about knowledge when I was in the garden day after day? I wrote about the preoccupation as I wrote about research issues. It was only some considerable time later that I could see that the issues I had been tussling with at the time were to do with breaking boundaries in research methodology. I had been living my research on a practical, gardening, level. I had been establishing clear boundaries to contain my fear of getting into the unknown.

The idea that everything is relevant is expressed in the concepts of harmonic convergence and morphic resonance (Sheldrake and Bohm 1982). These have their expression in the quantum physicist's concept of non-local causality, when in the sub-atomic sphere, two apparently unconnected events can be seen to be connected; or, on a global scale, when similar scientific discoveries are being made in different places by unconnected research teams at a similar point in time, or when there is a confluence of hitherto unthinkable political events, such as the break up of apartheid in South Africa, the destruction of the Berlin Wall and the break up of the Soviet Union, all happening during a brief three-year period in history.

I am not claiming categorically that everything is relevant to everything else. This is either tautological or unknowable depending on how you look at it. What I am concerned with are the consequences, in terms of our learning from experience, of viewing everything as if it were relevant. Even apparently totally unconnected phenomena may, given time, subsequently turn out to be relevant. What I am suggesting is that extending the range of what we consider relevant to any given situation opens us up to new insights. This happens, for example, when skilled workshop facilitators use an aspect of the interaction which others might consider irrelevant to move the group forward in its task.

The phenomenologist Edmund Husserl (1973) said that if you think you know, then you should look again. Too often we close off possibilities by not looking enough. This idea is embodied in Kolb's (1984) notion of the experiential learning cycle or Rowan's (1981) concept of research cycling, where we move from an experience to reflecting on and conceptualizing that experience to the formulation of explanations which are then put into practice and so on. Popper's (1959) notion of falsifiability in research method also contains the idea of revisiting theories while regarding them as always potentially refutable.

Looking again means always being open to seeing anew and differently. By revisiting the same issues time and time again, the objective is to see, in the sense of getting a true intuitive grasp or understanding of a phenomenon. The value to the experiential learning process of successively looking again should, by now, be obvious. It means that our knowledge is always contingent. In combination with a commitment to treat everything as relevant, new insights emerge. Used to pre-judging relevance, we need to learn to take on more and more potentially relevant factors. Only if we keep looking again can we practise this.

Often in experiential learning, we give way to the fear of what we do not want to know, to the fear of knowing ourselves, and perhaps to strong emotional attachments which have dictated past patterns of behaviour. In presenting the Yacqui way of knowledge, Casteneda (1968) describes the Mexican Don Juan's notion of 'unbending intent'. This has some of the sense of diligence, but it is much more than that. It means going on even when the going gets tough. Acting with unbending intent means not getting caught by what Pirsig (1974) calls 'gumption traps'. So often, he says, what gets you stuck is running from the stuckness. The notion of unbending intent reminds us that there is no sense in trying to circumvent the stuckness. It has to be gone through. It cannot be got round. This is what psychotherapy is often about.

Guided in an attempt to learn from experience by an intention to treat everything as relevant, to look again if we think we know and to press on with unbending intent does not lead to an accumulation either of knowledge or of experience. At least, not as we conventionally conceive it. Rather the reverse. In my own case, I found that the use of these three guidelines led me, along with the circumstances of my life which accompanied their application, to a state, not of knowledge, but of a recognition of my total ignorance. For me, the point of transformation came when I realized that all that I had learnt in education, in life, in study, from books and from research over some 35 years, was useless in helping me to face and solve a particular crisis in a relationship. I was in total ignorance of what to do, how to behave, what I needed, what I wanted, what the issues were that were informing the situation and with no idea of how to decide how to proceed. Everything I had learnt about my self and how I related to my environment and to other people had had to be completely unstitched. At times like this, when one's reality is completely upturned, the level of unlearning is acute. I'd had a jigsaw puzzle which was the reality I had made up, painstakingly built up over my lifetime, added to by my experiences and informed by what I had learnt. And now the jigsaw was undone. The new jigsaw which I was trying to put together had too many pieces missing to make any sense, and in any case meant I had to change past experiences in order to make the new ones fit together. When one part of one's reality becomes unstitched in this way, there is a process of trying still to do the old jigsaw with bits of the new appearing. But it can't be done up and there is still more unlearning to do before the new puzzle begins to make sense.

The process I am describing is not merely cognitive. To some degree, we choose what propositional knowledge we accept and what we reject. Where unlearning is concerned, our whole selves are involved, and there is no choice. The point of total ignorance is the point of transformation, but there is no choice in what we transform into. The only choice is to blot out the lessons unlearnt. This becomes progressively more and more difficult as they gather momentum, reaching the point of total unknowing. Once our reality is deconstructed, it cannot ever be reconstructed in the same configuration.

Through our educational process, we do come to understand the world and that knowledge does, after all, grow and develop. Why go deeper into ourselves? If it is possible to build up experiences and learnings over a lifetime, building up knowledge of how to cope with problems, why should we risk the uncharted waters of the process of unlearning? Why should we engage in such difficult processes? Psychology is, after all, no substitute for engineering – particularly when there is a bridge to be built. I'm not suggesting we study psychology instead of technology. What I'm suggesting is that this whole process needs to be turned inside out. Imagine our current knowledge as an old overcoat. At the end of one sleeve is knowledge of the external world and at the end of the other is knowledge of the inner world. What I am suggesting is not that we swop one sleeve for the other, but rather that the whole overcoat needs to be turned inside out. The turning and the overcoat are the process of coming to know.

I've been talking about an occasion in our lives when the whole of our definition of reality undergoes a fundamental shift. Such occasions are, fortunately, rare. But the same mechanism applies when, for example, we are forced by the actions of others or the possession of new information, to re-examine a particular area of our lives; for example, the environmental effects of driving a car or a change in the managerial structure of an institution in which we work.

When I first started writing this chapter, instead of sitting down and writing about unlearning from experience, I found myself in a situation which required just the kind of perceptual reordering of an aspect of my reality I have been describing. I was trying to write about learning from experience and how sometimes one experience shatters the depths of our knowing and changes even the past experience. What was happening to me at the time was an instance of that very thing. I was having to give up a project in which I had invested a great deal of time and energy. I didn't want to write about it because I suppose I'd wanted to appear strong. I found myself wanting to appear as if I had learnt something. Somehow, there seemed to be something a little shameful in never making progress. So am I saying that although a new experience can make us unlearn, nevertheless we do learn from the experience, i.e. we do progress.

One of the ways I think I have progressed is in having a greater repertoire of ways out of holes. Like I know what holes I tend to get into and I have a number of ways of getting out. One of the techniques is quickly to acknowledge that I have absolutely no idea how to act, or what to do. Floundering around in a sea of unknowing feels somewhat familiar now and I don't get out of the hole by trying to get out; by planning a strategy as it were. Perhaps I get out of holes by redefining the hole; by reordering reality differently in some way. I know better now that this has to be done. I am more familiar now with the old stuff which entraps me, which contrives to prevent me moving on from the state of unknowing. I suppose I'm saying that I'm coming to know myself. I want to explore this in a little more detail because again self-knowledge is often assumed to result from an accumulation of experiences. I am suggesting self-knowledge results from unstitching experiences, from unlearning. So what do I mean by coming to know myself?

To explore this, let's make a distinction between, on the one hand, knowledge which comes from outside, from our relationship with the world through our experience, through our study and so on, and, on the other, knowing which somehow comes from inside of ourselves. An example of this was when I was buying my house. Despite a collapsing chain of buyers, irate sellers and acute pressure from the selling estate agent, I knew I had stood in my garden. I knew that the lounge I had stood in was my room, i.e. the one I had seen in my mind's eye two years before. I was unnerved by the surface reality but the inner knowing was firm. It was real.

There's another distinction which needs to be made and that is between knowledge which resides in the head, probably in the form of ideas, imaginings, understandings, and so on, and knowing which is located somewhere in the centre of our being. I am not merely talking about what Polanyi (1958) called 'tacit knowledge', which is a set of commonsense non-articulated understandings through which we make sense of our world. The concept of inner knowing is a strange one within the context of western scientific knowledge. Yet I have found that when I have talked to people about their inner knowings, the concept has not been alien. In mystical traditions, it is commonplace. It is given expression in the practice of meditation and asceticism. It is akin to the knowing of the Hebrew prophets. They had knowledge of the social and political conditions of their day which came not from an analysis of the situation but from an inner spiritual source. They demonstrated the possibility of accessing this ground or source of being and knowing.

Note that I am talking about inner knowing. Philosophers from at least the time of the Greeks have sought to establish how we can have knowledge which is certain. It's embodied in Descartes' (1912) famous question: 'If I am sometimes deceived, how can I be sure that I am not always deceived?' The concept of inner knowings is not a question of believing or supposing. It is knowledge, therefore certainty is endemic to it. As I have said, knowing and being are allied. They are different facets of the same dimension. So of course knowing is knowing. The problem is that we may think we know in the sense of having access to our inner knowings, when actually we are deceived. We are entrapped by our own particular perceptual spectacles. Traditional inquiry has no way of differentiating genuine from false inner knowings. We can see the dangers of confusing the feeling of certainty with truth in, for example, the global phenomenon of the rise of fundamentalism. This suggests why it is important to continually look again.

I am defining inner knowing as coming from our intimate relationship to the cosmos. But this sounds as if it comes unconnected to the situations in which we find ourselves and more or less at random. This is not what I am wishing to imply. Our knowings are a function of who and what we are in the way that knowing and being are, as I have suggested, intimately related on a cosmic level. It's as if there is a dimension or hyperspace of knowing and being (Bohm's implicate order, Bohm 1980). We individually manifest aspects of knowing. What we access or tap into is defined by our being. We cannot know what we are not. In that we deny who we are, so we cannot access what we know. The sad thing about our educational process is that it teaches us to deny our inner knowings and thereby to deny our very being, i.e. who we are. Self-knowledge means we have unclouded access to our knowing. There is strength in giving expression to such knowings. They are important to us.

When we talk of learning something, we refer to grasping or getting hold of or possessing something we did not previously have, or changing an aspect of our view of the world. But inner knowings, as I have described them, in that they are tied to our being, are in us all the time. They are a part of who and what we are.

Earlier, I wrote about the way in which conventional learning can inhibit the process of coming to know ourselves. There is so much noise around in the sense of ideas and activities outside of ourselves that inner knowings become obscured. Indeed, as we have seen, this noise often supports our fear of knowing. The problem with inner knowings is that we do not have any choice about them. They represent knowing, not supposition, as when, for example, we know a particular job is not right for us but we persist with the application. They will not go away. They will not be silenced. They continually knock on the door of our understanding. We can try to ignore them, but we cannot escape from the problems and issues which they continually pose for us.

Through our experience, we learn to live with such problems. We learn to contain them. We may even have a sense of getting better at dealing with them. But unless we engage in the process, which earlier I described as unlearning, we will never eliminate them, because to do so means accessing knowings we would prefer to ignore.

By treating everything as if it were relevant, looking again and again, and proceeding with unbending intent, we come face to face with ourselves; with who we are. What that means is that we become less protected and have a greater chance of accessing our inner knowings. Paradoxically, unlearning in this sense leads to knowing, for we uncover what clouds our view. We progressively learn to unlearn.

So let's recap. I've suggested that conventional views make the assumption that learning, knowledge and experience are all cumulative. Changes in knowledge are relatively trivial in the sense that they are unlikely to have life-shattering consequences. Unlearning takes place when experiences necessitate a conceptual reordering of the whole or a part of one's world view. This process puts us in touch with our ignorance but it provides a basis for coming to know ourselves by coming to access our inner knowings. We can assist this process by treating everything as relevant, by the continual process of looking again, and by proceeding with unbending intent.

Society cannot be what its members are not. The direction society pursues is that pursued by its members. In coming to know ourselves, we transform ourselves. In transforming ourselves, we transform society. Sometimes the circumstances of our lives give us no option. But I believe there is a moral imperative to choose to go in this direction. The process of transformation is a continual one. There is no end-product, only the process. We successively uncloud our view but we are always in the act of unclouding. We are continually looking again. There is only the journey and once we are on the journey there is no going back.

What I have written in this chapter, I have learnt from my experience. But there is no way that I could have done this by trying to do it. I set out to explore the nature and limits of our knowledge, with an interest in knowing whether other forms of knowledge were possible. I could not have predicted the outcome, for this was a conflation not only of the research ideas going on in my head and supported, upheld and advanced by the literature I was reading, it was also a function of the events of my life which needed to be made sense of. Reason and Marshall (1987) suggest that when we set out on a process of self-discovery, we always get more than we bargained for. This suggests an open-endedness in terms of learning outcomes. What we learn is what we learn, not what we choose to learn, nor what we would have liked to have learnt. This is in contrast to some types of learning where situations are planned in order to bring about specific learnings.

The decision to treat everything as if it is relevant makes us open to a large variety of contexts for learning and an openness to learning content. What we learn and where and how we learn it are not only unpredictable, they may cover a vast range. There are no artificially imposed limits to what can be learned.

Wisdom may come through experience, but it does not come through an accumulation of experience. Unlearning is about being prepared to throw out what one has learnt and begin afresh. I'm inclined to say that it is the process of learning that is important; that there is only the journey, never the destination. However, I think what I am referring to is the process of unlearning: the attempt to access our inner knowings; the coming face to face, again and again, with our ignorance; with our not-knowing. The highest point of knowing is not knowing. Herein lies the paradox of learning from experience.

References

Bohm, D. (1980) *Wholeness and the Implicate Order.* London: Routledge and Kegan Paul.

Brew, A. (1988) Research as learning. PhD Thesis, University of Bath.

Casteneda, C. (1968) *The Teachings of Don Juan: A Yacqui Way of Knowledge.* Harmondsworth: Penguin.

Descartes, R. (1912) *A Discourse on Method: Meditations and Principles* (translated by J. Veitch). London: Dent (first published in French in 1637).

Heron, J. (1981) Philosophical basis for a new paradigm. In Reason, P. and Rowan, J. (eds) *Human Inquiry,* pp. 19–35. London: John Wiley.

Husserl, E. (1973) *The Idea of Phenomenology* (translated by W.P. Alston and G. Nakhninkian). The Hague: Martinus Nijhoff (first published in German in 1964).

Klossowski de Rola, S. (1973) *Alchemy: The Secret Art.* London: Thames and Hudson.

Kolb, D. (1984) *Experiential Learning: Experience as the Source of Learning and Development.* Englewood Cliffs, NJ: Prentice-Hall.

Kuhn, T.S. (1977) Second thoughts on paradigms. In *The Essential Tension.* Chicago: University of Chicago Press.

Pirsig, R.M. (1974) *Zen and the Art of Motorcycle Maintenance: An Inquiry Into Values.* London: Corgi.

Polanyi, M. (1958) *Personal Knowledge.* London: Routledge and Kegan Paul

Popper, K.R. (1959) *The Logic of Scientific Discovery.* London: Hutchinson.

Popper, K.R. (1963) *Conjectures and Refutations: The Growth of Scientific Knowledge.* London: Routledge and Kegan Paul.

Reason, P. and Marshall, J. (1987) Research as personal process. In Boud, D. and Griffin, V. (eds) *Appreciating Adults Learning: From the Learner's Perspective.* London: Kogan Page.

Rowan, J. (1981) A dialectical paradigm for research. In Reason, P. and Rowan, J. (eds) *Human Inquiry.* London: John Wiley.

Sheldrake, R. and Bohm, D. (1982) Morphogenetic fields and the implicate order. *In Revision*, 5(2): 41–8.

7

Experiential Learning at a Distance

Mary Thorpe

At first sight, distance education might not seem a sympathetic context for experiential learning. The negative critiques of distance education highlight the differences between the two, suggesting that a traditional pedagogy of 'chalk and talk' has been replaced by 'wall-to-wall' course units (Harris 1987). Distance learning is seen as flawed precisely because (so the criticism goes) knowledge is packaged, even predigested, via uniform course materials in which the course team's view dominates and takes the place effectively of what should be the learners' effort after independent thought.

As a result, a critical, reflective capacity is not developed by the learner, and it is reflection, which so many thinkers have identified as the means through which both concrete experience and abstract theory are transformed into knowledge, which the learners 'own' and can use in their own terms (Kolb 1984; Boud *et al.* 1985). Reflection thus plays a central role in both experiential learning and in conceptual understanding. Distance education is seen as flawed to the extent that it undermines the development of reflection by the learner. The culmination of this argument sees distance education (as indeed any other form of education or training) as saved for 'real learning' through the addition of reflection.

This (now familiar) critique of distance education makes a point of central importance about the quality of learning. However, when we come to look at particular courses, critiques operating at this level of generality about distance education may be unjustified. Taking the Open University as an example, a very wide variety of learning experiences is offered through a diverse range of courses, many of which make serious attempts to promote reflection through in-text activities, projects and audio-visual materials.

Distance education and experiential learning

But can distance education create opportunities for experiential learning where the learner gets away from head knowledge and involves herself or himself in a qualitatively different way with ideas, feelings and personal history? Distance education has demonstrated successfully that courses can be designed to stimulate student reflection on concepts and arguments, but can it integrate study of the experience its learners bring to course work?

My experience is that courses can be designed so that students spend a much higher proportion of study time than is usually the case working on activities and assignments which create direct experience to be 'used' within the framework of the course. This strategy can be very productive where students are taking courses relating to their occupation or their social roles, and thus bring into the course a wealth of experience for learning. In recounting the events and outcomes of this experience, I will be reflecting on the nature of my own experiential learning as a course team member and tutor in the Open University, and on the implications of this experience for course design, which suggests that experiential learning should not be considered a simple 'add on' to a conventional course package.

Reflecting on course team experience

During the late 1980s, I was a member of a course team designing a professional diploma for practitioners working in the field of continuing education and training. 'Professional' is an important qualifier here, and I felt that the module I was to author could not work within the academic paradigm with which I was familiar from the undergraduate programme. One of the bedrock assumptions of higher education as practised at the Open University (notwithstanding the critiques which have been made of its practice) is that its courses should enable students to demonstrate an independent and critical grasp of knowledge. Although many of its courses are innovative because of their interdisciplinarity, they aim at the conventional academic outcome by assessment through written work which demonstrates the student's critical grasp of abstract thinking and analysis.

The Diploma presented a challenge of a different order. Here we wanted something other than academic critique alone; we aimed at the development of the learner as a professional or practitioner (I use the terms interchangeably here), both in terms of their sense of identity with a field of theory and practice, and in terms of a changed awareness which would shape their intended practice in future. The courses written for Diploma students were to be innovative in that the usual amount of course material was cut by about a half, and the students' study time was made up by completing activities in the units, work for the assignment, listening to an audio-cassette, and readings from set books.

My main role as a member of this course team was to produce one of these courses, titled 'Approaches to Adult Learning' (AAL). This course required about 120 hours study including the assignment. I felt unsure how to design and to write this course initially, because the Diploma aimed for professional development of its students, not simply increased knowledge and understanding.

I solved my problem eventually by using myself as guinea pig, and engaging in a form of experiential learning. I thought about my own professionalism, not unreasonably since I shared the same profession as many of my intended students. I asked myself how I had developed as a professional over the decade and more that I had worked for (tutored for, counselled for, researched for, written for, staff developed for, but never, despite my title, lectured for) the Open University.

Having posed myself the question, the answer came in the form of a flood of memories, the most insistent of which concerned the biggest collaborative teaching effort I had been involved in at that time – the production of the course Third World Studies. The course team experience had been formative for me, as for so many others. Although my experience overall was positive, many of the memories involved difficulties, or experiences which I had found hugely frustrating at the time. There had been many course team meetings lasting the whole day, with quite a large and disparate group of people (anything from twelve to twenty) struggling to fathom how to create the first distance taught course about the third world ever produced, and how to come to terms with each other at the same time.

I remembered the pattern of my life at that time, where so often the drive back from Milton Keynes to my home in London provided a very necessary space in which to live through my feelings from the day's events, to calm down and to work out how things might go next time round. Occasionally, I shared my journey with a colleague who listened and offered his own non-institutionalized insights into what my experiences might 'mean'. At any rate, I was grateful for his distance from the events, and for the alternative interpretations he offered – though very tentatively (he being a psychologist by trade) and only when asked.

This period of my life presents itself as one of intense learning, during which I developed in a number of ways professionally and, if one wants to separate things out this way, personally. I felt I knew more and could do more by the end of the four years, but I also realized that I had made a qualitatively different acquisition. In some ways, my aspirations had been changed, I saw the possibilities of what might be involved in teaching and learning in my own institution rather differently. I had worked with people active in researching and teaching in a number of third world countries, and I saw how their engagement with a field of social action as well as theory, informed how as well as what they wrote. I learned how what at first sight might seem to me unimportant differences of opinion over 'mere' phrasing, was for those inside the disciplines and social networks of their field a manifestation of important differences in approach to theory and practice. I was involved in the production of what has been termed 're-searched teaching' (Drake 1979).

Reflection on this experience brought the realization of how much I was prepared to learn and to persist despite difficulties which were unpleasant and stressful when I liked and respected the people with whom I worked. At the time, it was the goal of producing the course which seemed the galvanizing factor, but looking back I remembered how much it was also the stimulus of people which generated the effort and the learning. There was something here about the degree of intellectual engagement with the situation being linked with emotional engagement; I felt involved in an enterprise which mattered, not only to us, but to a wider penumbra of communities outside the course team.

There were other areas to reflect on, such as the disputes within the university about the value or otherwise of course teams (Blowers 1979; Costello 1979; Drake 1979). These highlighted the tensions between producing high-quality materials and meeting the targets required for print production in time for student mailings. Some consider the process of collegial discussion and commenting on drafts to be time-consuming and ineffectual. My own experience, by contrast, had been more positive. My reflection reminded me of how much my own writing had been polished – as well as demolished – by my colleagues. It is true that criticism can be damaging. I am told by my colleagues of one particularly sardonic occasion when the speaker began his demolition job with the words: 'this unit is crap' (adding hastily) 'but I don't mean that in a pejorative sense'. Nevertheless, course teams are also capable of providing much support to individuals and after all, it is better to know the worst that might be said of one's work before it is published, than afterwards when it cannot be changed.

My own experience of feedback on units I have written has been the occasion for some of the most intensive learning I have experienced. Indeed, I have always felt that extensive commenting on my own units has been an act of generosity by my colleagues, given the time it takes and the pressures under which many of us in higher education now work.

In sum, this reflection back over my own professional development crystallized a number of learned outcomes for me:

1. The importance of people and the quality of the relationships we have with our colleagues, in directly affecting the quality of what we produce.
2. The need to trust that collaborative decision-making will have valuable outcomes and should not be lightly cast aside in favour of more managerial methods for course production.
3. The necessity for a degree of mutual generosity if you are going to produce the highest quality teaching and learning experience – during course production, as well as for students studying the course afterwards.

Applying reflection to course development

This reflection on my own experience had been stimulated by the impasse of my writing for the professional diploma. How did it help with that? Essentially, it enabled me to solve my course design and writing block, because I felt as a result of what I had got out of my own reflection, that I had to somehow recreate the same or a similar process of reflective engagement for my students. This would be a process of reflection on their own experience, both prior and concurrent, and on the relationships between it and the content of the module I was to create.

I also realized that my learning had had at least two stages: that which occurred at the time of the experience, and that which I had just undertaken, thereby identifying more clearly what had been learned which was verified subsequently. I named what I had learned from experience, and thus made it a more explicit part of what I knew, more 'to hand' for future application. In both stages, I had been engaged in a very active processing of my direct experience, though in the first stage much more intensely and with the added dimension of having to handle the immediate emotional charge of experiences. This 'thinking about' or reflection was the process through which I learned from my own direct experience, and accordingly I saw how I must make it central to the module I was to write. I realized not only how much I had indeed learned 'on the job', but the extent to which I had been 'formed' by my experience. This learning had significance for my own identity; I was prepared to give it the serious consideration it deserved, and to encourage my students to do so in relation to their own experience.

Reflection as the key concept

Looking back on this process of reflecting on my own professional experience, I see how I used it to shape my teaching in a number of ways. First, it directly affected the content of the module, since it led me to present reflection as the key process in professional learning and as central in learning in adulthood generally. This emphasis appeared early in the text, linked to the theoretical work on reflection in professional development (Schön 1983) and on reflection and experiential learning (Boud *et al.* 1985).

A process-oriented teaching approach

Secondly, it directly influenced how I wanted to teach, and led me to a process-oriented design for the module as a whole. I concluded that the best way to encourage the professional development of my students was to build in the process of reflection to their study of the module. I wanted them to become interested (if they were not already) in their own learning as but one instance of how adults learn generally. Their experience would be different from the classic undergraduate approach referred to above of how adults learn, because they would be asked not only to reflect throughout, but to use their own direct experience as a resource for thinking critically about the ideas and theories presented in the module. This is not a new idea, but I believe it was applied with a degree of consistency and to an extent which is not often found in assessed courses. Let me present some evidence in support of this.

The module text has activities which ask the learner to rehearse their prior experience and reflect on it. For example, the second activity in the text asks the students to pause from their reading of definitions of learning and of the nature of 'learning on the job' to engage in an exercise which you will now recognize as a reconstruction of my own reflection prior to producing the module:

> Looking back, would you say that your own approach to teaching and learning has changed? If so, can you relate these changes to particular people, events, circumstances or activities? You might find the questions below helpful as a prompt:
> a. How did the change(s) come about? Was the change triggered by particular events, circumstances or people? Was an agency involved – such as an external examining body, like City and Guilds?
> b. Do I perceive these changes as improvements, or not? Do they represent increases in confidence for me?
> c. Was my learning stimulated by feelings of satisfaction/dissatisfaction, success or failure in my own performance?
> (*Approaches to Adult Learning* 1988)

The students were also asked to reflect on their own learning process as it was happening. They were, for example, asked to become aware of and to evaluate their own learning as it progressed, by working through a self-evaluation exercise at particular points in the text. These took the form of a number of questions, posed informally, thus:

> Thinking about your work on the preceding sections:
> a. Aspects which interested me were . . .
> b. Things which I would have liked more/less of . . .
> c. About myself: how well did I work? Am I feeding in my interest? Am I using my own experience?
> d. Are there any implications for how I approach learning in the rest of the module?
> (*Approaches to Adult Learning* 1988)

The students were asked to record their thoughts in answer to these questions and to the activities in a journal or portfolio. The idea for this was introduced through the experience described by Walker (1985) of using a portfolio as a means of enabling learners to work through their ideas and feelings, as they relate to their coursework. For Open University Diploma students, the value of keeping a portfolio was stressed but left as a voluntary activity, with the option that it could be shown to the tutor or students, if they wished. The idea was suggested that writing can be a way of capturing thoughts and feelings, and working with them more consciously. Writing was presented as a way of structuring and of using reflection strategically, for intentional learning:

> The distinguishing feature about the portfolio is that it is for you, and therefore that it should offer a release from the kind of inhibitions which plague more "public" writing – "how will it sound?", "they will

think I'm stupid if I say that", "what I've got to say is still so incoherent, so unworked out". In fact your portfolio is precisely for work at this more difficult, semi-coherent stage of thoughts and feelings, even if you also decide to use it to make notes on the content of the module and offprints as well.

(Approaches to Adult Learning 1988)

An 'experiential' assignment

This idea of writing as an opportunity to crystallize and sort out thoughts and feelings was also linked to the continuous assessment component of the course. It was suggested that the assignment could be seen not just as a hurdle required by the institution, but as a rather more formal version of the kind of capture and reconstruction of thinking just described. Since the written assignment is a formal submission for assessment, more stress was put on the value of this kind of writing for the construction of coherence and clarity in thought and its presentation.

The assignment also provided a distinctive third feature (in addition to reflection and writing in a journal) in the experiential nature of the course. It included options where students could set up interviews or group discussions and thus engage in a form of designed experiential learning as part of assessed coursework. One option, for example, required that students interview about half a dozen learners, drawn in all probability from those known to them in their own institution, in order to explore the ways in which individuals differ from each other as learners. Whatever their choice of assignment, however, all of the students were required to reflect on what they got out of completing it. They were required to write about 500 words in reflection on 'the value to me of completing this assignment and whether changes in its design would have made it a more productive exercise for me'. This requirement embodied the process-oriented approach of the module, in asking that the students reflect on their learned outcomes and communicate their thoughts to their tutor in a written addition to their assignment.

A conversational style

Finally, I believe that my own reflection on experience in a course team affected the style of what I wrote, which had a degree of personal involvement and directness which it might not otherwise have had. The text manifests the characteristics of what Holmberg (1989) has called a 'guided didactic conversation'. It retains the stance of a practitioner addressing other practitioners, and in places refers to my own experience. It has a conversational and informal style, and frequently directs back to the reader, questions about their own response. The activity to which I drew attention earlier, for example, was followed by a comment which drew on my own reflection, and illustrates the kind of style Holmberg is referring to:

Thinking back to my own response to the previous activity, I realise that I used only work experience, and that initially, only positive instances came to mind. But I can also list "negative" or less successful things which have changed my own practice – often in very specific ways, as when one thinks "well I won't do that again", when something we do goes badly wrong or misfires.

(*Approaches to Adult Learning* 1988)

This is one example of a textual style intended to reflect Holmberg's criteria for guided didactic conversation:

. . . invitations to an exchange of views, to questions, to judgements of what is to be accepted and what is to be rejected.

Attempts to involve the student emotionally so that he or she takes a personal interest in the subject and its problems. Personal style including the use of personal and possessive pronouns: I, my, you, your, etc.

(Holmberg 1989)

The students' response

Since the module was first presented in 1988, about 200 students have taken it. An evaluation was undertaken with some of the students who studied the module during 1988, and the findings suggest a generally positive response by students, with particularly strong appreciation for some of the conceptual material, and for the assignment.

Valuing theory

First, the students did value the theories of adult learning to which they were introduced, especially the work on reflection and experiential learning, individual differences in learning, and barriers to learning or 'learning blockages' (Downs and Perry 1984).

I've always worked with adults, but this is actually giving what I see as the technical back-up and specific knowledge about my experiences and its slotting in together very nicely and very helpfully, and it means that I feel that I can actually talk with more authority about adult learners.

(Field Officer, Open Learning)

I think that as far as I'm concerned, knowledge is giving one confidence . . . it gives one the confidence to know that I'm not stupid and I'm not just practical – I've been being practical, working practically for years – and I can do this theory business.

(Self-employed Education Adviser)

The students welcomed rather than rejected the theory introduced in the module, which they saw as relevant to their immediate work experiences. In this regard, there is a divergence with the literature around in-service education for school teachers. Much of this literature tackles the mismatch between teacher experience and values, and theories of schooling and learning derived from psychology and sociology. Why are these practitioners in post-compulsory teaching not equally alienated by academic theorizing? Two factors are suggested by the evidence here.

The first is that much of the content of the module presented *applied* research undertaken in contexts with which the students could often identify. The selection of material, and the depth of coverage, was found by the students to be both valid and relevant. This suggests that these students were not necessarily intrinsically more theory-oriented than school teachers, but that the selection and mode of presentation of researched or theory-based material influences whether students react positively or negatively to it. The second factor which may account for their reaction derives from differences in the social position of practitioners in continuing education and training. Practitioners in this area are a very heterogeneous group with very undeveloped structures for professional training and progression. The entrenched positions on contentious issues, which characterize school education, are not as yet mirrored in the post-compulsory area. If anything, there is a dearth of theory which can in any way be seen as relevant to an age range of students varying from 16 to 96, learning in contexts as diverse as the workplace, an open learning centre, nurse education, higher education and so on. In this context, a modest amount of theory is welcomed, even for legitimizing practical experience whose value is not necessarily widely recognized.

Valuing reflection

In association with the welcome given to the theoretical framework of the module, the students also valued the legitimacy it gave to finding the time for their own reflection. Students have valued the opportunity for extensive reflection on themselves and their practice. The theory in the module helped them feel justified in finding the time for something which it is only too easy to push to one side under everyday pressures. The process-oriented features of the text were seen therefore as more than just desirable teaching devices, because they were reading at one and the same time about theories and research which provided a rationale for their intrinsic value in learning. Theory and practice in this sense worked together to create a much more convincing whole, than either on its own:

> ... it does give you a chance to actually stop still and think about what you're doing. It makes you focus in a bit more, not on the minutiae of what one is doing every day, but it gives you the chance

to sort of take an overview . . . it certainly helped me to actually re-examine a lot of my teaching techniques and approaches and so on that I've taken for granted.

(Deputy Head, Community School)

Many students did talk about the ways in which they reflected more, and more intentionally, than before. Many said they did record their thoughts, if not always to the extent intended in the guidelines on setting up a portfolio:

Well, I can remember writing down things like I felt isolated and I felt on my own, I wasn't sure what I was doing . . . And then gradually, as I started to work through the course, then it finally clicked that I was actually learning quite useful skills by having to be on my own and to sort things out myself . . .

(Adult Basic Education Tutor, part-time)

Valuing experiential learning

Another major outcome was linked with what students got out of their work for the assignment. The most popular option has proved to be that in which students interview a number of individuals (often their own students or learners with whom they are working) about their approaches to learning. For many, this has proved little short of a revelation:

The most important part of studying AAL was the assignment that I did because I interviewed people for the first time ever on tape. I did an assignment concerning the different ways in which adults learn, and it suddenly made all sorts of pennies drop for me. I could actually suddenly feel something that I could understand that I hadn't understood before, which was that people who had done well at school and so on, it hadn't just happened. They'd actually had a way of doing it. The people I spoke to who had been "successful" learners had had actual strategies for doing it, even when they were just at school, and they developed those strategies as they got older . . . I used [Boud et al. 1985] extensively in the assignment because it just fitted in exactly to what people had said. I could underline bits and say "Kate said this" and "Helen said that": and these are all people that I knew reasonably well and it was quite fascinating to do it, so I really enjoyed doing the assignment.

(Technical College Tutor)

This appears to be a classic case of the difference between knowing a thing and experiencing it. Propositions about the dimensions of diversity among adult learners may come across with the obviousness of common sense – and risk thereby having virtually no effect on what people do as facilitators. But by using their assignment to interview a number of learners, students have gained direct experience of this diversity and a commitment to change their practice the better to recognize their new awareness.

So the module had a number of positive outcomes for many students, associated with both the concepts of reflection and experiential learning, and with the opportunities for themselves as learners to engage in various forms of experiential learning as a legitimate component of course study. However, students vary in the degree to which they respond, to both content and style, and there are less successful areas of the module which suggest that the use of experiential learning needs development. Many students, for example, have neither enjoyed nor come to terms with the information-processing model of learning (Gagne 1977), which was also used in the module. Only one of the students interviewed said that she used writing as a way of tackling her difficulties with the ideas and working them out. Reflection at a distance appears to have been a relatively weak tool where ideas do not find an immediate fit with practitioner experience. A welcoming style in the text was not enough to encourage the students to work with their difficulties in their portfolio, or to sort out questions to put to their tutor to help resolve their difficulties.

Effect of the students' responses

Part of the rationale for introducing the idea of a portfolio was to encourage the students to use their own writing as an opportunity for learning. Looking back, and reading through the interview transcripts of my students, and through their assignments and examination papers, I have to admit that I committed the original sin of all teachers (well, perhaps almost all), of assuming that the way I learn is desirable for everybody else. In this respect, I had not taken enough notice of my own teaching, which stressed the need to recognize the differences between all learners. Some people, perhaps most people, do not enjoy writing, and while they might be persuaded to see it rather more positively than they have done in the past, it is probably too much to expect that they transform their settled attitude towards it completely, and suddenly start to use it as a major medium for their own learning. Although group work was suggested, there were very few opportunities for group discussion and so reflection in ways other than writing was under-emphasized.

However, the feature which most students commented on spontaneously and positively was the assignment where they interviewed other learners. This led me to reflect on the significance of experiential learning for distance education more generally: first in relation to student independence, one of the key concepts in distance education (Juler 1990), and, secondly, in relation to the implications for course design.

Making time – and place – for experiential learning

Course teams who want to incorporate experiential learning to a significant extent need to rethink some conventional norms about the materials they produce. First, it is not enough to invite the students to reflect on their experience, while producing exactly the same amount of course material for study. A reduction in the study time required for materials is necessary and, in many instances, this will mean a reduction in text. This legitimates the time spent by the students in working actively with course ideas, and reflecting on their own experience.

Secondly, courses should seek to create opportunities for students to gain new experience in contexts away from the authority of the teaching institution. These are, in effect, opportunities for empowerment, in which students can find out for themselves, account for what they discover, and its implications, and thus take on some of the roles conventionally assigned to the teacher. This requires independence in the sense that students need to set up activities or investigations which they carry out on their own, using help provided by course materials and their tutor. It does not necessarily mean the kind of independence which some institutions may have in mind, where students can study effectively with very little help from a tutor at all.

All this may require a shift in orientation for the course team, from the idea of creating a 'tutorial in print' (Rowntree 1974) to that of designing how the student uses the study time required for course completion, and creating opportunities for new forms of direct experience. However, written texts are generally less effective than facilitative persons in giving back to the learner opportunities to discover for themselves and to produce accounts of their experience. Within distance education, texts have been used more often to initiate a kind of dialogue at a distance between author/course team and learner, than to enable learners to create their own texts independently.

But texts can be used, as in the AAL module and in project-based courses, to outline projects and tasks which set the learner off on experience designed for learning, undertaken independently of the institution. This can, as described here, involve the learner in extensive interaction with people not in any way connected with tutors or the course team. None the less, as has also been documented here, students can make connections between this experience and the concepts of their course work. When this happens, the learning seems to take on a particular force and legitimacy. In the comments students have made about AAL, it is where personal experience and insight is legitimated and illuminated by theory that there is greatest commitment to learning and its outcomes for changed future practice.

The implication of this for practice in distance education is that course teams may have to reduce both the amount of text and possibly also stylistic features designed to encourage dialogue, if these threaten to leave no space in which students can develop their own thinking and thus create their own texts. Strategies which increase the amount of text produced by course team authors, reduce the amount of time in which students can work out what they think and feel, and carry out their own projects, including projects explicitly designed to create opportunities for experiential learning. Institutions of education and training need to timetable time and space for experiential learning if students are to take it seriously.

In relation to these requirements, distance education is neither more nor less good as a site for experiential learning than conventional face-to-face education. It is as possible for the learner to be dominated by the verbal mastery of a teacher in the face-to-face context, as by the text in distance teaching. Further, by attending an institution, the possibilities for creating experiential learning are reduced to what can be generated within the classroom. Distance learners often spend hardly any time in the classroom, and are in a position to integrate study with the outcomes of continuing experience going on in parallel.

The value of this is perhaps most apparent in the kind of professional development course work I have been describing, in which the content of course work is relevant to day-to-day experience at work, thus suggesting that for some kinds of learning, factors of both place and time are important. Some would argue indeed that this is one of the greatest contributions which experiential learning has made – to focus attention on the fact that much valuable learning occurs away from sites of institutional provision of education and training.

However, where experiential learning is designed to contribute a significant proportion of the study time on a course (in the example discussed here, 25 per cent at least), both the content and process of the course are changed in a number of ways. The subject matter and referential focus of the course is changed by the inclusion of explicit references to the experience the learners brings with them. Its purpose is also modified because it includes the idea that the substance of what is being taught should not only be accurately learned, but subject to a critical integration with the learners' experiential learning.

The role relationships and pattern of interaction between teacher and learner are also changed, perhaps radically, by the legitimacy given to the learner's perspective. The only expert where experiential learning is concerned is the learner whose experience it is. 'It is the learner's interaction with the learning milieu which creates the particular learning experience. While facilitators, and others, can help create the milieu, it is the learner who creates the experience' (Boud and Walker 1990: 62).

More of the learners' attention is likely to be focused, in any case, away from the processing of abstract knowledge and information, onto the implications for themselves of what is in the course materials. Learners turn away, metaphorically speaking, from the teacher and institutional authority, to focus on the particularity and meaning of their own experience, in the light of the ideas they have been studying.

This can also lead to a literal change of place for learning, where learners incorporate planned periods of new experiential learning as part of course work. This is to overturn the classic epithet for distance education as 'home-based learning', because learning clearly may take place wherever the students' experiential possibilities take them, in or outside the home. Along with a change of place will often go an expansion of the number of people who play an important role in what is learned – the learner's colleagues, students, friends and family, for example.

Thus it is possible to see how two courses on the same subject or theme, one incorporating experiential learning the other not, offer two very different *domains* for learning. Both types of course, however, can be taught at a distance, and distance education is not anti-experiential learning in any intrinsic sense. It does indeed offer the potential for a rich learning experience through the integration of conceptual thinking with experience from a particular milieu. The students in this study appeared to value conceptual knowledge highly, without necessarily prioritizing it over their own direct experience. Indeed, course work appeared able to nourish new forms of experience and to validate intuitive knowledge.

Perhaps the greatest challenge to distance educators who wish to incorporate more experiential learning in their courses, will be to cut down on the amount of direct course text they produce, to hand back some space and time to students, and to respond appropriately to the texts their students produce, especially where experiential learning is presented for assessment. Distance education offers a rich and challenging environment for experiential learning, both by course teams and by students.

References

Approaches to Adult Learning (1988) Professional Studies in Post-Compulsory Education, Module 1. Milton Keynes: The Open University.

Blowers, A. (1979) Carry on course teams. *Teaching at a Distance*, 16, Winter: 54–7.

Boud, D. and Walker, D. (1990) Making the most of experience. *Studies in Continuing Education*, 12(2): 61–80.

Boud, D., Keogh, R. and Walker, D. (eds) (1985) *Reflection: Turning Experience into Learning*. London: Kogan Page.

Costello, N. (1979) The curse of the course team: A comment. *Teaching at a Distance*, 16, Winter: 53–4.

Downs, S. and Perry, P. (1984) Developing learning skills. *Journal of European Industrial Training*, 8(1): 21–6.

Drake, M. (1979) The curse of course teams. *Teaching at a Distance*, 16, Winter: 50–3.

Gagne, R.M. (1977) *The Conditions of Learning*. New York: Holt, Rinehart and Winston.

Harris, D. (1987) *Openness and Closure in Distance Education*. London: Falmer Press.

Holmberg, B. (1989) *The Theory and Practice of Distance Education*. London: Routledge.

Juler, P. (1990) Promoting interaction, maintaining independence: Swallowing the mixture. *Open Learning*, 5(2): 24–33.

Kolb, D. (1984) *Experiential Learning*. Englewood Cliffs, NJ: Prentice-Hall.

Rowntree, D. (1974) *Educational Technology in Curriculum Development*. London: Harper and Row.

Schön, D.A. (1983) *The Reflective Practitioner*. New York: Basic Books.

Walker, D. (1985) Writing and reflection. In Boud, D., Keogh, R. and Walker, D. (eds) *Reflection: Turning Experience into Learning*, pp. 52–68. London: Kogan Page.

8

Learning from Experience in Mathematics

John Mason

My aim in this chapter is to put forward a description of a disciplined practice derived from, and designed to promote, intentional learning from experience. I use the word *intentional* because I have become convinced that 'One thing people do not learn from experience, is that they do not often learn from experience alone.' In order to learn intentionally from experience, some action is necessary. The extra action needed amounts to what Khan (1983) called '*the epistemology of self-experience*' and what I call '*the discipline of noticing*' (Mason 1991). My examples will be drawn from mathematics, but more general application may be detected by practitioners in other fields.

From doing to construing

It is extremely tempting to launch into analysis and distillation of thirty years experience of teaching mathematics, but to do so would be inconsistent with what I have learned. I therefore invite you to bear with me, and to consider the following sequence of observations:

$$2 + 2 = 2 \times 2$$

This is surely an unexceptional observation. What about

$$3 + 1\tfrac{1}{2} = 3 \times 1\tfrac{1}{2}?$$

Don't rush on, think about it, savour it!
And if that is followed by a third expression,

$$4 + 1\tfrac{1}{3} = 4 \times 1\tfrac{1}{3}$$

and a fourth,

$$5 + 1\tfrac{1}{4} = 5 \times 1\tfrac{1}{4}$$

then even if you are not very confident with checking the computations, if you look at the sequence of expressions

$$2 + 2 = 2 \times 2$$

$$3 + 1\frac{1}{2} = 3 \times 1\frac{1}{2}$$

$$4 + 1\frac{1}{3} = 4 \times 1\frac{1}{3}$$

$$5 + 1\frac{1}{4} = 5 \times 1\frac{1}{4}$$

then I *know* that you *know* what will appear next.

Am I not right? It would be worthwhile spending a few seconds considering what you think is going to come next, and if possible, to try to say it to someone near you. Don't be bashful. Try to make a conjecture, because that is an extremely important part of mathematical thinking – having a go and then being willing to modify what you think, rather than waiting until you are sure you have it right, or deciding that you cannot do it and therefore doing nothing. Conjecturing is painless; it is releasing and playful because there is no commitment.

My conjecture is that you recognize that the next expression will start with a 6. Then there will be a plus sign. Then a 1, sitting beside a fraction. And you probably also know what that fraction is going to be, and what the other side of the equality sign is going to be. Pause now and work out what I would write next.

What I would write if I started off with $17 + \ldots$? How might the first expression be rewritten in order to bring it into line with the others? What about $100 + \ldots$? What about $4317 + \ldots$? What about *blah* $+ \ldots$? Or *Oomph* $+ \ldots$? Or *numb* $+ \ldots$? Or $n + \ldots$?

The mathematics which can develop from this simple start is interesting, lying at the heart of that school topic which is the watershed for so many: algebra. But much more interesting in this context is what you noticed about yourself. No matter what your reaction to what has happened so far, you have just had an opportunity to observe yourself, and this is essential in order to learn from experience intentionally.

You may have been put off by the presence of mathematics in this chapter, in which case you have the opportunity to observe your reaction. I don't mean telling yourself some explanatory story about a childhood experience which places blame somewhere. There may indeed be feelings aroused, which may possibly reflect vibrant childhood experiences, but they may equally well be triggered interpretations of natural and positive physiological changes such as increased heart rate, adrenalin flow, restricted breathing, etc. (Mandler 1989). By observing, I mean re-entering the experience of the moment, observing without judging or explaining, without indulging or indwelling; trying to describe it to yourself or to a colleague briefly-but-vividly, without judgement, amplification or explanation. There is plenty of opportunity for accounting for – for explaining – later.

It may be that you allowed your eyes to pass over the mathematical expressions, *looking at* each one in turn, but without *looking through* them, seeing each one but not seeing them in relation to each other. This behaviour is common among students, who early in their school careers learn to *work through* a series of exercises, but often never discover what it means to *work on* a series of exercises. It is as if they believe that doing the task the teacher sets, with a minimum of investment on their part, will produce the learning that the teacher is supposed to provide. This attitude is most unlikely to lead to intentional learning from experience.

On the other hand, it may be that you had a sense of developing pattern. This might even have begun to come to expression, either in actions (where you feel that as you write something down you are filling out a form of which you are partly aware) or in words (where as you start to say what you see, more detail emerges). I call this *expressing generality*. If you recognize any of this pattern seeking or expressing, then you have direct experience of the supremely mathematical experience of *generalizing*. That, too, is worth re-entering and savouring, even describing briefly-but-vividly verbally or on paper.

Now consider whether you recognize what you observed in this instance in some other recent experience, whether the act of generalizing, reacting to a task by some displacement activity, or working through but not on, or something else. It need not be mathematical, since every discipline involves generalizing in characteristic ways, and there are many opportunities to indulge in displacement activity or to work through. The important thing is to try to relate your current experience to past experiences, because this builds up a rich network of interconnected memories, which in turn can provide access to alternative behaviour in the future.

Most people, confronted with a task, either engage with it, or else find some reason to avoid or modify it. In either case, they are caught up in doing – doing the task or doing something else. But people often fail to pause and try to construe, to make explicit sense of what they do. Instead, they are left with unconnected fragments of stimulating ideas, stirred emotions and either successful or failed actions. By chance, these memory fragments may be resonated in the future, even summoning clear recall of the event. But intentional learning through experience requires more than trusting in haphazardly metonymic triggering of randomly stored memories.

I can't count the number of times I have been in a meeting, seminar or workshop, and thought to myself, 'That's a good idea, I must try that, use that, see about that, follow that up.' And yet, the moment I head for the door, I am caught up in thoughts about the next event, whether it is food, or another meeting or something else I have to do. Within seconds I find it impossible to recall what only moments before was vibrantly alive inside me. Even when I make notes, once they are out of the context of the session they lose their vibrancy. They suddenly become like all the other notes I have taken in the past. I gave up regularly reading newspapers when I realized that at the end of the reading, I had not the faintest idea what I had read, nor did I care. I find the same with radio and to some extent television. I have great difficulty recalling what I have heard, once there has been a change in the programme. To learn from these experiences, something more is required than passive presence.

The action necessary usually takes the form of storytelling, of accounting for fragments by weaving at least some of them into a coherent tapestry. This action may be based in cultural practices such as discussing last night's programmes at school or work the next day, or in disciplined cognitive reconstruction, in which you intentionally give brief-but-vivid accounts of fragmentary details, and then once these have been negotiated and agreed, weave these into a global story. The event then becomes the story which accounts for the remembered fragments. *Reconstruction* is a one-word descriptive label for the action which could take place in any situation, not just reading newspapers or attending sessions. When developed into a disciplined practice which exploits the human powers of mental imagery, and which involves developing a range of reflective practices such as story weaving, it becomes a means to learn intentionally from experience.

Reflective interlude: What has happened so far?

Recall your reaction to the aphorism and its corollary: the one about learning from experience. Can you recall it, or has it been overlaid with the mathematics which followed? If you paused and considered whether you agreed with them, you quite likely tried to find some examples in your own experience against which to test their validity. Mathematicians call this *specializing*, that is, applying a generality to particular test cases. They consider specializing (seeking confirming instances or possible counter-examples) to be intensely mathematical behaviour, but their version is only a disciplined version of what people do perfectly naturally all the time.

Specializing and generalizing are part and parcel of coming to know something, or what might be called *natural epistemology*. The word *natural* is of course controversial, because it appears to deny other epistemologies such as recourse to higher authority. I use it to signal that it is something which people very often do quite naturally despite any other avowed methodology. The purpose of specializing is both to see whether the proposed generality speaks to experience, and also to try to detect what the generality is saying by applying it to specific instances and then re-generalizing for yourself.

I invited you to undertake a mathematical task. But that task could be engaged in on at least three levels: (1) a mathematical response was possible, by doing the task while attending to what Tahta (1980) called its *outer meaning* in trying to predict a pattern; (2) activation of mathematical awarenesses was possible, such as transition from the particular to the general, and multiplicity of expressions with the same value, and these could have metaphoric as well as mathematical content (what Tahta called *inner meaning*); and (3) taking the opportunity to become aware of how you engaged and what you did – in short, to observe yourself, without judgement or criticism (*meta-meaning*).

I then broke off the mathematical activity and invited you to become aware of what you had done. This was an explicit move on my part to shift attention away from doing towards construing. There may have been many other things which you were attending to, including physiological changes, emotional responses and so on. But I have enough experience of using the 2 + 2 task to know that most people are caught up in the pattern in the moment.

I then offered a label for the awareness of pattern seeking and of expressing that pattern, namely *expressing generality*, or more simply, *generalizing*. I did more than simply offer a label. I invited you to consider whether you recognized that thinking process in your own experience, and I used that opportunity to make a few remarks which were intended to resonate with the experiences summoned up by working on the 2 + 2 exercise.

In a mathematical education context, I might then suggest that you think ahead to some situation likely to arise in the classroom soon in which generalizing could play a part. If this seemed attractive, you might then consider whether it would be worthwhile to be explicit about drawing your own students' attention to generalizing, or to act in some other novel way which would support students in employing their generalizing powers.

The mathematical activity was parallel to the aphorism about experience. As well as illustrating what I mean by intentionally learning from experience, I was providing two different contexts in which to carry out the same actions. I offered a fulcrum about which to shift your attention from the overt task and outer meanings, to inner- and meta-meanings, with the expectation that you would probably (but certainly not necessarily) observe something about your cognitive actions in testing a generality against experience.

By way of contrast, I introduced a pedagogic distinction between *looking at* and *looking through*, and between *working through* and *working on*, but in an abstract and laconic manner. What little sense you have of these as they went by provides further grist for considering the sort of support for reflective construal that is possible, perhaps even necessary. Further work on any of these notions would involve exposing you to more situations in which they were relevant, and gradually making my prompts less and less explicit, until you were observing them and acting upon those observations for yourself.

I have tried to indicate specific practices which comprise active and intentional reflection. By having your attention focused on specific recent experience, labels such as specializing and generalizing can become richly meaningful terms which remind you not only of your past experience, but possibly also will remind you in the future of some way of working that you would like to remember to do.

This process, this cycle of activity, reflecting on recent experience, relating it first to the past and then to the future, and then validating that against the experience of others, is, I suggest, the essence of how people actually do learn from experience. When I observe people outside of their professional capacity, I observe the same processes but employed in an *ad hoc* fashion. When I listen to what lies behind the posturing of professionals about their methodology, I hear the same processes being described. But to do it intentionally, to be methodologically and systematically effective, requires personal discipline.

Noticing

To notice something is to make a distinction, for without distinctions there are no boundaries, no edges. But distinction-making is non-trivial, as it requires previously undifferentiated past experience upon which to draw. That is why I began, as I almost always do, with a participatory exercise.

Noticing can be passive, and it can be active. Some ten years ago, when reading a book on mathematics education, I came across a reference to incidents in which children, when asked something like 3×4, responded with 7, but when then asked for $3 + 4$, immediately replied with 'oh, 12'. (Note the account of an incident.) The author claimed (accounting for) that the children were clearly responding to the first question; that their attention had been focused on the operation by hearing a similar question with the operation changed to that which they had already given the answer. I immediately recognized this *displaced response* phenomenon, because my son Quentin was doing exactly the same thing at the time. I had been vaguely aware that that was what he was doing, but had not reached a point of being able to articulate it myself. My experience included becoming aware of a distinction between *recognizing* and *remarking*.

Some ten years later, Quentin and I spontaneously developed a game not too dissimilar from *I Spy*, which makes this same distinction, this time between *recognizing* and *marking*. One person asks the other if he has noticed a particular something (a pattern in brickwork, the flow of hair on a dog, etc.), or if he had also marked it, that is whether he could have taken the initiative to remark upon it himself. In the latter case, the respondent will often give the observation a 'mark' out of ten, signalling marking through the pun. The game highlights differences between recognizing what the other remarks upon without having been able to remark upon it oneself, and having been in a position to remark upon it oneself.

Through having played this game with him, I found myself sensitized to other examples. I was asked recently to take a mathematics class at very short notice, in which the topic was to review a few technical terms like 'complementary angles'. At one point, I asked if anyone knew a name for the relation between a certain pair of angles. No-one did. I could have been caught in a typical 'guess what's in my mind' sequence of questioning, but instead I simply announced the usual technical term. One boy said, 'Oh, I knew that', and several nodded in assent. I chose in that moment to make an observation about his remark. I mentioned the distinction between *recognizing* and *remarking*, and the students all indicated that they indeed recognized(!) the distinction. I was able then to talk with them about various aspects of learning, and it turned out that they were fascinated. No-one had ever talked to them about their learning in this way before. That discussion was only possible because I was sensitized to the distinction between recognizing and remarking, and had alternative available behaviour to employ on the spur of the moment.

A particularly effective means for awakening a sensitivity in the future is to use labels and slogans as succinct summaries. The word *mark* and its associates have, for example, become a trigger which resonates the *recognizing– remarking* distinction in me currently. Labels which involve names or words which are likely to arise in similar contexts are particularly useful for awakening sensitivity in the future. Resonance of the distinction then provides access to associated behaviour patterns among which I can choose.

Moving from passive noticing to active marking is not an easy matter. One very hot summer afternoon I was faced with a group of about thirty students who had signed up for a tutorial session on partial differentiation. It was a topic that most tutors (myself included) found difficult, not to say students. I decided to try to get the students visualizing the surfaces that were used in the text as examples. Suddenly, I stopped and said to them, 'Try saying what I just said to someone near you'. There was a sudden burst of energy despite the previous heat-lethargy. I used this gambit several times in the session, and remarked to a friend later that it was so successful I was going to use it again. In the event, it was some two years before I managed to use that gambit again in a session. Often I would remind myself about it before a session, but never did I think of it in the midst of the event.

The word *noticing* applies to several different moments in that story. On the hot day I noticed an opportunity. There was a convergence of appropriateness and possibility. I noticed an opportunity, in the moment, to use a gambit. On later reflection, I realized that I heard of the notion of getting students to work in pairs, and had made a mental note to try it, but I had not envisaged how to initiate it. The making of a mental note also deserves the description *noticing*. I had marked it, but did not then have it available for use. It required some considerable internal and subconscious processing before it emerged as a possibility. When it did emerge, I was unaware of the source of the idea; it seemed entirely spontaneous. However, as a stratagem it was hard to make use of again immediately.

This sort of thing happens quite often. Sometimes in meetings or in workshops, something that is said or done stands out sharply in my awareness. It is as if bright light is cast upon it; I stress certain words, while the mass of other words are entirely ignored. This, too, is a form of noticing, but it is destined to fade away unless something is done about it to crystallize it.

Despite the implications of a gerund derived from a transitive predicate, *noticing* is not something that can be turned on and off at will. It is more akin to a state which can be fostered, but which comes and goes. One moment I feel aware of what is happening around me, and some time later I wake up to the fact that I have little recall of what was happening, that I have subsided into a trance-like state (Neville 1989) of waking sleep.

Long-distance driving typically produces this state, when I suddenly realize that I have no idea how I got through the previous few miles. (The word 'realize' signals a shift of awareness.) With great effort I may be able to reconstruct some of what happened, but mostly I have been operating on automatic pilot, reacting in pre-set ways.

Unfortunately, waking-sleep applies not only to driving, but also to meetings and to teaching, indeed to any aspect of life. I am in an event of some sort, perhaps in a meeting, or in front of a class, and I suddenly realize that I have just interrupted a pupil, or just repeated what they said back to the class: something that I had resolved I would not do again. In a meeting, I spoke out when I had intended to remain quiet and listening, or I didn't speak out when I had intended to participate. But I notice this only after the fact, *retrospectively*. Such retrospective noticing is helpful, but only if it can be used, because in order to alter my behaviour it is necessary to notice in the moment, *spectively*. Noticing my own actions usually begins as retrospective awareness, which, with luck and intentional acts, can gradually involve less and less time delay until it turns into spective awareness. Retrospective noticing often induces judgements, because the fact of not having learned from experience has meant that undesirable behaviour has taken place 'yet again'. Such negative judgements (captured by the tone of 'yet again') serve only to dissipate the energy acquired from noticing.

If I notice in the moment, spectively, I have an opportunity to participate in choice to act differently. For me, there is real freedom, perhaps the only real freedom, in just that one moment; the moment when I am awake and alive to a possibility. If my attention is fully caught up in the task at hand, then there may be none left over to pay attention to the overall direction, to guide and monitor progress, to recognize opportunities to do other than react in habitual ways. Hence the automatic pilot. Hence the observation that much of what happens in a classroom was proformed years before when the teacher integrated various coping strategies through repeated performance.

The notion of an inner monitor awake to possibilities has an ancient pedigree. For example, the following stanza translated by Rhadakrishnar (1953: 623) from one of the oldest recorded writings of any culture mentions the idea explicitly.

> Two birds, close-yoked companions,
> Both clasp the self-same tree;
> One eats of the sweet fruit,
> The other looks on without eating.
>   Rig Veda

It is a vibrant image, because the depiction of two such birds can be found in many places, on cards, on carpets, and in carvings, ancient and modern.

Noticing in the moment requires that there be part of me which is *doing*, eating the sweet fruit, and it requires part of me to be *observing*, looking on without eating of the sweet fruit. Without that, it is impossible to notice in the moment, and therefore very difficult to change my standard reactions to whatever situation I am in.

Disciplined noticing

The 'discipline of noticing' is an attempt to outline a systematic form of personal and collective enquiry into how to sharpen moments of noticing so that they shift:

- from the retrospective 'I could have . . .' or the judgementally retrospective 'I should have . . .',
- to the present indicative and choice-making spective 'I could . . .',
- by means of the descriptive but non-judgemental postspective review 'I did . . .', and the prospective preparation of 'I will . . .',

by imagining myself in a similar situation in the future, entering that moment as vividly as possible, and mentally carrying out each of the actions among which I wish to choose in the moment.

I have identified four component actions which seem to be essential in most intentional learning from experience: (1) systematic reflection; (2) recognizing choices; (3) preparing and noticing; and (4) validating with others. The following account is based on a version by my late colleague Joy Davis (1990). Any presentation has to begin somewhere, even though the four aspects are mutually intertwining in practice.

Systematic reflection involves apparently simple acts such as keeping little accounts of things that have happened to me that I've noticed; seeking threads in what seems to be similar and what seems to be different about those accounts, but avoiding accounting for them or justifying myself in any way. For example, I wish that I'd done something differently in some situation. Perhaps in working on a mathematics problem I wish that I'd thought to specialize, or I wish I'd thought to generalize, or I wish I'd thought to draw a diagram. Perhaps in a meeting I wish I had held my counsel a little longer until other parties had had their say; perhaps I wish I had spoken out earlier.

It is critical in account keeping to stick to accounts of what is noticed, and not to embroider, judge or otherwise elaborate or explain away what is observed. Noticing releases energy. Judging or justifying dissipates that energy and nullifies the act of noticing.

Observing is like accumulating data. But data about the past is of little value unless there is some indication of what could happen in the future. Thus an important aspect of noticing is recognizing choices that could have been made, accumulating them as alternatives, and identifying and labelling those alternatives.

I use *identify* in the sense of distinguishing and bringing into existence. Labelling makes use of that ultimate human ontological act of providing a name for something which gives you the feeling it exists, at least temporarily.

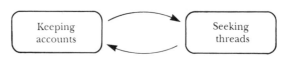

Figure 8.1   Systematic reflection.

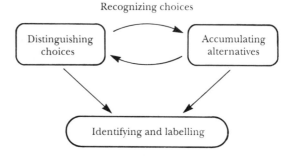

Figure 8.2   Recognizing choices.

The role of the label is to help you to identify situations in the future, so choices of labels which involve words that are likely to arise in relevant situations are more likely to trigger remembrance of intended action than are random labels. Sometimes labels which are richly associated with vivid experiences turn into slogans, and these slogans can become internalized and integrated so that you are barely aware of the chain of awareness triggering that leads to actions.

There is a big difference between 'could happen' and 'happening'. Thus it is important to spend time preparing to notice possibilities and choosing how to respond: imagining possibilities in which a fresh response is triggered, and trying to notice possibilities in the moment for fresh action.

Now this so far all looks as though it could be done entirely by an individual, but, of course, it is absolutely critical to verify and validate my experience with others. Validity lies in participation in a sizeable community of like thinkers, of people working in a similar disciplined fashion, who constantly check the appropriateness and informing quality of distinctions signalled by labels and slogans.

One of the ways of doing that is by describing salient moments, little significant fragments of experience to other people and seeing if they can find some resonance in their own experience, some example of their own which is similar. For me, education is as much a personal journey within a social context as it is a collective journey. Although Plato, and thousands after him, if not also before him, have articulated the fundamental tensions in teaching and learning, it is essential for each generation to seek fresh vernacular expression, as part of their own journeys.

Preparing and noticing

Figure. 8.3 Preparing and noticing.

Validating with others

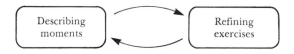

Figure 8.4 Validating with others.

Such recognizable moments can be used to construct and refine exercises (tasks like the ones at the beginning of this chapter). Working *on* those tasks is a matter of recognizing meta- and inner- as well as outer-meaning, negotiating similarities between different descriptions, and supporting each other in strengthening sensitivities for informing future noticing.

For me, validity is relative to time, place and participants. If others recognize events which are salient for me, and if they can turn those into salient events for them, then so be it. If others do not recognize events which are salient for me, then either my descriptions are insufficiently vivid, or their sensitivities are not yet attuned to such incidents, or I may be deluding myself. My experience is that some distinctions seem important at the time, but fade rapidly away, while others have a long-lasting effect, and are taken up by others. Thus validity is for me a constant checking against my own experience and that of colleagues, in an ecology of survival of the most informing.

The essence of the 'discipline of noticing' therefore is the following. To be a real teacher, to work with a pupil or colleague, requires that you are able to enter the experience of the other. In order to enter the experience of the other, it is critical to be able to enter the experience of oneself (or, more accurately, one's selves). And so, everything comes down to entering one's own experience. But this apparently idiosyncratic and self-centred focus requires the support of colleagues. It is almost impossible by oneself. Brief-but-vivid descriptions of salient moments from classrooms not only provide grist for discussion with colleagues and for personal reflection and sensitization to potential noticing in the future, but also enable threads of common experience to be detected. Often what people think they are interested in is not actually what they are sensitized to!

I suggest that as organisms, we need – indeed cannot escape from – experiences in a socio-cultural milieu, analogous to the primordial ooze in which it is thought that biological life began. Life developed in a biological soup, and selves develop in a socio-cultural analogue.

Early experience is undifferentiated, undistinguished, inchoate. Just as for a neonate on first entering the world, there is a profusion of sense impressions for which no meaning is possible, so too for adults, we are aware only of what we have become sensitized to. Meaning is the sense of connection, which already assumes boundaries and separateness so that there are *things* to connect. Thus meaning only arises when distinctions are possible. Maturana and Varela (1978) describe the coming into existence of a cell as an act of autopoesis, or *self-forming*, because it is not the act of some outside agent, but rather a self-creating act which creates a boundary, a self. In the biological case, the self is a cell which forms a boundary. The boundary distinguishes the cell from the rest of the soup. In the psychological case, the boundary is personality, the little quirks and defences which we build in order to distinguish ourself from the rest of our psycho-social milieu.

I go further and find it helpful to think in terms of myself as a multiplicity of selves constructed or formed in response to social and psychological forces in order to defend the core emptiness from exposure to the outside world. For example, the self which dominates in the classroom is not the self which answers or responds to a researcher's questions. The self which reads an article is not the self who writes one, nor the self who presents a paper at a conference. Personality is the many community of selves which shield one's emptiness from everyday awareness. Multiplicity evolves because each social context involves a collection of practices which define participation. These practices produce behaviour which can be read as indicative of beliefs and perspectives, but which may or may not be explicitly acknowledged or even compatible with what individuals say about themselves. Different selves have different perspectives, different distinctions, different things to say. When each is dominant, it acts as if it was the sole self.

Salient moments, or fragments of experience available to recall, are indications of a degree of presence or awareness in the moment. At other times, we simply are not sufficiently present to build an accessible memory or to notice an opportunity. Some periods of waking-sleep are due to being so intensely involved in action that there is no attention available for metacognition, while other periods arise because attention is diffused and unfocused.

Sometimes, differentiated experience can be integrated directly into practice. This is typical of the expert who garners and develops awarenesses of details of their craft, without really being aware of it. For example, in Zen instruction, students may spend long periods of apprenticeship apparently doing irrelevant or menial tasks in the presence of the master, only to find much later that they have actually integrated certain awarenesses into their being without being aware of the process. Dewey (1933) put a case for this sort of learning, which he called *collateral*: 'Perhaps the greatest of all pedagogical fallacies is the notion that a person learns only the particular thing that he is studying at the time. Collateral learning . . . may be and often is much more important than the lesson.'

By far the major part of effective learning is integrated into one's being through explicitly *working on* ideas, i.e. through explicit awareness of, and reflection on, experience. There are a variety of ways in which such reflection can be undertaken, some of which will be described shortly. Schön (1983) refers to the same idea as the acts of the *reflective practitioner*, the individual who reflects upon or tries to make sense of his or her experience.

Theorizing and abstraction are often sneered at as abstruse and even unnecessary processes beloved of academics but of no-one else. As long as theorizing is divorced from practice, then perhaps there is some point to the criticism. But theorizing and abstracting are essential parts of everyone's life just in order to cope. Those who do it intentionally and explicitly get better at it. Those who work hard at it rise to the top of their profession. For *theorizing* is based on the Greek root *theoria*, meaning *a way of seeing*, and *abstracting* has as one meaning the search for or distillation of essence or structure. Every time someone utters a generality (and in speech it is impossible not to), they give evidence of abstracting, of generalizing, and hence theorizing. What they say tells you as much about their current way of seeing as it does about what they see.

To theorize requires a standing back, a separation in attention, in which doing and awareness of doing carry on simultaneously (or at least in rapid succession). Perhaps it is from this experience of an inner separation that we get the notion of objectivity of observation, because that which is observed becomes an *object* of attention. When what is observed is external to ourselves, the objectivity of objects seems not in doubt, though of course a deeper analysis draws even this impression into question. When what is observed is internal, when an inner monitor develops, then there is a corresponding sense of objectivity, which is enhanced by comparing descriptions with colleagues and learning from their experience as well as from my own.

References

Davis, J. (1990) The role of the participant observer in the Discipline of Noticing. In Seeger, F. and Steinbring, H. (eds) *Proceedings of the 4th SCTP Meeting*. Materialien und Studien series. Bielefeld: IDM.

Dewey, J. (1933) *How We Think: A Restatement of the Relation of Reflective Thinking to the Educative Process*. London: Heath.

Khan, M. (1983) *Hidden Selves: Between Theory and Practice in Psychoanalysis*. London: Maresfield Library.

Mandler, G. (1989) Affect and learning: Causes and consequences of emotional interactions. In McLeod, D. and Adams, V. (eds) *Affect and Mathematical Problem Solving: A New Perspective*. New York: Springer-Verlag.

Mason, J. (1991) Epistemological foundations for frameworks which stimulate noticing. In Underhill, R. (ed.) *PME-NA XIII*, II, 36–42.

Maturana, H. and Varela, F. (1978) *The Tree of Knowledge: The Biological Roots of Human Understanding*. Boston, MA: Shambala Press.

Neville, B. (1989) *Educating Psyche*. Melbourne: Collins Dove.

Rhadakrishnar, S. (1953) *The Principal Upanishads*. London: George Allen and Unwin.

Schön, D.A. (1983) *The Reflective Practitioner: How Professionals Think in Action*. London: Temple Smith.

Tahta, D. (1980) About geometry. *For the Learning of Mathematics*, 1, 2–9.

Part 3

Introduction

The questions that remain are as important as those which have gone before. In this section, several of the contributors pose questions about groups: How do groups learn, as a group? How can group learning be fostered? How can individual learners be helped in their learning by a group context? This section also explores broader issues about the relationship between the individual and the society and culture in which the individual is situated. By linking one's private and social worlds, insights can be gained into how society and culture affect experience and learning. Finally, the section raises some fundamental questions about experience and learning. What is the relationship between meaning and experience, between language and experience, and between discourse and experience? What is the difference between learning from experience and experiential learning? How can we recognize how our own experience can be a trap which limits learning?

The chapters by Miller and Kasl, Dechant and Marsick and placed together because both are concerned with learning in groups. Miller takes up the group relations laboratory learning method as a way of bringing together her concerns as a sociologist, as an adult educator and as a feminist. Her reflections centre around her own transformation from her initial experience in T-groups and demonstrate how she has subsequently applied these learnings to her own group work. She illustrates how her explorations in experiential group work have helped her focus a number of personal, professional and political preoccupations. Reflecting on a common project, Kasl, Dechant and Marsick explore how the group, as a group, evolves in its own learning, and they propose a model of group learning. The process of developing the model together not only sheds light on their common project in a rather unexpected way, but also illustrates their working together as a team. They acknowledge the personal aspects of their professional experience and find this to be a rewarding methodology.

The social influences on experience and learning is the focus of Criticos' chapter. He reflects on the social and political conditions of South Africa and shows how apartheid affects the experience and learning of all members of the society. He shows that in this context of oppression it is especially important to work with our experience to expose the socially conditioned assumptions which shape it. Through an example of his work in a fishing village, we are able to identify some of the political realities which are so pervasive. The final chapter by Usher is placed here both as an appropriate conclusion to what has gone before and as a challenge. He draws our attention to the use of language and reminds us that meaning is relational and contextual. Usher offers some significant reflections on experience, he alerts the reader to important questions about learning and experience, and provides a basis for future exploration of the relationships between them. What more do we require in order to learn from experience than experience itself?

9

How the T-Group Changed My Life: A Sociological Perspective on Experiential Group Work

Nod Miller

How my life was changed

On a dark Sunday evening early in the new year of 1983, I set off for my first T-group laboratory. It was organized in a residential centre in Leeds by the Group Relations Training Association, and was advertised as 'an experiential event focusing on group and community dynamics, personal behaviour and group membership, interactive skills and social processes'. I hoped during the event to enhance my understanding of how groups worked and perhaps to pick up some ideas which I might apply in my teaching in a university department of adult education. I took along a large briefcase bulging with papers with which I intended to deal during the free time. I also resolved that if the event was too dull, I could escape across the Pennines back to Manchester with little lost.

Five days later – although it felt more like five years later – I returned home. I had not opened my briefcase, let alone dealt with the papers inside. I had, however, learned a good deal about processes of inclusion and exclusion in groups; about inter-group conflict and the formation of subcultures; about power, influence, authority and leadership; about gender and class stereotypes and the difficulty of dismantling them. Many of the insights which I gained came from the extension of theoretical understanding into the lived experience of the laboratory environment. I had experienced wild extremes of emotion and what I have since labelled 'the Brillo pad effect' – a feeling akin to having the inside of my head scoured out with an abrasive substance. This is an uncomfortable process, but one which leaves me feeling sparkling. To many seasoned T-group participants, this would probably sound like a pretty average T-group experience.

Since 1983, much of my time has been spent exploring ways of applying the learning from T-groups to my own professional practice. I have participated in and organized many experiential events, laboratories and workshops. I have sought opportunities to meet and work with pioneers of group relations training across several continents. I have researched the history and development of T-groups, produced a television programme featuring T-groups for the Open University, and spent three years as chair of the Group Relations Training Association (GRTA). My work on early drafts of this chapter coincided with preparations for the 1992 GRTA Annual T-Group Laboratory, of which I was Dean (senior staff member).

My aims in this chapter

Since I discovered the T-group, it has seemed to me that the group relations laboratory learning method represents a way of bringing together my concerns as a sociologist, as an adult educator and as a feminist. In this chapter, I shall try to demonstrate how my explorations in experiential group work have helped me to focus a number of personal, professional and political preoccupations.

The field of experiential learning is one where confusions of terminology abound, so perhaps I should make it clear that I am using the term 'group work' to refer to the practice of those who work as trainers or facilitators in settings where there is an explicit focus on group processes. I see T-groups, the nature of which I shall discuss in detail shortly, as constituting a particular form of experiential group.

An important item on my personal learning agenda has been the development of my sociological imagination; I shall explain my understanding of this key feature of social scientific experience, and indicate why I believe the T-group laboratory provides a suitable environment for its exploration. I shall pinpoint some specific examples of the learning I have derived from group relations laboratories, and describe some of the training events I have organized in which I have tried to build on and develop the methodology of the T-group. I shall go on to tease out some of the ways in which the values underlying my own practice differ from those of traditional T-group culture, and conclude with some pointers as to how laboratory training needs to develop in order to maintain its social relevance.

Stimulating the sociological imagination

In reflecting on my identity and values as a sociologist and my activities in facilitating learning about social science, I am seeking to understand the development of my sociological imagination, and to assess the effectiveness of my attempts to help others to develop this quality, which was defined by C. Wright Mills in the following way:

> . . . a quality of mind that will help . . . [people] to use information and to develop reason in order to achieve lucid summations of what is going on in the world and of what may be happening within themselves.

> The sociological imagination enables its possessor to understand the larger historical scene in terms of its meaning for the inner life and the external career of a variety of individuals . . . the sociological imagination enables us to grasp history and biography and the relations between the two within society.
>
> (Mills 1970: 11–12)

I believe that it is this potential for linking the personal and the structural, individual life-histories and collective social movements, private and public worlds, which makes sociology such an exciting and powerful discipline. And yet Mills's clearly expressed insight seems often to get lost in the way in which sociology is written and taught. Certainly, much of my early experience as a student of sociology led me to doubt whether the subject had much at all to do with my life-experience as a member of a working-class family and as a woman.

I became a student of sociology because I wanted to find a way of making sense of how groups worked and how people communicated. In particular, I wanted to make sense of my own experience, in terms of the tension between the culture of my class of origin and the middle-class culture into which I started to become assimilated in the course of my passage through grammar school. I was puzzled and exasperated by the tendency of those who taught me to dismiss personal experience as merely 'anecdotal', and to discuss social class in such abstract terms as to suggest that it only existed 'out there', miles from the lecture-room and detached from the lives of sociology students.

I came to believe that experiential laboratory methods could enable students to develop their sociological imaginations and to understand some of the connections between their personal experience and the social structures within which they operate. Furthermore, my experience as a female – and feminist – academic, my involvement in the women's movement, my contact with other feminist sociologists, and my reading of contemporary feminist literature had led me to a belief in the notion of 'the personal as political'. The T-group, with its potential to link personal experience with social processes, seemed to provide a way of furthering feminist research and practice.

What are T-groups, anyway?

The 'T' in T-group stands for training, not therapy, as is often supposed. What happens in T-groups is sometimes referred to as 'sensitivity training', since the aim is to sensitize participants to their own patterns of behaviour within a group by encouraging them to observe, comment and reflect on these patterns as they emerge. A T-group is typically composed of between eight and twelve members who are strangers to one another at the outset. The group meets for several hours at a time, and the focus is on the here-and-now experience of participants. T-groups often take place over several days in a residential setting, and a course of T-group training is generally referred to as a laboratory, to draw attention to the opportunities offered to experiment with new behaviours and ways of communicating. A laboratory will generally include other forms of group activity, such as large group meetings and inter-group exercises, as well as T-groups.

Some early exponents of the T-group method described it in the following way:

> A T-Group is a relatively unstructured group in which individuals participate as learners. The data for learning are not outside these individuals or remote from their immediate experience within the T-Group. The data are the transactions among members, their own behaviour in the group, as they struggle to create a productive and viable organization, a miniature society; and as they work to stimulate and support one another's learning within that society. Involving experiences are a necessary, but not the only, condition of learning. T-Group members must establish a process of inquiry in which data about their own behaviours are collected and analyzed simultaneously with the experience which generates the behaviours. Learnings thus achieved are tested and generalized for continuing use.
>
> (Bradford *et al.* 1964: 1–2)

Bradford *et al.* are here drawing attention to several features of T-groups which I believe make them a suitable setting in which the sociological imagination may be fostered and developed. A central part of my own professional activity has been the creation of microcosmic versions of social systems, where all members have a face-to-face relationship with one another and can therefore compare their perceptions and interpretations of the microcosmic 'reality'. The subject matter or research data in a T-group is personal experience, but personal experience which is contained within boundaries of time and space, and conducted in a setting where the process of reflection on experience, and the development of theory from that experience, is initiated and fostered.

Pioneers of the T-group suggested that T-group experience needed to be separated from everyday life, and that a laboratory should be conducted on a 'cultural island' where participants' ties to their regular relationships were minimized and established some distance from participants' daily routines. Trainers do not lead a T-group in the conventional manner generally expected of teachers, but behave in a way which participants often find disconcerting to begin with. Peter B. Smith, who has written extensively about T-groups, acknowledges that a clear conception of a T-group is hard to come by for those who have not participated in one, and describes the departure from everyday social convention in the following way:

> Whereas leaders of groups are normally expected to structure activities, facilitate decision procedures and so forth, T-group trainers usually decline to undertake these activities. Instead they express interest not in what the group does, but in how it is done. If a group decision

is arrived at on some issue, the leader may focus on how members feel about the decision, who they perceive as taking what roles in its achievement, or how the decision affects their own position in the group. The focus is on the process whereby the group members are interacting with one another.

(Smith 1980: 10)

While it may seem paradoxical to create a cultural island in order to further understand patterns of communication and relationships in the outside world, exponents of the T-group method argue that the T-group operates as a sort of microcosm, within which such issues as power, influence and leadership within groups, and gender and cultural conflicts, may be lived out and explored.

The puzzlement expressed by many participants during the early stages of a T-group reflects the difficulty of gaining a fresh perspective on interpersonal interaction, when such interaction forms the taken-for-granted fabric of people's lives. One psychologist, commenting on the fact that we are steeped in group relationships every day, likens the role of the sensitivity trainer to 'teaching fishes what water is' (Houston 1976: 177).

The model of learning on which the T-group laboratory is based is that of the experiential learning cycle. An underlying assumption of this model is that group behaviour is best understood from the experience of participating in groups and observing group processes as they occur. Theory-building about group behaviour takes place on the basis of reflection on that experience. The laboratory environment allows for experimentation with new forms of behaviour, which in turn become the object of further reflection and theory-building.

How precisely did the T-group change my life?

I began this chapter with a reference to my first, life-changing experience of a T-group laboratory, and I will try to identify more precisely some instances of my learning from that event. I should explain that I had had some acquaintance with experiential group work some ten years earlier, when I attended a group dynamics course which was organized according to what I later identified as the Tavistock model (for a full description, see Shaffer and Galinsky 1974: 164–88). While I found this course both stimulating and absorbing, I also experienced extremes of confusion, irritation and frustration. I found the behaviour of the group leaders, who said very little apart from the occasional gnomic aside about what they thought the group was doing, remained impassive in the face of extremes of distress or hilarity among participants, and left the room at the exact moment the group was scheduled to finish, utterly mystifying.

On one or two occasions, my discomfort with the organization of the Tavistock course surfaced in the form of comments in the group about the navel-gazing nature of the activity in which we were engaged, and remarks to the effect that the group was entirely made up of middle-class people and hence not representative of 'real life'. It was extremely frustrating not to be able to make comments about the conceptual model without being reinterpreted inside the framework of the model itself. It seemed to me that built into the Tavistock model was an automatic antidote to doubt: try to step outside and your behaviour is interpreted from inside.

My unease with what I saw as the narrow cultural base of the Tavistock course, and the lack of opportunity to explore social and political issues, meant that I confined myself to treading around the periphery of group work culture over the next ten years, and, no doubt limited my expectations of the 1983 laboratory. In the event, my negative expectations were not confirmed. I found the T-group much more user-friendly than the Tavistock study group, with much less emphasis on expert interpretation and greater opportunity for the development of shared understandings. The 1983 laboratory featured meetings of reference groups, which were self-chosen groupings based on some shared social role or identity. I found that this aspect of the design enabled me to explore and develop my understanding of social processes and structures with which I was preoccupied. I was a member of the feminist group, which became the focus for much of my learning during and after the five days of the laboratory.

One source of interest was the way in which the feminist group was viewed by other members of the laboratory. Reactions included curiosity, puzzlement and hostility – this last reaction being expressed by some of the female, as well as male, participants. The exercise to set up reference groups resulted in the formation of a women's group as well as a feminist group, and, when the members of my group discovered this, we suggested to the members of the women's group that we join forces. They declined, on the grounds that they saw feminists as 'extremists' and 'man-haters'. This seemed ironic in view of the fact that the feminist group included two men (and, indeed, recruited several more in the course of the week).

I learned a good deal from discussions in the feminist group, and from inter-group encounters between the feminist group and other reference groups, about, for example, differing constructions of sexual harassment and the operation of stereotypes of gender and class. At one point, I was shocked when one of the male participants in the laboratory announced that I should be seen as a 'failed feminist', since he felt that I did not fit his image of a feminist (as 'butch-looking' and aggressive). I was upset at the time, but on reflection I recognized that revising firmly fixed categorizations is painful and difficult. This caused me to reflect on other experiences of the tendency to cling to stereotypes in the face of countervailing evidence.

I was also moved to confront some of my own stereotyped constructions. At one point in the laboratory, the members of the feminist group were working to reach some shared meanings in the sphere of sexual politics by trading autobiographical stories. During this process, I became aware of being forced to rethink my attitude towards one of the men present. I had felt rather dismissive of some of his earlier contributions, not so much on grounds of gender, but rather on those of social class, since he spoke with what I had labelled a 'posh' accent. As he sketched his personal history, it emerged that he was an actor who had been born into an economically deprived working-class family, but whose mode of speech had been modified as a result of his social mobility through education and his theatrical training. His life-history, in fact, mirrored my own in a number of respects. This experience pushed me towards a closer examination of my own class prejudices and categorizations.

Promoting change in group work culture

Following my first concrete experience of a T-group laboratory, I was encouraged to seek out further experience of this kind through immersion in the group relations culture. I then began to delve into the literature on T-groups in order to aid my own reflection and theory-building. I was excited by the possibilities for using experiential methods to bring alive the teaching of social science and to link immediate, individual experience with wider social, economic and political structures, but I became critical of certain values and behaviours which I observed within the subculture of group relations practitioners.

I was exasperated at the individualistic focus of much contemporary experiential group work, and frustrated at the exclusion of such issues as socio-economic differences between participants by the focus on the here-and-now in the T-group. I shared the concern, expressed by several other practitioners in this field (see, e.g. Duke and Sommerlad 1981; Hudson 1983) that an over-concentration on personal growth within such work had distracted attention from issues of social and political change.

Working with Jim Brown, a colleague who was also critical of the thrust of much group work practice, I designed and organized a number of events in which the intention was to promote learning about features of social structures through the adaptation of laboratory methods. In some cases, we used the concept of the 'Street' (discussed in Potter 1981); a Street laboratory is a large group event which usually takes place in a large open space with fixed geographical and time boundaries, enabling people to experiment with a variety of roles and identities. The metaphor of the street clearly carries differing connotations for different people, ranging from community space to urban battleground. I have seen participants acting out roles such as those of beggar, prostitute, mugger, political demonstrator, neighbour, market stallholder, funeral director and passer-by. Each session is followed by a period of reflection and review, but is otherwise unstructured.

Two events which employed this model were 'Beyond the T-group', which we organized in Leeds in 1984, and a GRTA conference held in 1987 on 'Power and Leadership in Groups'. The first event involved the creation of an unstructured, leaderless environment in which the only fixed points were start and finish times, and midday and evening meals. The nineteen participants, including myself, clung fiercely to the few elements of time-structure which there were, arriving promptly for meals *en masse*, and generally appeared to be deeply confused by the experience. The second event marked the fortieth anniversary of the birth of the T-group, and attracted 120 people. The conference design was left open and negotiable so that the participants could explore the themes of power and leadership experientially during the life of the conference. Throughout the event, there were regular meetings of what came to be referred to as the Large Group and several workshops and small groups were initiated, including 'situational leadership', a non-verbal workshop, an art therapy workshop and 'dressing for power' – a workshop on clothing and style.

On other occasions, we conceptualized whole conferences as micro-cosmic social structures; an event viewed from this perspective appears as a seamless web of interaction bounded by time and space rather than a compendium of workshops, meal breaks and free time. We experimented with aspects of their internal organization; a notable example of this approach was the establishment of a nightclub and a newspaper at the 1984 GRTA conference, the subject of which was 'The Whole Person'. The newspaper, which reported on events and people at the conference in a scurrilous and often sensational fashion, was used as a vehicle to challenge the dominant value of unconditional positive regard which pervaded this event, and its personal growth orientation. My four days as a tabloid newspaper editor significantly enhanced the theoretical understanding of journalistic ideologies which I had researched as a non-participant during my years as a graduate student of mass communication. Since then, newspapers, with their potential for subversion and provocation, have become a regular feature of the conferences I organize.

Jim Brown and I developed an economic model of interpersonal and group behaviour which was explored in several workshops and events, the most thorough-going example being the 'Mini-Economy', a residential laboratory held in 1985, described in detail in Miller (1989: 202–240). This involved the creation of an economic system in miniature; we developed an economic structure whereby participants were allocated 'money' with which to purchase resources in the conference community, such as food, drink, bedroom accommodation and use of the lavatories. The allocation of money was based on the real-life income and wealth of the participants. The community had to deal with the fact that some individuals did not have the resources to afford a bedroom, whereas others had enough to exist very comfortably. It had to reach decisions about, and implement, changes in the economic structure. The outcome was captured neatly in a description of what happened given by one participant shortly after the event: 'During the first 24 hours we managed to condense five centuries of social change; we lived through capitalism, revolution, socialism and feudalism.'

We saw the mini-economy as a radical departure in the field of experiential group work. The event had a strong impact on all who took part in it, and one of its effects was to leave me with a strong desire to know more about the historical development of laboratory learning. Eventually, I worked my way back in the history to the origins of the T-group in the work of Kurt Lewin (documented in Benne 1964, 1976), and began to reassess my own professional practice and to redefine what I had seen as a radical rebuilding as an archaeological expedition back to my social scientific roots.

The social relevance of T-groups

It became clear from my reading of the history of experiential group work that critiques of the T-group as becoming detached from social and political issues similar to those that I had mounted had been rehearsed several times. In the 1970s, two leading practitioners in the group work field were expressing doubts about the relevance of T-groups to problems of contemporary society.

Cary Cooper, who was an early proponent of the T-group in Britain, writing at a time when unemployment, hyperinflation and economic crisis dominated the wider political agenda, saw the needs of industry and business for T-group applications diminishing along with job mobility and economic growth. He remarked on the need to resolve the tension between the Anglo-American social science environment with its 'empiricist and pragmatist tradition, reflecting a positivist approach to data and an experimental approach to phenomena' (Cooper 1979: 264), of which the T-group was essentially a product, and the more theoretical European tradition. He linked the development of the T-group with the shift of focus towards personal issues and the idealistic ideologies of the 'baby boom' generation of the 1960s, which, ten years later, he suggested might be becoming increasingly obsolescent. He also noted that a typical participant in a T-group tended to be of middle-class origin.

Gurth Higgin, another pioneer in experiential group work, also argued that in order to maintain its relevance, the T-group culture would have to address demographic, environmental and development issues. He felt that experiential groups had potential for fostering the sort of changes in consciousness, attitudes and behaviour which he saw as essential for humankind to deal with contemporary social and ecological ills, but asserted:

> I don't believe a lot of the traditional sensitivity training activities are relevant in this setting any more. The old T-group with its focus on the numinous but at the personal and interpersonal level is fine as fun, but there's not much new reality-making that way. No, it's the mini-society learning that I believe provides the most useful approach. It is through the confrontation of groups having shared perceptions in the old reality that the unreality of the old can be exposed and the possibilities of the new can be perceived.
>
> (Higgin 1973: 131)

I share Higgin's scepticism about the usefulness of an approach to experiential group work where the focus stays exclusively on the interpersonal
level and where the primary aim is expressed in terms of intrapersonal
development. However, I believe that laboratory designs which move beyond
the T-group are worth exploring. My own preference is for the mini-society
laboratory endorsed by Higgin, with the opportunity which it creates for
inter-group exploration. This type of event explicitly sets out to create a
microcosmic society and hence enables current social issues to be explored
and analysed (see Higgin 1972; Hjelholt 1972).

The values underlying my own practice

I shall now move on to a consideration of the values and assumptions
underlying my own practice, and, in particular, try to ascertain to what
extent this practice has taken me beyond the T-group. A period of study
leave in 1988 afforded me the opportunity to reflect upon the guidelines
which I have evolved as a basis for my activity in the field of experiential
group work, and my journal records the following list of rules:

1. Minimize/simplify structure.
2. Use inter-group as well as interpersonal communication – in
   order to enable people to explore structural as well as individual
   similarities (in perception, material interests, etc.).
3. Import (selected?) bits of "real world" into the laboratory
   environment.
4. In designing laboratories, keep in mind at all times how things
   work in "real life".
5. Encourage intervention/confrontation (e.g. through the asking of
   questions) as well as self-disclosure.
6. Use metaphors (e.g. economic ones) to explore interpersonal
   behaviour.
7. Remember that past and future are experienced in the present.
                                              (Journal entry, 29 April 1988)

The analysis of the values underlying conventional T-group practice which
I have found most helpful is that provided by Cooper:

> The most basic value is a strong emphasis on involvement – encour-
> aging the group members to be intimate, warm, and fully integrated
> with one another. A second value is on interdependency – encourag-
> ing mutual co-operation, effective decision-making, and the creation
> of a group structure that is adapted to the individuals' needs. A third
> general value is on the development of awareness – the individual
> becoming aware of his impact on others and others' impact on him.
> Other values also emerge in some groups, though not all. For example,
> some groups place an emphasis on the members' relation to the outside
> environment, whether this is a specific institution or a more general

context. In this case, what happens inside of the group is partly related to its effects in the outside environment. This type of value is
likely to emerge in groups where members come from a specific
environment (e.g., students, managers, social workers). Another value
which is mostly associated with personal expression groups, and which
is often unstated, is a testing of social taboos, often with the individual
being encouraged to develop a greater tolerance towards unconscious
feelings and behaviour.

(Cooper 1979: 261–2)

The values embedded in my own practical experiments in group work
represent, to some extent, departures from the value system outlined by
Cooper. The testing of social taboos has been part of my design in a number
of projects. This was explicitly the case, for example, with the setting up of
a newspaper to challenge the dominant culture of the 'whole person'
conference. As far as relations with the outside environment are concerned,
I think that my work has placed greater emphasis on the relationship between what takes place within a group and the implications of that behaviour
for what happens in the 'real world' than is generally the case in T-groups.
As my journal entry above shows, I have been aware of trying to import
elements of the outside world into the laboratory, in order, for example, to
understand more fully the micro- and macro-reality of economic relations.
In the course of my early explorations in the T-group, I experienced
frustration at what one of my colleagues has succinctly labelled the 'here-
and-now chute', down which disappear, for example, economic inequalities
as well as important differences in historical experience. The mini-economy
represents my most thoroughgoing attempt to import structural differences
into a laboratory environment, but I have tried to break down the boundaries
between the laboratory and its outside environment in a number of other
events and to set up (minimal) structures to aid the application of learning
to life in the outside world. I have found the use of reference groups to be
particularly helpful in this respect.

In relation to the development of awareness among participants, this is
certainly an important aim in the workshops I run; I am concerned to
encourage participants to observe the impact of their behaviour on others
and vice versa. At the same time, I recognize the limited nature of my ability
to ensure that an increase in self-awareness comes about, and the general
difficulty of predicting outcomes of learning events. I am also in favour of
interdependency, in the sense that I believe in the value of collective experience and learning.

It is with the emphasis on involvement that I have most problems. While
it has been my hope to create 'involving' experiences in the sense that I
think it is desirable for activities to arouse intellectual and emotional interest in order to promote learning, I am less sure about involvement if this
means, as Cooper (1979: 261) suggests, 'encouraging group members to be
intimate, warm and fully integrated with one another'.

While I have no desire to stir up conflict in a group for its own sake, it seems to me that a T-group laboratory becomes nothing but a fantasy island if intimacy, warmth and openness characterize all relationships. I should also note that my emphasis on the importance of asking questions represents a departure from convention in terms of the practice in most experiential groups. The Theme-Centred Interaction Group, a close cousin of the T-group, explicitly excludes the asking of questions; one of its five ground rules is 'give the statement behind your question' (see Shaffer and Galinsky 1974: 258). The implication behind this rule is that confrontation or 'interviewing' is undesirable, and that self-disclosure is an activity to be encouraged. Although my journal entry does not make this quite explicit, my stress on the need to 'encourage intervention/confrontation . . . as well as self-disclosure' has come in part from my recognition that one person's self-disclosure is another's receipt of an unwelcome emotional burden.

While the guidelines set out above relate primarily to my practice in running group relations workshops, I should stress that they also now inform my work as a university teacher of communication and media studies. My experience in the T-group has changed my life in relation to the way that I conduct the whole of my professional life. The MEd course which is the central focus of my job, and which I designed and developed, aims to integrate theoretical and practical studies in communication, and elements of the course deal with mass communication theory, media production and interpersonal communication.

One feature of the course is a rich mixture of cultures, religions, races, age groups and occupations. There are, for example, nineteen nationalities represented on my current course. I try to encourage the use of class meetings as laboratories for learning, where the participants reflect upon their interaction with one another in order to extrapolate understanding of social processes such as the construction of cultural identity and difference.

I have moved from struggling to keep abreast of academic developments relevant to the varied interests of all my students to the recognition that what counts is the creation of opportunities to share and reflect upon experience. The course in interpersonal communication is structured around reflection groups, where the task of the group is to reflect upon and review the patterns of interpersonal communication between group members as these patterns emerge. The media course, although making more use of external referents, still places strong emphasis on the use of experience and the process of learning through the communication which takes place within the course group.

Reconciling social science and group work

I hope that I have succeeded in conveying in this chapter something of the learning which I have derived from my explorations in experiential groups.

In relating my own journey through group relations culture, I have tried to apply C. Wright Mills's model of the sociological imagination as linking history and biography. In conclusion, I want to reassert that experiential groups have much to offer the sociologist in that they provide a model of action research as well as a methodology to promote learning about the nature of the discipline.

Alongside my conviction that sociologists may derive much benefit from laboratory training, I wish to place my belief that sociological insights can be employed to good advantage in the development of group work methodology. I would argue that it is necessary for exponents of experiential group work to develop a self-reflexive practice and to scrutinize the ideological assumptions underlying their activities and the styles of interaction embedded in their culture so that group work practice may maintain its contemporary relevance.

I have no doubt that an understanding of group relations is as necessary as ever in a world where the '-isms' of class, sex, race and age persist – but, if they are to promote that understanding, group work practitioners need to address the social divisions within their own culture and to guard against operating within a discourse which derives exclusively from the concerns of white middle-class Europeans. My own participation in experiential groups, where the majority of participants are black non-Europeans, has pushed me towards a realization of, for example, how very differently gender relations or processes of teaching and learning appear when viewed from the perspectives of participants from Ethiopia, Egypt or Ecuador, and I believe that the development of group work practice would be aided enormously by an injection of diverse cultural viewpoints.

Psychological models have proved helpful in the examination of the process of experiential learning and the evaluation of the effectiveness of group work as a training methodology. I believe that sociological perspectives need also to be employed to raise questions about the ideological bases of group work practice and its explicit and implicit values.

References

Benne, K.D. (1964) A history of the T-group in the laboratory setting. In Bradford, L.P., Gibb, J.R. and Benne, K.D. (eds) *T-group Theory and Laboratory Method: Innovation in Re-education*. New York: John Wiley.

Benne, K.D. (1976) The process of re-education: An assessment of Kurt Lewin's views. In Bennis, W.G., Benne, K.D., Chin, R. and Corey, K. (eds) *The Planning of Change*, 3rd edn. New York: Holt, Rinehart and Winston.

Bradford, L.P., Gibb, J.R. and Benne, K.D. (eds) (1964) *T-groups Theory and Laboratory Method: Innovation in Re-education*. New York: John Wiley.

Cooper, C.L. (1979) *Learning from Others in Groups: Experiential Learning Approaches*. London: Associated Business Press.

Duke, C. and Sommerlad, E. (1981) Experiential small group learning and the human relations movement. In Haines, N. (ed.) *Canberra Papers in Continuing Education*. Canberra: Australian National University.

Higgin, G. (1972) The Scandinavians rehearse the liberation. *Journal of Applied Behavioral Science*, 8(6): 643–63.

Higgin, G. (1973) *Symptoms of Tomorrow: Letters from a Sociologist on the Present State of Society*. London: Plume Press/Ward Lock.

Hjelholt, G. (1972) Group training in understanding society: The Mini-Society. In Cooper, C.L. (ed.) *Group Training for Individual and Organizational Development*. Basel: Karger.

Houston, G. (1976) *All in the Mind: The Making of an Interpersonal Group in a Television Series*. London: BBC Publications.

Hudson, A. (1983) The politics of experiential learning. In Boot, R. and Reynolds, M. (eds) *Learning and Experience in Formal Education*. University of Manchester: Manchester Monographs.

Miller, N. (1992) *Personal Experience, Adult Learning and Social Research: Developing a Sociological Imagination In and Beyond the T-group*. Adelaide: University of South Australia Centre for Human Resources.

Mills, C.W. (1970) *The Sociological Imagination*. Harmondsworth: Penguin (first published 1959).

Potter, S. (1981) Reclaiming the group. Unpublished MEd thesis, University of Manchester Faculty of Education.

Shaffer, J.B.P. and Galinsky, M.D. (1974) *Models of Group Therapy and Sensitivity Training*. Englewood Cliffs, NJ: Prentice-Hall.

Smith, P.B. (1980) *Group Processes and Personal Change*. London: Harper and Row.

10

Living the Learning: Internalizing Our Model of Group Learning

Elizabeth Kasl, Kathleen Dechant and Victoria Marsick

The purpose of this chapter is to describe the authors' experience of learning together as a research team and to analyse how our experience enhanced our understanding of our own research. We tell our story of group learning based on two experiences. The first story describes our effort to analyse case study data during a week we spent at a seaside resort; the second story is about a day we spent in a university conference room eight months later.

The three of us – Elizabeth, Kathy and Victoria – have been working together for two years to build empirically based theory about group learning. Kathy and Victoria have worked together even longer; their interest in workplace learning led them to conceptualize and initiate the research in which the three of us are now involved. Their original premise, based on individual projects of their own, was that the key to understanding organizational learning lay in understanding small-group learning. At the time Kathy and Victoria were planning our research, Peter Senge's (1990) book about organizational learning had not yet been published. His words, since published, sum up their originating premise: 'Team learning is vital because teams, not individuals, are the fundamental learning unit in modern organizations. This is where "the rubber meets the road"; unless teams can learn, the organization cannot learn' (Senge 1990: 10).

In essence, Senge argues that because organizations have a need for team learning, team learning exists. He uses logical analysis to identify particular conditions that he argues must exist if team learning is to happen. However, Senge does not provide descriptive information or empirical data about the process of team learning. We feel that although Senge's argument about the importance of team learning lends credence to our research rationale, his book has not filled the need for which our research was designed. Our research purpose is to collect descriptive data that can illuminate the dynamic processes of small-group learning.

Our choice of the label 'group learning' instead of 'team learning' is deliberate. By using 'group' instead of 'team', we intend to communicate the possibility that our model is applicable to groups who are not function-ing as units of organizations, such as community action groups, research teams, self-help groups, etc.

Our research as context for our learning

This case-study research was carried out in two profit-oriented corporations. Our first case study was in a petrochemical company that had been recently formed through merger. Some fifty-five groups or 'synergy teams' planned and helped implement this merger; subsequently, various teams and groups worked at carrying out the design for the new company. Our interview sample included twenty-eight employees who represented a diagonal, cross-functional slice of the new organization; many of our interviewees had participated in these groups. In the manufacturing company that was the site for our second case, we were able to interview twenty-three of twenty-five members of a data-processing unit that had recently reorganized itself into three self-managed teams. Self-management by work teams was new to this unit and to the company as well.

Kathy and Victoria began planning the research in 1989 and made their first field visit to the petrochemical company in early 1990. Shortly after completing the interviews for the first case study, they invited Elizabeth to join the research team. They felt her knowledge about adult development and learning would complement their expertise in organizational devel-opment and workplace learning.

In the spring of 1990, as a team of three, we coded an initial sample of the petrochemical interview transcripts, using ideas from the literature and concepts inductively derived from individual analyses and ensuing discusssion. We created four families of codes: learning outcome, learning process, type of learner (individual, small group or organization) and contextual con-ditions. During the summer, Kathy and Elizabeth collected most of the data for the second case study; Kathy and Victoria finished coding the first case's interviews and created a model of group learning. Based on the data and their own theoretical beliefs, they derived four phases of group learning which they called simply: phase 1, phase 2, phase 3 and phase 4. We eventually named these phases contained, collected, constructed and con-tinuous, respectively. Currently, we define the four developmental phases of group learning as follows:

- *Phase 1: Contained learning*: a group exists, but learning, if any, is con-tained within individual members.
- *Phase 2: Collected learning*: individuals begin to share information and meaning perspectives. Group knowledge is an aggregate of individual knowledge; there is not yet an experience of having knowledge that is uniquely the group's own.
- *Phase 3: Constructed learning*: the group creates knowledge of its own.

Individuals' knowledge and meaning perspectives are integrated, not aggregated.

- *Phase 4: Continuous learning*: the group habituates processes of transforming its experience into knowledge.

We describe these phases as developmental to indicate progression and growth in learning, but we do not intend to indicate that groups never regress. Individual groups can cycle through the learning phases, starting at phase 1 with each new learning task. However, it is likely that as groups develop skills as learning bodies, very little time, if any, is spent in the first two phases of group learning.

Our week on Cape Cod: Learning ebbs and flows

Although a lot was accomplished during our first spring and summer working together, little progress was made during the next year. Not only did we have difficulty getting the interviews from the second case study transcribed, but we each were absorbed by the demands of the academic calendar. It was not until late in the spring of 1991 that we were finally able to work with the second case. Summer arrived. We decided to spend a week at Kathy's vacation home on Cape Cod, a resort area on the seashore in the northeastern United States. Our purpose was to closet ourselves with the research and make the kind of headway that uninterrupted effort could allow.

Our contained learning phase: Beginning the learning process

Once we made our plan to spend a week in uninterrupted work, we wanted to prepare adequately. Our goal was to have all the coding finished when we arrived at the Cape so that we could concentrate on analysing the data and conceptualizing how to write up the research. We decided to divide the interview transcripts from our second case study into three groups. We refreshed our ability to use the petrochemical coding categories through a process of duplicate coding and discussion; then each of us took a group of transcripts that included all the interviewees from one self-managed team. Our assignment was to code the team's transcripts and write a summary report of the team's learning. We anticipated using these individual reports to craft an analysis of the second case and to attempt cross-case comparison between the petrochemical and manufacturing companies.

July arrived. We packed Elizabeth's Toyota van with books and journal articles, flip charts, transcripts, a computer – and beach chairs. We looked forward to working hard, but taking afternoon beach breaks. During the fifteen months we had been working as a team, we had developed respect for each other's abilities and an easy camaraderie. Occasional full-day meetings at Kathy's house in Connecticut had been productive and we anticipated that six contiguous days would reward us with rich accomplishment. Our spirits were high as we set off; the four-hour drive slipped away in animated conversation.

We settled into Kathy's vacation home, shopped for groceries, and started work by orally summarizing our written reports. To our dismay, our effort had not borne the expected fruit. Only Victoria's report seemed on target – she had used our coding categories to describe her team's learning processes, learning outcomes and contextual conditions that enhanced or impeded learning. She included an interpretative analysis of how the team's learning seemed to follow the four-phase model of group learning that had been posited from the petrochemical company data.

Kathy had been unable to create a similar report. The 'problem', she explained, 'is that this team really didn't experience group learning. There was not much individual learning either. So I coded the conditions and tried to analyse how they impeded the group from learning.' Elizabeth said she didn't do the assignment in the same way as the other two. 'So what else is new', quipped Kathy with a smile. Our group had grown used to Elizabeth's perspective being different. 'I tried to use the coding categories', Elizabeth said, 'but this team's experience is so complicated that the coding doesn't capture the group's learning in a meaningful way'. She continued, 'What I did instead was lay out a chronology of critical events that affected the group's learning.'

We may have been disappointed that our prepared assignments hadn't accomplished what we hoped, but we were basically undaunted. The luxury of having a week working together seemed full of promise.

Our collected learning phase: Aggregating information

The next few days were mixed with free-wheeling explorations in search of analytical frameworks and quiet times for individual reading and thinking. Our group discussion was stamped by our individual styles. Kathy likes to use flip charts to capture ideas as they are generated, or to test analytical frameworks by drawing diagrams. Newsprint gradually covered the walls. Victoria processes ideas by making summary notes periodically on a computer. The Macintosh and printer perched permanently on the dining table. Elizabeth is easily distracted by detail. Her interest in small points often sidetracked discussion.

Awareness of our different styles has marked our work together. For example, we often joked about Elizabeth's concern with detail and Kathy's and Victoria's leaps to generalization. Elizabeth observed, 'I sometimes can't imagine where you two get these ideas', and Victoria smiled back, 'You mean our intuitive leaps? It's good we have you to keep us honest.' We were aware during our search for analytical frameworks that the differences among us were enriching our discussion, if also making consensus difficult.

Although we could apply the petrochemical coding categories to the second case study, we were not making the progress we had envisioned. Two questions that had been plaguing us since the beginning of the project remained unanswered: How do these learning processes that we are coding relate to each other and to the phases of group learning described in the model? How does what we are describing as group learning differ significantly from the descriptions of group process and development that are in the group dynamics literature?

One afternoon we decided to give each interviewee a pseudonym. We knew the task had to be accomplished eventually to protect confidentiality, and we thought we should get in the habit of calling the interviewees by fictional names. We also needed a change of pace from the intensity of our discussions. Although we did not realize it at the time, the activity of choosing names for the research subjects enabled us to break through barriers that had been inhibiting our progress and allowed us to move into the next phase of group learning. Therefore, we describe the process in detail.

Our constructed learning phase: Making meaning together

We remained seated at the table, but the tenor of our effort changed. The papers that surrounded us – piled on the table and under it, heaped on unoccupied chairs and scattered into the living room – were forgotten. Pencils and magic markers lay idle, the Macintosh switched off. Our conversation meandered at a leisurely pace as we shared stories from our personal and professional lives that explained associations we made with particular names. We chose pseudonyms based on people whom we knew in common. We giggled when one of us explained an association that made a name 'absolutely perfect' or 'not at all right' for a particular interviewee. We gossiped. We relaxed and had fun.

During this process, each of us used the intimate knowledge of the interviewees' attitudes and personalities that we had acquired from coding the transcripts and writing our pre-Cape reports. Our unstructured conversations also elicited memories from the interviews which had frequently been conducted by someone different from the person who coded the transcript and wrote the report. Our process was peppered with comments like, 'I remember her vividly because she was so critical and negative. She whined about everything. Whine. Whine. Whine.' Or, 'He seemed so arrogant. He didn't have much respect for his co-workers and showed little concern for how his actions affected them.' Or, 'This man was so thoughtful and caring and gentle. He has been at the company longer than the others. I can see why they look up to him.'

When we finished naming the twenty-three interviewees, each of us had a much better understanding of the characteristics and experiences of the two teams we had not coded. Our leisurely discussion, filled with meandering explanations and associations, had brought the three teams to life in a way that the written reports had not.

Before we named the interviewees, our discussions had been marked by heavy reliance on each researcher as a content expert for the team she had coded. Each of us generated ideas that were mostly tied to the frame of her own team's experience. When we did attempt an observation about a different team, the content expert often corrected, 'No. That isn't quite how it happened.' Sometimes the content expert would be cued to share new information: 'You're right! And now that you point that out, I see how it connects to something that I didn't put in my report . . .'. After we named the interviewees, each of us was able to pull ideas from the entire data-set, not just her individual piece.

With our new perspective on the full data-set, we soon discovered that the three self-managed teams corresponded in their typical ways of work to three of the phases in our group learning model. Kathy's team, where each individual kept his or her learning tightly bounded, clearly operated in the *contained* learning phase. Elizabeth's team, which did not create meaning as a group, although individuals shared information and ideas, fitted our definition of the *collected* phase. In contrast, Victoria's team had created meaning together and could be characterized as operating most of the time in the *constructed* learning phase; her team even took some actions that we characterized as phase 4 behaviour.

We had created our first bit of group-constructed knowledge. Although we did not understand it at the time, our research team had shifted from aggregating information to integrating perspectives. We had moved into the third phase of our model of group learning.

With a clear understanding that each of the three self-managed teams typified one phase in the model, we now had a concrete strategy for examining how the learning processes manifest themselves at each phase of group learning. Before the Cape, we vaguely understood that each learning process changes qualitatively as a group moves through the phases, but we had not been articulate in describing those changes. A careful examination of how the learning processes manifested themselves in each team was the key to answering a question that had been nagging at us: 'How do these learning processes that we are coding relate to each other and to the phases of group learning described in the model?' When we left the Cape, Victoria used our insight to draft a paper that described how the learning processes developed (Marsick *et al.* 1991).

Heading home with a sense of accomplishment

Driving home from the Cape at the end of the week, we felt happy with our progress. We had recorded carefully all of the ideas that were generated during those free-wheeling discussions. The pad of flip chart paper was filled; the computer disks brimming. We still could not answer the second nagging question: 'How does what we are describing as group learning differ significantly from the descriptions of group process and development that are in the group dynamics literature?' Although we still had no answer to this question, we were optimistic that the answer was present in rudimentary form among the records of our discussion and that we could pull the ideas together easily in the Fall.

Interim months of frustration

We met at Kathy's house to critique Victoria's draft of the paper on group learning processes and felt very pleased that our Cape experience had been so productive. Based on the vision laid out in the paper, we were able to identify a conceptual problem with the model and constructed a different understanding of how phase 4 should be defined. Our new bit of constructed meaning was integrated into the paper. We felt confident and self-congratulatory.

Then, we turned to our major agenda item – laying out a conceptual framework for journal publications. Lists and diagrams began to cover the walls of Kathy's kitchen, but the sense of free-wheeling jubilance that had characterized our Cape discussions was missing. The spirit of confidence ebbed as we felt ourselves sinking into a swamp of ambiguity and confusion. During the Fall, we grappled half-heartedly with the ambiguity. Each was busy, Victoria in particular because of a weight of administrative responsibilities. Progress was at a dead halt. We attributed our lack of progress to hostile conditions. Only as we met to plan this book chapter did we realize that hostile conditions were not the heart of the matter.

Eight months after Cape Cod: The dawn of consciousness

Our team of three had not met for two months. The task that brought us together was this book chapter. Kathy and Victoria had submitted a draft that was rejected because the focus was not personal. As we convened in New York, we understood our task was to create a story from our own experience about how we learned from experience.

Using the model to name our own experience

We were meeting in a small conference room at Teachers College. As we settled ourselves at the formal conference table and commiserated with each other about work overload, we reminisced about our week on the Cape and spoke wistfully about the contrast between the two sets of working conditions. It became immediately clear that we might analyse our Cape experience in order to write this chapter.

Victoria had brought newsprint and magic markers from her office; as always, Kathy took charge of recording our ideas. Quickly we named the conditions that had enabled us at the Cape to produce generative insights: Kathy's vacation home was beyond commuting distance. Thus, we were separated from our daily lives and relatively free from distraction. We came to the Cape with a shared agenda and an attitude of openness to exploring both the meaning of the data and approaches to analysing it. We liked, respected and trusted each other. These personal feelings made risk-taking and self-disclosure possible; we could express our doubts and ignorance without fear of embarrassment. We had a large block of time that allowed us a sense of freedom to meander off-task during what we perceived as work time. In addition to freedom within work time, we shared informal moments as we cooked, ate and cleaned up. We also had planned time for recreation (although we did not actually make it to the beach until we had been there two days!).

With the conditions listed, we decided to sort through our experience in search of learning processes from our model of group learning. The conceptualization of these processes, strongly influenced by Donald Schön (1983), is as follows:

- *Framing ⇒ reframing*: framing is an initial perception of an issue, situation, person or object based on past understanding and present input. Re-framing is a process of transforming that perception into a new under-standing or frame.
- *Integrating perspectives*: synthesis of divergent views, such that apparent conflicts are resolved through dialectical thinking, not compromise or majority rule.
- *Experimenting*: reflective action undertaken for hypothesis testing, move-testing or discovery.
- *Crossing boundaries*: communication between two or more individuals and/ or groups.

As we reconstructed our experience in search of learning processes, we remembered our three very different approaches to our pre-Cape reports. Victoria had completed the assignment as planned; Kathy had analysed learning conditions; Elizabeth had created a chronology of events but not the expected interpretative analysis. We remembered that Kathy and Victoria were impressed by the chronology and thought it would be useful if they could do the same thing for their teams. After an hour's effort, they had pronounced the experiment a failure: 'It just doesn't work. Our teams didn't have the same kind of long-term history as Elizabeth's team.'

We appreciated our good fortune at having stumbled into the activity of giving the interviewees pseudonyms. Although we had not realized it while at the Cape, we could now see how this process was a catalyst for our realiz-ation that the three teams corresponded to three phases of the learning model. Before the catalyst activity, our individual perspectives afforded ample clues about individual differences among the teams. Kathy had observed about her team, 'The problem is that this team really didn't experience group learning.' Kathy and Victoria pronounced their attempt at chronology a failure because their teams were too 'different from Elizabeth's'. Yet, before the pseudonym activity, we had not connected different team experiences with the idea of different phases in group learning. Each of us was too mired in the perspective of a single team's experience to be able to see the larger picture in our data.

As we reviewed our Cape experiences, we realized for the first time that our experience as a research team could be explained by our own model of group learning:

- *Phase 1: Contained learning*: we experienced this phase when we coded our own data and wrote our pre-Cape reports.
- *Phase 2: Collected learning*: we presented our reports to each other and discovered we each had taken very different approaches to interpreting the task. Kathy and Victoria attempted to redefine their data by using Elizabeth's strategy, but this attempt to force fit the data failed.
- *Phase 3: Constructed learning*: together, we created a new understanding of the relationship between learning processes and phase of group learning.
- *Phase 4: Continuous learning*: we did not yet think about ourselves as continuous learners.

We consulted our post-Cape paper to see how our own learning processes matched what we had written. For the learning process of *integrating perspectives*, for example, our paper suggests that the move from the collected phase of group learning to the constructed phase is marked by a move from a position where 'different views [are] exchanged but only partially integrated' to one in which group members 'struggle to listen, hear, accept, and integrate viewpoints to construct a shared view' (Marsick *et al.* 1991). From our analysis of personal experience, we elaborate what we wrote. At the beginning of our Cape experience, we 'exchanged' views by sharing our written reports; we made a good-faith effort 'to listen, hear, accept' each other's work. However, the effort did not provide us with the understanding that we acquired from our pseudonym activity. We now understand that before groups can integrate perspectives to construct shared knowledge, each individual needs to understand the others' perspectives with enough depth and complexity that those perspectives can be readily called upon during discussion.

Our experience with moving from collected to constructed group learning through the developmental process of integrating perspectives raises an important issue regarding how groups can learn to learn. This issue is the knotty problem of finding a balance between individual knowledge and group knowledge. Our research team did what many task-oriented groups do. We delegated tasks in the interest of efficiency. Yet, our strategy was ultimately dysfunctional. Our content-specialist's knowledge of only a piece of the picture interfered with our ability to choose an appropriate frame for viewing our data and achieving our ultimate goal. Our interviewees described the same phenomenon in the context of their work as systems experts. They reported that attempts to work together were often frustrated because their knowledge as individuals was so specialized and disparate that it interfered with their team's ability to find a common language for co-operative efforts. Plans to 'cross-train' within their teams were continually abandoned because there 'wasn't enough time'. In essence, learning for long-term gain was sacrificed in favour of accomplishing tasks for short-term objectives.

In the case of our research team, we had given ourselves the gift of time. We had our week of isolation and a mind-set that was open to experimenting. The easy give-and-take of the naming activity, with its associational thinking and freedom to ask questions, is unlikely to have happened in the normal press of our working worlds. Yet, without that activity, we might never have created the new frame that proved so valuable to our conceptual analysis.

Our day in New York led us to another important insight. We realized that we consistently explained our different approaches to the data as differences in personal style. The frame of individual differences through which we viewed our work as a team interfered with our capacity to be open to alternative explanations for what we were experiencing. For example, it was easy to assume that it was Elizabeth's attention to detail that led her to write a pre-Cape report that was a detailed chronology instead of a conceptual analysis. With the old frame broken, an entirely different interpretation of our Cape experience became visible: the differences in the written reports were caused not so much by differences in personal style as by different assumptions about the purpose of the pre-Cape assignment. Elizabeth had assumed that she was to make the story of her team's experience accessible to the other researchers so that all three could engage in analysing her team's learning. In essence, she was trying to organize the raw data. The presupposition on which Elizabeth's assumption was based was that the model derived from the petrochemical data was specific to that case and that the same inductive process would be repeated on the second case. She expected a new or amended model to emerge based equally on the two cases. Kathy and Victoria had assumed that the assignment's purpose was to apply the petrochemical coding strategy to the new data in order to test its efficacy. Their presupposition was that the second case was being used to test theory that had been developed from the first.

The fundamental dynamic that underlay what happened raises two issues that are critical to understanding how groups can learn to learn. The first issue is about group memory. Elizabeth had not been involved in developing the first model; it is not surprising that she experienced neither the depth of understanding nor the sense of ownership that Kathy and Victoria did. When she observed on the Cape, 'I sometimes can't imagine where you two get these ideas', she was making a literal statement that had more meaning than anyone realized at the time. Questions raised by reflection about group memory include: When work is accomplished while one or more members are absent, how is group knowledge-making affected? What strategies can enable the group to move forward with confidence about shared meaning?

The second issue concerns group heterogeneity. Elizabeth was recruited into the group because she brought a different perspective, yet the diversity of perspective that was created made group consensus more difficult. Questions raised by reflection about this issue include: How do groups balance their need for richness in perspective with their need for closure? How can groups learn to recognize when it is dysfunctional to sacrifice consensus for expediency? How do groups learn the skills of dialectic thinking that enable integration?

Our continuous learning phase: Reframing ourselves as a learning group

We were bringing our meeting to a close. Kathy was summarizing, '. . . and we have seen how we moved from the collected to the constructed phase of learning'. She paused and seemed to wonder aloud, 'are we continuous learners?' We had just drafted a paper in which we connected our concept of continuous learning to Senge's concept of generative learning (Kasl *et al.* 1992), and the diagram lay on the table in front of Kathy. She spotted the word 'generative' and said, 'Did we experience generative learning? Let's see if we can name generative learning.' Victoria and Elizabeth were stacking books and papers, getting ready to leave. It was late Friday afternoon and each was thinking about the lateness of the hour. Startled and somewhat disbelieving, Victoria asked, 'You mean now?' 'Yes, now' came Kathy's reply.

We settled back into our chairs, silent, each pondering the question. Victoria observed that we were becoming 'more facile at learning'. Her language signalled a clear change in our usual references to 'getting a lot accomplished' or 'making progress' with the task. We remembered how we had often commented about language at the petrochemical company. Interviewees continually referred to their 'learnings' or 'sharing the team's learnings'. Language that described the outcome of team efforts as 'learnings' had been integrated into the new organizational culture.

We do not know whether institutionalizing language about 'learnings' was an intentional, pre-planned effort at the petrochemical company, but we believe that deliberate consciousness of a group's identity as a learning group is critical in the dynamics of group learning. We believe our own group's development was enhanced when Victoria's remark about our group's learning skills framed our research team's identity as a learning group.

This reflection helps us begin to form an answer to the question that has been plaguing us since the beginning of this project: 'How does what we are describing as group learning differ significantly from the descriptions of group process and development that are in the group dynamics literature?' Our answer emerges: When a group frames itself as a learning group, its experience and effectiveness is changed qualitatively. This conclusion is grounded in the work of Jack Mezirow (1991), who is influenced by Gregory Bateson and Edward Cell. All three theorists posit progressively complex forms of learning in which increased potency in learning is accounted for by increases in the learner's consciousness of self as a learner.

Although Mezirow, Bateson and Cell are writing about individual learning, we believe their principle can be applied to groups; we use Mezirow's term 'meaning scheme' to explain the process. A meaning scheme is a composite of 'knowledge, beliefs, value judgments, and feelings that constitute inter- pretations of experience' (Mezirow 1991: 5–6). Actions are governed by meaning schemes.

When a group's meaning scheme constitutes its identity as a task-oriented group, it perceives its goals to be task achievement. Although the group may concern itself with stages of group development and the nature of interactions among group members and the roles they play (Gladstein 1984), the root concern is getting the task accomplished. If the group shifts its meaning scheme and frames itself as a learning group, the goal-action becomes, in the petrochemical company's language, to generate 'learnings'.

A goal of 'learning' is more open-ended than 'getting the task accom- plished' and encourages generative thinking in at least two ways. First, individuals who are released from the pressure of task accomplishment feel more freedom to engage in associational thinking. We believe it is signifi- cant that our research team's most important conceptualizations can be traced to associational thinking. Secondly, individual group members may find it easier to dissociate themselves from their own meaning schemes if they feel they are trying to learn rather than find the 'best solution'. Both Mezirow and Senge insist that the ability to engage in transformative or generative learning depends on the ability to identify and suspend as- sumptions in order to subject these assumptions to rational evaluation. To dissociate oneself from treasured ideas is easier to prescribe than actually do. We believe that by framing a group's goal as a learning goal rather than task, it becomes easier for individual members to dissociate themselves from particular visions of the ultimate group product or task achievement. A learning frame may increase members' openness to other perspectives as well as their capacity to identify their own assumptions. In the long run, as both Mezirow and Senge imply, this capacity to dissociate the self from treasured ideas or envisioned solutions expedites accomplishment of task at a higher level of quality.

Summary and conclusions

In this chapter, we used our own research-based model of group learning to describe our experience as a research team. Writing this chapter turned out to be not just a simple report of how we applied our model to our own experience, but a learning process that yielded new insights about the model itself.

From our experience of analysing our own experience, we reframed our group identity and for the first time perceived ourselves as a learning group. This new frame enabled us to formulate an answer to the nagging question, 'How does what we are describing as group learning differ significantly from the descriptions of group process and development that are in the group dynamics literature?'

From our experience of formalizing our analysis by committing it to paper, we can more clearly articulate another question that has been implicit in the model from its inception: What propels a group from one phase to the next? We offer an answer which we have crafted from our own experience but for which we find tentative confirmation in our case-study data:

• Groups move from the contained to collected phase when particular learning conditions are present. These conditions include mutual trust, respect and regard among the participants, as well as a perception that association in the context of a group can bring personal benefit.

• Groups move from the collected to constructed phase when members listen carefully and respectfully to each other, and understand each other with enough depth that multiple perspectives can be integrated to construct shared meaning.

• We tentatively suggest that the energy that propels a group from constructed to continuous learning is created when the group *frames its identity as a learning group* and becomes conscious of monitoring its processes as *learning processes*, rather than the processes of interpersonal interaction and role fulfilment that are described in the group dynamics literature.

We believe that these learning processes are dialectic integrations of reflection and action, and that the processes described in our two stories – one at the Cape, one in the conference room – are examples of that dialectic integration.

References

Gladstein, D.L. (1984) Groups in context: A model of task group effectiveness. *Administrative Sciences Quarterly*, 29, 499–517.

Kasl, E., Marsick, V. and Dechant, K. (1992) A conceptual model for group learning. In *Proceedings of the 33rd Adult Education Research Conference*. Saskatoon, Saskatchewan, Canada, May.

Marsick, V., Dechant, K. and Kasl, E. (1991) Group learning among professionals: The Brewster Company case study. In *Proceedings of Professionals' Ways of Knowing and the Implications for CPE*. Commission for Continuing Professional Education of the American Association of Adult and Continuing Education, Montreal, Quebec, Canada, October.

Mezirow, J. (1991) *Transformative Dimensions of Adult Learning*. San Francisco, CA: Jossey-Bass.

Schön, D.A. (1983) *The Reflective Practitioner.* New York: Basic Books.
Senge, P. (1990) *The Fifth Discipline: The Art and Practice of the Learning Organization.* New York: Doubleday.

11

Experiential Learning and Social Transformation for a Post-apartheid Learning Future

Costas Criticos

South Africa and other countries struggling to escape oppression and poverty seem to have a deep understanding for education that liberates. Education in these settings becomes a defence against oppression and a preparation for a future free of the constraints and practices that disempower citizens.

Decades of schooling constructed by the present regime reinforced the apartheid lie that most South Africans were inferior and in need of special (segregated and inferior) treatment. Society was segregated so that each race group had its own curriculum, schools, homes, hospitals and even prisons. These ghettos of privilege and oppression ensured that people did not engage in conversation or encounter experiences that would contradict the lie. It is not surprising, therefore, that Whites felt themselves to be superior and Blacks felt themselves to be inferior. Two of the most important institutions in South Africa that challenged this lie and allowed conversations to continue are the church and the universities. Certain of these were, however, instruments of the regime which gave theological and academic support to policies of oppression.

In my own experience, my segregated and privileged life was first challenged during discussions at Christian youth meetings. Later, my university education led me to a more critical and analytical examination of the pathology of apartheid oppression. The learning that I experienced was a learning of tension; a tension between contradictory experiences and contradictory explanations of society. The mechanics of this learning resides in the conversation, negotiation and argument that takes place between people or in the internal wrestling over the tension between competing experiences and competing explanations.

Apartheid, as explained by Nationalist Party propaganda – and later, school textbooks – is a policy of 'self-determination'. This explanation stands in strong contrast to theological and political science perspectives that explain apartheid as racist oppression. In my own case, learning did not take place when I accepted one or the other position, but when the tension of contradictory explanations forced me to be reflective and generate a personal understanding. The moment at which I resolved or explained the contradiction, is when learning took place and knowledge was constructed.

Since these personal discoveries I have sought ways of working, teaching and learning that expose contradictions and promote tension between taken-for-granted explanations. These interests have brought me to experiential learning, participatory video and other ways of working that promote critical and collective examinations of experience. This chapter will explore the emancipatory character of experiential learning and its growth in South Africa. I conclude this exploration with an account of my work in documentary production and primary school teaching which have incorporated an emancipatory interest.

Educational foundations

The revolutionary climate of resistance in South Africa created a popular interest in an education that advanced democracy in contrast to the domesticating education that maintained the *status quo* of oppression. At the heart of this emancipatory education is an alternative view of knowledge itself: knowledge is not something fixed which is transferred to learners. The epistemology of emancipatory education is a perspective which regards knowledge as being constructed by learners. Learners in emancipatory education are creators rather than consumers of knowledge. The debate about epistemologies is not a peripheral interest, but rather a central issue that impacts on the way we teach, learn and view our role in the educational process:

> ... the way we know has powerful implications for the way we live. Every epistemology tends to become an ethic, and every way of knowing tends to become a way of living. The relation established between the student and the subject, tends to become the relation of the living person to the world itself. Every mode of knowing contains its own moral trajectory, its own ethical direction and outcomes.
>
> (Palmer 1990: 107)

There is no doubt that there are two major competing epistemologies. The dominant epistemology underpins most of mainstream education. This dominant epistemology, an analytical and objective way of knowing, does not tolerate experiential learning, action research, holistic medicine and other alternative ways of knowing and working.

Tim Stanton, Stanford University academic and experiential learning advocate, explains why the work he does is necessarily marginal in traditional higher education:

... the dominant epistemology of knowledge, which informs higher education is based on a sense that replicability is the final test of truth, that knowledge is analytical, abstract and logical. The task of education is the distribution of knowledge, or the "banking" method of education. Random experience is inadequate as a means of knowledge. We are taught to distrust personal experience as a guide, to identify universal truths from logical, preorganized, abstractions.

(Stanton 1986)

Emancipatory education has an alternative epistemology, which, in contrast to an objective knowing, is based on a connected knowing. This is an education which is generative not consumptive, concerned with perception not reception, searching not researching. In such a system, intelligence is a process not a product, and intelligence equals intelligent behaviour (Stanton 1986, 1990).

Habermas's theory of how fundamental human interests influence the social construction of knowledge is a valuable contribution to this examination of the foundations of education. He rejects the dominant view of knowledge that is separate and discovered by the individual in favour of a knowledge that is constructed in communal action. For Habermas, what separates humans from other animals is speech, and that within speech (discourse) an interest in rationality is discernible. The fundamental interest, survival, is based on life that is organized through knowledge and human action. He posits three ways of knowing – empirical-analytical, historical-hermeneutic and critical:

The task of the empirical-analytic sciences incorporates a technical interest; that of the historical-hermeneutic sciences incorporates a practical interest and the approach of critically oriented sciences incorporates the emancipatory cognitive interests.

(Habermas 1972: 308)

While the technical and practical interests are concerned with control and understanding, respectively:

... the emancipatory interest is concerned with empowerment, that is, the ability of individuals and groups to take control of their own lives in autonomous and responsible ways ... At the level of practice the emancipatory curriculum will involve the participants in the educational encounter, both teacher and pupil, in action which attempts to change the structures within which learning occurs and which constrains freedom in often unrecognised ways.

(Grundy 1987: 19)

In South Africa, the structures of education were designed specifically to constrain freedom. Education was divided on racial lines and the curricula were designed to reinforce the lie of white supremacy. Whites were prepared for positions of management and high-technology, whereas Blacks were prepared for positions of subservience. In addition to school texts which perpetuated the lie of apartheid, the type of education that was typical in schools did not give pupils opportunities to be critical of their own learning. Teaching styles in classrooms are typical of what Paulo Freire has called 'banking education' – the depositing of knowledge into the heads of passive learners.

Opposition to apartheid was waged in a low-level civil war of armed resistance on South African borders, townships and industrial settings. In parallel to armed resistance, there was oppositional activity in educational settings. Schools became sites of struggle as 'banking education' which disempowered through its contents and methods was rejected. In the place of 'banking education', emancipatory alternatives such as 'People's Education' was popularized by the National Education Crisis Committee and other groups that sprung up following the education-focused protests. Educational authorities and the police tried to control this resistance through harassment and imprisonment of education activists.

South Africa is not unique in experiencing attacks on an education that liberates. Highlander Folk School, the educational pulse of the labour and civil rights movement in the USA, focused on allowing people to make meaning of their experiences (Bell *et al.* 1990: xxiii). In 1957, Martin Luther King was photographed while he spoke at the 25th anniversary of the Highlander Folk School. Those photographs were used by segregationists to construct posters with the caption 'King at Communist Training School'. The school was closed and its teachers were harassed by the authorities who described them as troublemakers.

These reactions were not surprising, since Highlander was advocating an education for change. This type of education flowers in harsh circumstances; it is based not on the formal scholarship of the textbook, but on the scholarship of inquiry – an examination of ourselves and the society we live in. If the society we live in is oppressive, then the oppressors get very nervous when the oppressed become empowered by understanding, documenting and challenging that oppression.

In South Africa, Paulo Freire's (1972) *Pedagogy of the Oppressed* provided a theoretical framework to challenge oppression. His writing seemed to be directly addressing the South African situation and it offered liberation via education. The security forces were not slow to realize the danger that Freire's writing presented – so Freire's books were banned. The interest in Freire's work was spread through the University Christian Movement and from there to the South African Students Organization.

Neville Alexander, a Black South African who was imprisoned for his political beliefs, examines the history of emancipatory education and the central role played by the works of Paulo Freire:

> Although the government banned Freire's works, about 500 or more copies of *Pedagogy of the Oppressed* made the rounds at the "bush colleges" (segregated universities established in the "homelands" as part

of grand apartheid) and were eagerly studied by the young activists of the Black Conscious Movement. In Freire's works, they saw the mirror image of that which they rejected in the Bantu-Education system as well as the possible way out of the cul-de-sac.

(Alexander 1989: 6)

This explanation was given by Alexander during an address at the First National Conference on Experiential Learning in South Africa. As the keynote speaker, he had been asked to examine the reasons why experiential education was so popular in the education of resistance. He cited four key reasons why Freireian methods and experiential learning were popularized:

- Freire's anti-capitalist social theory concurs with analyses of educationists in South African liberation movements.
- The context in which Freire's pedagogy was formed was similar to that of oppression in South Africa.
- Freire's linking of education with conscientization.
- The demand for and interest in democratic practices by grassroots organisations reinforced the interest in Freire.

Reflective experiential learning

The interest in experience is not new; it has been valued universally and not only in situations of crisis. Folklore and educational common sense tell us that experience is valuable. We often say, 'you learn from experience'. We nod our heads in agreement with the Chinese proverb, 'I hear and I forget, I see and I remember, I do and I understand'. There is, however, far more to experiential learning than the simple analysis of the proverb.

If experience in itself was so valuable, then humans who are enmeshed in experience ought to be more knowledgeable than they are. Sadly, the only conclusion that can be reached is that we do not learn from experience. Experience has to be arrested, examined, analysed, considered and negated in order to shift it to knowledge (Aitchison and Graham 1989: 15). These reservations and cautions about the value of experience led Torbert (1972: 7) to ask:

Why do some people appear to learn from experience – increasing the effectiveness of their action, increasing the accuracy of their beliefs about patterns in experience, and increasingly accepting their emotions as significantly related to situations – while others repeat habitual patterns without learning?

Although many early educationists and learning theorists have alerted us to the value of experience, Dewey was the first to give the interest any substantial theoretical and philosophical defence. In his 1938 classic, *Experience and Education*, he alerts us to the variable value of experience: '. . .

that all genuine education comes about through experience does not mean that all experiences are genuinely or equally educative' (p. 25). What, then, makes experience educative? It is surely not the quality of the experience itself but the quality given it by the learner. Unless an experience is examined and reflected on it has no educative value. I believe it is this engagement that makes experience in Dewey's terms 'genuinely educative'.

For Torbert, experiential learning involves the awareness of 'qualities, patterns and consequences of one's own experience as one experiences it' (p. 8). Indeed, the absence of this awareness might even be regarded as a form of personal or social dysfunction. The term experiential learning has been used in a much broader sense than Torbert's definition. It has been used to describe everything associated with learning and experience. To make some sense of the terminology I distinguish three major types of learning along this continuum of meaning: practical training, experience-based learning and reflective experiential learning. The key distinction relates to the central role of reflection in reflective experiential learning. Only if we make this distinction can we understand the women and men who report on the difficult and even painful experiences as valuable learning. Was the experience itself valuable? Not at all – what was valuable was the intellectual growth that follows the process of reflecting on experience. Effective learning does not follow from a positive experience but from effective reflection.

This view was confirmed by a moving documentary in which the camera is locked on three men talking about their life on Robben Island, the prison for South African political prisoners. In the film, *Robben Island: Our University*, three ex-prisoners – Neville Alexander, Fiks Bam and Max Kwedi – unpack the reasons why they regard the Island as the University of the liberation struggle. The Island was the place where some of the prisoners encountered African history for the first time – their school history spoke only of colonial conquests. They were a community of intellectuals who held discussions and tutorials in the midst of their work details in the rock quarry or during exercises. The principal texts were their own experiences and their common purpose to liberate South Africa. In addition to the political debates and discussions, many prisoners studied for higher degrees through UNISA, the distance education university in South Africa. These students formed discussion groups with prisoners who were leaders in their own fields, such as Neville Alexander for History, Nelson Mandela for Law and Denis Brutus for English.

The prisoners had a high regard for the Island because they were in control of their own learning – they constructed knowledge out of their personal and collective experience. An important lesson which I learnt from this film and through my discussions with Alexander is that the learner is not free of the responsibility of making every experience educative. It was intended that Robben Island should constrain the prisoners – instead, they grew more powerful.

The story of Robben Island is an exception to the rule. Learners conditioned to value objective knowledge and the expert position of the teacher are intimidated by a demand that they move from passive consumers of knowledge to active creators of knowledge. Such learners not only resist animation but they also value passivity.

The value given to passive education is frequently illustrated in the schoolyards of rural areas in South Africa. In many of these schools, there are too few classrooms, so classes may need to meet out in the open. Rather than sit in a circle, the students often attempt to reconstitute the traditional classroom. In one such meeting, the students lined up along the perimeter of an imaginary classroom, demarcated by stones, and waited until the teacher walked in through the imaginary door. When they were called by the teacher, they marched 'in', stood by the imaginary desks, and then greeted the teacher before sitting in neat rows on the dusty ground. What was so attractive about the traditional classroom that led to this practice? Why did they choose to sit in neat rows similar to their peers in the real classroom? For them, the only person who can teach is the teacher and the only place of learning is the classroom – such is the pedagogy of domestication!

Such entrenched views of education present major obstacles to the development of a learning culture. A 1988 research project revealed a disturbing statistic of very high resistance by black students to classroom activities that make demands on critical skills. The students who brought education to a standstill and marched with banners proclaiming 'NO DOMESTICATING EDUCATION' and 'PEOPLE'S EDUCATION FOR PEOPLE'S POWER' have not welcomed the demands of an emancipatory education. The research by Gilmour showed in a sample of over 1000 teachers and high school students that:

> ... there is a deep-seated individualism amongst students in the sense less of personal assertion, and more in terms of the internalisation of values consistent with capitalist ideology. These include an instrumental view of education in the sense of preferring goals that are extrinsic to the learning process itself. Secondly, a belief in meritocracy as manifested initially by a down-playing of the goal of equality, and further by the ways in which success and failure are perceived. The lack of concern with syllabus changes as a major task of reform, and the low ranking of independent learning, illustrate an instrumental view of knowledge that is reinforced by both examination orientation and teachers' behaviour.
>
> (Gilmour 1988: 21)

What I have attempted to argue is that People's Education does not materialize by edict or the application of specific methods. Instead, it follows from a world view or perspective rooted in an epistemology of connected knowledge. This perspective does not focus on schooling, alone, but rather illuminates all our social activity. In my own professional work, such a changed perspective led to a change in my practice.

Practising participation

Emancipatory interest is a theme that extends beyond education to other disciplines such as anthropology, history, geography and others which have accepted participatory action research as an alternative to traditional experimental research. My own training as an educational television producer equipped me to be creative as an individual and make executive decisions about the 'texts' that I created. As I became involved in working with community organizations, I was influenced by their democratic styles of working. I found my expert and directive style of working to be inappropriate. My training gradually yielded to participatory approaches that were consistent with the democratic interests of the organizations and unions that I was serving. Initially, this yielding was simply satisfying a 'customer's whim'. Very soon, however, I embraced this approach. In addition to the moral imperative for participation, there is a different quality to the work. While there is no technical advantage in this approach, the distorted power relationship between producers and subjects is addressed.

Working in a participatory manner, founded on an epistemology of connected knowing and democracy, is not something that can be picked up as one of the tricks of the trade. It is rather an overriding way of working. My initiation into participatory video led to an interest in the theoretical underpinnings of this approach and its symbiotic association with reflective experiential learning. Instead of approaching a subject with a shooting script, we establish production collectives made up of production workers and members who are the subjects of the video. This way of working demands that we determine collectively the outcomes in a dynamic manner.

Hanging Up The Nets is the latest production of our unit, the Media Resource Centre. It was a considerable success, as in addition to the completed documentary the production process itself was a valuable educative experience. The documentary was initiated at a meeting of seventy descendants of an Indian fishing community. The fishermen and their families were no longer actively fishing because a variety of council and national (apartheid) rulings had moved them away from the traditional fishing sites. The meeting had been prompted by a few fishermen who expressed an interest in documenting their struggle to maintain a viable fishing community.

As is usual in our work, we requested that a meeting be called to consider how we ought to proceed. We met in a local temple where the researchers showed samples of previously produced work and the preliminary interviews of the fishermen who had invited us to produce a documentary. The fishing families and the descendants of the pioneer fishermen brought photographs, newspaper cuttings and letters illustrating their lives as a fishing community.

It was at this meeting that the first discourse which had been established by the researchers was challenged in the face of their commitment to the principles of community video. Initially, some of the fishermen and their descendants were cautious about the project. In the past, they had been filmed by commercial companies on many occasions without their consent and without any knowledge of the purpose of the filming. The initial distrust lead to the fishermen withholding information because of a lack of trust. The public showing of these preliminary interviews at the meeting resulted in the fishermen being more critical of themselves and the researchers. For instance, one fisherman rejected the footage of his interview accusing me of having 'got it all wrong'. 'Why did you only ask part of the story?' 'Why didn't you ask me about my experience when I was a child?' The error of asking 'only part of the story' lay in the attempt to extract certain answers about the community's history, based on our previous research, rather than to arrive at an understanding of this history through dialogue.

Nevertheless, the meeting proved to be crucial to the success of the project. It established a collective intent to produce a video and it served to rekindle interest among the descendants of the pioneer fishing community that they were a 'community' with a 'history'. It was here that the 'community' was revitalized and, through dialogue with the researchers, the conditions of the project were established. A production collective which included a social geographer, two members of the fishing community and myself was formed. The meeting gave us both a mandate to proceed and some specific directives – the granddaughter of one of the famous pioneer fishermen was nominated to be the narrator. The narrator had no professional training – so this added to the many educational demands that are part of any participatory approach.

Bearing in mind what we learnt from the meeting, we continued to record oral testimonies but worked less at asking questions than in allowing the participants to tell their stories. As the work progressed, a sound cooperative relationship evolved among the fishermen, their families and ourselves. When we had completed the bulk of the interviews, we put together a draft film in the form of a continuous chronological narrative of the oral history. Again, this approach was determined by the impression of the community which we had built up over time and which had been endorsed by the fishermen, their families and descendants.

Finally, we produced a full script of the interviews and the narrator's text which was presented to the community representative and others for comment. Once the revised script was returned to us, we completed the sound recording and started to edit the film. We edited the film using the approved script and used our own judgement only when there were errors in the editing script or the requested footage was damaged.

The completed video was then shown to representatives of the community. They requested minor changes such as editing and caption errors which we then corrected in a revised version of the video. The final draft of the video was shown to the community at a meeting held in a local library, where it was discussed and where it received the full support of the community. In particular, the participants made an explicit claim of 'ownership' of the video.

There were, however, tensions during the meeting. Kamla, one of the interviewees and daughter of a pioneer fisherman, expressed her dismay at not having received a presentation copy of the video. Videos were presented to members of the production team and elected community representatives. This was resolved eventually when it was decided to give Kamla a presentation video. In addition to the issue of the videotape, Mrs Billy, the community co-ordinator, reported that she and some of the community were unhappy with a sequence which shows a dirty pit latrine structure as typical of the latrines in the fishing village. She said that those toilets implied that they, as a fishing community, were dirty and that this was not 'the sort of thing to show school children'. After some informal discussions with the production collective, Mrs Billy conceded that the footage was indeed an accurate representation of the latrines.

The video is now being circulated to schools to present an alternative account – a history from below – which has not featured in the history lessons in South African schools. The video has also been instrumental in convincing the city council to guarantee the fishing rights of this community and promote the video through the museum and library services of the city.

Apart from the role of the video as an educational and political tool, the process of production was itself extremely valuable. The fishing community developed an understanding of the production processes of video. Some of the community, with direct production roles, such as the narrator, developed specific production skills. I expect them to be less intimidated by the demands of commercial crews that will film them in the future. With the fishing fleet reduced to a single boat operated by part-time fishermen, the community is no longer united in the common interest of fishing. The production, which took three years to complete, reconstituted the community in their common interest to document their history.

This production alerted me to the way in which my questions 'silenced' people and yielded only the answers that I had anticipated. Although we had used meetings in previous productions, this was the first production in which we used large public meetings. The principal value of these meetings was the animation of community interest and involvement of people that smaller meetings might have missed. Wherever possible, I now attempt to use this approach to encourage collective reflection, public scrutiny and accountability.

The lessons we learnt in this documentary production and others have also influenced my work in other areas. In a workshop on newspaper production for twelve-year-old schoolchildren, the class is divided up into groups representing a typical newsroom. The paper is planned, and stories researched and written. Working in groups, these children experience the tensions of contested meaning and competition for space. The magic of the newspaper, and the notion of objective reporting, is undermined as the complex process that lies behind the product is revealed. The pupils experience at first hand the industrial character of the press and the way news is 'manufactured'. The advantage of public scrutiny was used in this workshop by making the newspaper a giant enlargement that covered the entire wall of a school hall. Each newspaper column was printed by hand onto a roll of newsprint – a nine-column newspaper when pasted to the wall was nine metres wide! The pupils wrote more carefully as their work was subjected to the scrutiny of their classmates and others who would come into the hall later on. An interesting development in this workshop was that the pupils wrote the lead story, which they gave the title Tuckshop Beggars, on the practice of older pupils harassing young pupils during the lunch break. Complaints by the young pupils to teachers and prefects had not been heard or taken seriously in the past – now these pupils planned to expose the harassment as a lead story. The newspaper would be seen by teachers and parents when the hall was to be used for a meeting on the same day. Apart from experiencing the tension of the newsroom, the children also learnt about the power of the press.

Conclusion

The examples I have given of the documentary production and the newspaper workshop show some ways in which a whole community or a whole class may learn. Furthermore, collective learning and social engagements enable and encourage conversations which are often silenced by social and school constraints.

Although emancipatory education, the rallying cry of the student protests in the 1980s, is not attractive to students who have been schooled by rote learning and examinations, there is some encouragement. Many organizations and teacher bodies are making concerted efforts to develop materials, curricula and educational programmes that are founded on a connected epistemology and an emancipatory interest. The long and arduous journey towards a post-apartheid learning future is already underway.

References

Aitchison, J. and Graham, P. (1989) Potato crisp pedagogy. In Criticos, C. (ed.) *Experiential Learning in Formal and Non-Formal Education*, pp. 15–21. Durban: Media Resource Centre, University of Natal.

Alexander, N. (1989) Liberation pedagogy in the South African context. In Criticos, C. (ed.) *Experiential Learning in Formal and Non-Formal Education*, pp. 1–13. Durban: Media Resource Centre, University of Natal.

Bell, B., Gaventa, J. and Peters, J. (eds) (1990) *We Make the Road by Walking: Conversations on Education and Social Change/Myles Horton and Paulo Freire*. Philadelphia: Temple University Press.

Dewey, J. (1938) *Experience and Education*. New York: Collier.

Freire, P. (1972) *Pedagogy of the Oppressed*. Harmondsworth: Penguin.

Gilmour, N. (1988) Shortages of skills or skilled shortages? A comparison of employer, pupil and teacher expectations of education. Paper presented at the Kenton Conference, Cape Town, South Africa, October.

Grundy, S. (1987) *Curriculum: Product or Praxis?* London: Falmer Press.

Habermas, J. (1972) *Knowledge and Human Interest*, 2nd edn. London: Heinemann.

Palmer, P.J. (1990) Community, conflict and ways of knowing: Ways to deepen our educational agenda. In Kendall, J. (ed.) *Combining Service & Learning*, Vol. I. Raleigh, NC: National Society for Internships and Experiential Education.

Stanton, T. (1986) Private correspondence from Tim Stanton on the marginal role of experiential education in mainstream education.

Stanton, T. (1990) Think piece: Field experience and liberal arts education. Paper presented at the Annual Conference of the National Society for Internships and Experiential Education, Boulder, Colorado, July.

Torbert, W.R. (1972) *Learning From Experience*. New York: Columbia University Press.

12

Experiential Learning or Learning from Experience: Does it Make a Difference?

Robin Usher

Is there a difference between learning from experience and experiential learning? The former happens in everyday contexts as part of day-to-day life, although it is rarely recognized as such. Experiential learning, on the other hand, is a key element of a discourse which has this everyday process as its 'subject' and which constructs it in a certain way, although it appears to be merely a term which describes the process. Here, then, I think that there's a difference that makes a difference. For those of us located in the discourse of experiential learning we assume, for example, that giving an account of experience is significant. Accounts are, of necessity, discursive, they are cast in and communicated through language and are understood by us in terms of our discursive frameworks. Yet the discursivity of accounts and the discursivity of our interpretations of accounts is given virtually no weight. Instead, we focus on things like authenticity, going on voyages of discovery and getting rid of the baggage of false consciousness.

Now I don't think it's either coincidental or 'natural' that we focus on certain things rather than others. Once we start analysing something, once we make something the object of our investigation, we do so within and through a discourse. It gives us a vocabulary, a set of concepts and pre-understandings, a motivating focus and direction for our investigations – above all a disciplined and systematic way of 'talking about'.

A discourse doesn't discover objects of knowledge, but through its disciplined and systematic way of seeing, thinking and acting constitutes or 'makes' them but without appearing to do so (Foucault 1972). The discourse of experiential learning is thus a body of knowledge about learning from experience based on constituting experience as a form of knowledge. The everyday process of learning from experience becomes 'experiential learning', a 'theory' and 'systematic' practice embodied in a 'literature' of written texts. This book is itself an example.

If one takes the recognized and respected texts of this discourse (e.g. Boud *et al.* 1985; Boud and Griffin 1987; Weil and McGill 1989), the implication of experience in language and the discursive constitution of experiential learning fall out of view. Of this there is a silence. A discourse has the power to delineate the sayable and thus by implication the unsaid, what cannot be said. For me, therefore, the main problem about experience, a problem which precedes questions about how we can learn best from experience, lies in a double unsaid: a silence about the implication of experience in language and a silence about the implication of experiential learning in discourse.

Experience, language and reading

I want to argue for a different way of seeing where understanding experience is seen as a process of reading. I realize that I am speaking metaphorically, but the discourse of experiential learning is loaded with metaphors, for example 'the voyage of discovery'. I want to highlight the prevalence of metaphor in order to bring something that is largely unacknowledged, viz. the influence of language, into the open. Furthermore, drawing attention to metaphor shows how seeing learning from experience as 'experiential learning' is a discursive construction rather than a descriptive label placed on 'reality'. Of course, my metaphor lacks power, since it is not part of a systematic discourse. However, like all metaphors, it is a resource for seeing things anew. With it, we can start to weave a different text about the textuality of experience.

To read is to interpret, to give meaning. The key feature of experience is that it has meaning. Thus the meaning of experience depends on an interpretive process. Now meaning is always understanding as, a projection requiring something to project from and in relation to. The metaphor of reading therefore immediately suggests the notion of positioning, that understanding experience is to be positioned as a reader in relation to a text. Furthermore, like a text, an experience does not have its own intrinsic meaning waiting to be discovered. Experience can have meaning because there is a meaning system. Meaning is relational, a meaning 'means' only in relation to other meanings, ultimately to the whole 'chain of language'.

Meaning is also contextual. When we interpret 'our' experience, we do so from a particular context or standpoint. The context is both a material and linguistic location, a bank of cultural significations, deposits of already existing meanings including the meanings of one's own experiential history. It is from this bank that interpretation draws in projecting meaning.

What we draw from this bank are 'prejudices' or pre-understandings (Gadamer 1975). Thus I understand my experience through the pre-understandings which situate me, which make me the kind of person who projects the kind of meanings I do. Now in the sense that these pre-understandings are 'mine', I am going to interpret my experience in a 'personal' way. In another sense, however, they are 'other' to me because they 'belong' to language and culture. Language by virtue of its belonging to everybody belongs to nobody. The 'personal' meaning that my experience has is always conditional upon meanings which are not personal.

I want now to show how this relates to my metaphor of understanding experience as reading by taking the reading of a book as an analogy, let's say a book entitled *Perspectives on Experiential Learning*. Once I take the trouble to start reading it, the presumption is that I want to try and understand what it says. I anticipate that the book will not only have a meaning but a meaning of a particular kind, so from the very beginning, before I have even started reading it, I project a meaning onto it. Perhaps if I am familiar with the discourse of experiential learning, the title will help me do this.

Of course, what is crucial is the fact that the words of the title already have a meaning within a language and a particular meaning and significance for me because I am a practitioner located in a discourse of experiential learning. My pre-understandings are therefore linguistic and discursive, they 'situate' me as a reader and enable me to read. However, although they are very much 'present' in terms of their effects, since I use them rather than being consciously aware of them, they are effective as an 'absence'.

Of course, my initial projection of meaning may be confounded if the book, for example, turns out to be an elaborate satire. More likely, however, my initial projections will be strengthened, modified, elaborated or possibly even radically changed as I address myself to the subject matter of the book. The more I 'get into' it, the more my developing understanding of its meaning will alter my pre-understandings, in effect will give me a new set of pre-understandings from which I can further develop my understanding and so on potentially *ad infinitum*. What's at work in reading, therefore, is meaning as a circular process of dynamic change.

I want now to foreground certain aspects of this process and in doing so 'cash in' my analogy to show the usefulness of the metaphor of reading in relation to experience. First, my pre-understandings may be such as to make me quickly lose interest in the book. Or I might, because of them, have very clearly defined expectations which if not quickly realized might lead me to reject it. Or I might reject it because it presents such a radical challenge to my pre-understandings that my personal stability is undermined to an unacceptable degree. In all these cases, pre-understandings are closed with the consequence that reading fails – it either never gets off the ground or is terminated with limited outcomes. Reading as a giving of meaning remains within the realm of already given meaning.

All of this could equally be said about the understanding we have of our experience, our reading of the text of our experience. How often do we find ourselves in a situation where we make little effort to understand our experience? We either can't be bothered or we find it too difficult or too painful. We prefer to remain as we are; the 'text' remains closed or only superficially or partially read. Of course, this doesn't mean that our experience doesn't have meaning for us. Some of our experience must have some meaning some of the time. It does mean, however, that our pre-understandings remain safe and unchallenged, that the meaning of our experience remains unchanged within a closed and static circle of understanding.

However, the situation is quite different when our pre-understandings are open to challenge and change. As we read a text by addressing ourselves to its subject matter, both our pre-understandings and understandings change. Correspondingly, when we read our experience, we address ourselves to the actual 'stuff' of our experience. An initial meaning is projected, but the more I address myself to my experience the more this initial meaning changes as my understanding unfolds. If my pre-understandings are open, the more I will come to understand my experience in a radically different way.

There is, however, another aspect to this. Having open pre-understandings means recognizing that understanding is not a process which has a terminus, a final destination. At any one point in time, a meaning has to be fixed, but that's not the only meaning possible for all time. There is a way of reading which strives to find a meaning but is never quite sure that the meaning found is the only possible one. I can settle on one particular meaning at any one point in time, but can I ever be sure that that's the end of the story? I think this is what O'Reilly (1989) is pointing to when he argues that experience is incoherent, that it doesn't come in neat packages of pre-determined meanings. This is not to say that it's meaningless, but simply that meaning is often multiple, at times contradictory, and although temporarily fixable always has an undecidability, an excess of meaning about it. In effect, it can always be re-read and every reading is a reading differently.

Experience, it seems to me, always says less than it wishes to say – there is always more that can be read into it. Its meaning is never exhausted, it never reaches a 'destination' of total clarity and definitiveness. As readers, therefore, we can never fully master it, never render it completely 'present' – although if our pre-understandings are closed we invariably try.

How often do we feel that the texts which 'speak' to us most are those that have an 'otherness' about them? They seem strange, elusive and perplexing. They challenge our safe and unquestioned pre-understandings, disrupt our easy confidence that we will always get the better of them. They require the work of interpretive effort because they resist our attempts at mastery. Yet we seem unable to resist our desire to master them. Isn't it the same with those experiences that we feel 'speak' most significantly to us? They too require interpretive effort; they too possess this quality of 'otherness'. Isn't it precisely this rather than any cosy quality of 'belonging' and 'owning' which makes coming to grips with one's experience, wanting to master it, such a difficult, often painful, yet exciting and transformative undertaking.

Now my argument for the text that 'speaks' having no one definitive meaning might seem to suggest that reading is totally subjective. Certainly, such a text seems to 'speak' in a subjective, personal way. The recognition of a text's multiple meanings may not be shared by others; indeed, there may be a general resistance to such a possibility. The experience of disconfirmation which negates current understandings is where one sees anew and differently and is inevitably something personal in the sense that it very often cannot be 'objectively' justified.

However, the process of reading openly and critically, although personal, is not thereby to be labelled 'subjective' either in the sense of arbitrary and whimsical or in the sense of belonging exclusively to 'me'. Any reading, whether it be the reading of written texts or of the text of experience, depends on an interpretive culture, a discursive 'tradition' within which our pre-understandings are located. Without such a tradition, of which language itself is the most obvious form, the interpretive process would never get underway. We would lack the linguistic and cultural tools to carry out the work of reading.

Although we are part of tradition in this sense, or more precisely it is part of us, we are not its prisoner. It is not the 'dead hand' of the past. It can be oppressive, but it also constitutes the substance of our critical resources. Any critical interpretation, any attempt to understand our experience contrary to dominant understandings, any reading which leads to a disconfirmation and review of existing understandings, can only be carried out through an interpretive culture. When we speak critically, when we seek new experience or a new meaning of experience, or when we invoke our experience to challenge oppression or injustice, we are not standing outside of all tradition but are interrogating a dominant tradition through harnessing the critical potential which is always present in it. It is this location in, and consequent reading through, a tradition which provides the 'objective' dimension.

But there is more to it than simply this. As our interpretations change, as we read 'differently, as we give new and disconfirming meanings to our experience, so too the meanings of the tradition within which we are located also change. The interpretation and reinterpretation of 'tradition' is mutually interactive.

When Boud and Griffin (1987: 9) say 'We know that all we experience is filtered through the lenses of our personal versions of reality, our frames of meaning', I agree with them about the 'frames of meaning' but not that these are 'personal' in the sense of mine and mine alone. I would argue that they are both personal and 'traditional', mine and not mine. I 'know' my experience through my pre-understandings which appropriate and draw from tradition. In this sense, my pre-understandings make possible a personal reading. But even the most personal meanings, where 'I' seems to speak most authentically, are discursive articulations, interpretations through which tradition 'speaks' and the 'I' is spoken of.

Equally, however, although understanding experience is 'objective', experience is not objectified. With the systematization of experiential learning, experience is submitted to methodical reflection and analysis as a means of revealing its true meaning. It's difficult to see how this 'true' meaning is to be found if the meaning of experience is situational. Consequently, the methodological search for such a meaning simply turns experience into a lifeless commodity whose only use is to be exchanged for credits in the educational marketplace.

Experience, therefore, can be said to be objective and subjective. This apparent contradiction is an effect of reading and ultimately an effect of language, for after all what is language other than something which is at one and the same time both a part of me and apart from me. The very notion of a realm of the personal, of an inside in contrast to an outside, of things belonging to the self sharply distinct from those that are 'other' to the self, is an effect of language, a (arte)fact of our Western cultural tradition.

Understanding my experience means 'giving' it meaning, but the means to do this arise from a source outside of me, a bank of pre-existing yet changing significations and cultural meanings. Experience is personal be- cause there is an 'other' to the personal, a social 'other' which works through the constitutive power of language. Experience is the site where the personal and the social intersect and intertwine and through which each gives a constantly changing meaning to the other.

Experience, learning and writing

My metaphor of reading suggests a way of looking anew at the process of how experience is understood, how it comes to be meaningful. Now I want to change the metaphor slightly in order to look anew at the process of learning from experience. While still retaining the notion of textuality, I shall do this by using the metaphor of 'writing'. One of my purposes in doing so is to suggest a distinction between learning from experience as 'writing' and the writing in 'experiential learning'.

The place of writing in 'experiential learning' is a place whose signifi- cance is, once again, marked by silence. Yet the body of knowledge and systematic practice which is experiential learning could not be recognized and accepted without it. The history of the experiential learning 'movement' shows only too clearly that one either writes or is written of(f). Without a written text there is no discourse, and without a discourse experiential learning dissolves into the flux of everyday experience. Learning from experience is an aspect of this flux; experiential learning, in so far as it seeks to systematically know it, is not.

Writing, in its literal sense, is not an 'innocent' or naive activity, a recording in graphic form of the ideas, thoughts and feelings 'in our heads'. For one thing, we always write in and through language and language is more than just a tool for describing the world. For another, when we write, we do so in terms of a textual strategy. How to write always involves a choice, al- though the choice is not always consciously made. If language delimits the sayable, then textual strategies shape the sayable in particular ways. A written text is therefore constructed and, through its particular mode of construction, a 'world' is created. Experiential learning, through its implication in writing, creates a world to be discovered.

The kinds of textual strategies used make all the difference. A textual strategy of narrative realism, much favoured in 'experiential learning', effectively hides its own being as a textual strategy. By 'putting myself into it', the text appears to be merely a vehicle for expressing my 'truth', a faithful reflection of the reality of my experience, its meaning fully present and accessible both to me and to all readers as methodically derived 'learning outcomes'.

In the metaphorical sense in which I am using writing, learning from experience is a kind of 'writing' that creates a world, a fictional text, in which we are the central character of the story. A text is woven, creating the self as a character in its own story, from the 'raw material' of our experience, our being-in-the-world. In effect, learning from experience is a process where we textually create and recreate ourselves but without being confined to one textual strategy.

Let me try and illustrate what I have in mind here by telling my own story about writing, a story which centres around the question of what is to be taken as most authoritative – learning from experience or learning from written texts? As a practitioner located in the humanistic discourse of experiential learning, I was aware that this is a difficult problem, but my pre-understandings disposed me to see it in terms of a binary opposition where the poles 'learning from experience' and 'learning from written texts' were mutually exclusive. In humanistic discourse, the opposition is a weighted one, with the 'learning from experience' pole privileged. What became embodied in my practice, therefore, was rejection of written texts as a source of learning motivated by the fear of an external and imposed authority which distorted and corrupted the 'pure' authority of personal experience.

Operating with this framework, it's perhaps hardly surprising that all my classroom experience seemed to confirm this. Given that my pre-understandings were safe and unchallenged, I interpreted my experience in a humanistic way and thus my humanistic framework was reinforced through the 'evidence' of my own experience. However, at the same time, I was placed in a dilemma. As a practitioner, one cannot avoid written texts. Every practitioner, no matter how practice-centred, at the very least reads books which purport to be practice-centred. One does so in the hope of deepening one's understandings and improving one's practice. One has to have a written tradition, an unseen community, from which to draw sustenance, ideas and exemplars. In my case, I read Carl Rogers, specifically *On Becoming a Person* (Rogers 1967).

Rogers' 'message' is that he writes about what he knows and everything he knows comes from his experience. He argues that nothing can be taught that is not already known. People teach themselves, learning is a matter of 'realizing' what is already there. However, the other aspect of his 'message', which is perhaps less obvious but nevertheless crucial in determining its effects, is the way he conveys it in a clear, transparent and 'down-to-earth' style. Rogers wants to tell us about what he knows from his experience in a direct and unmediated way. He seeks to convey what is 'inside' him to the 'inside' of his readers.

In effect, Rogers writes as if he is not writing. The vehicle for conveying his experience, the written text, becomes transparent. We feel as readers that Rogers doesn't need to write, a feeling which echoes Rogers' often stated wish that he could convey what he wants to say other than through the distorting medium of a written text. What he conveys privileges the unmediated and 'natural' voice of experience against the textually mediated, 'unnatural' process of writing about experience. His style, the writing that is not writing, is an attempt to embody this.

Yet Rogers does write and indeed has to write. He wants others to know about and be persuaded by his 'message' and the only way he can do this is through a written text. He thus finds himself in a situation where his message about experience, founded on a distrust of writing, must necessarily take the form of a written text. He can only privilege the natural voice of experience through the unnatural process of writing.

Now it could be argued that Rogers is well aware of this and, recognizing that he has to write, nevertheless does so in a style which still allows experience to speak in an unmediated way. Unfortunately, this argument cannot be sustained because his style is itself an effect of writing. Rogers, whether unconsciously or not, utilizes a textual strategy. His text is constructed, the words don't just 'pop into' his mind. Words are put together in such a way as to achieve the appearance of transparency, of a faithful reflection of the 'reality' of experience. They have certain significations rather than others in helping the reader to 'make sense' of the text. They appeal to and draw upon a certain discursive tradition which the reader is assumed to share or at least be aware of. They evoke a subjective response of empathy and identification on the part of the reader.

My argument is that all these effects which make meaning and indeed a certain kind of meaning possible depend for their achievement upon the use of certain textual strategies. If Rogers' text was obviously literary, a work of fiction, we would have no problem recognizing this. It's simply harder for us to recognize, let alone accept, that this is also the case with non-fictional texts. Because Rogers' text presents itself as a work of non-fiction, we think we see through the words and the way they are constructed to the reality which lies beyond them and which they purportedly describe. Yet Rogers' text, because it is constructed, is as fictional as any 'fiction'. His message about 'reality' depends on writing.

Rogers writes in an autobiographical way, but his writing doesn't appear to be situated. But, of course, he is situated; he is gendered, he has an ethnicity and he is formed by the tradition of an interpretive culture. His text, therefore, is inscribed in this situatedness. What 'speaks' in Rogers is not simply the unmediated 'truth' of his experience, but the significations he gives his experience through the 'truth' of his situatedness. No matter how much he may reject the authority of the latter, and he spends much of his time doing precisely that, he is informed by it 'beyond his willing and doing'. The interpretive culture in which Rogers is located produces and reproduces itself through the dissemination of texts. It makes itself 'known' through intertextuality, the traces of texts upon other texts, traces which form the already known and from which the yet-to-be known is formed.

A text 'speaks' to other texts in the same interpretive culture, often confronting and interrogating them by using the critical resources potentially present within it. Rogers' text rejects written texts as an authoritative way of knowing. Yet the written texts of the 'authoritative' culture in which he is located are the condition for him knowing from his own experience. Thus he cannot know only from his own experience and he cannot show this in his text. In the end, he cannot exemplify what he says. Writing, the sign of authority, the feared and rejected other, is already 'inside' him.

Rogers' text is only one example from the literature of experiential learning, yet it exemplifies a common position of rejecting yet depending on written texts, seeking to inscribe yet being already inscribed. Experiential learning as a body of knowledge and systematic practice depends on the authority of its written texts, without which it could neither communicate its message nor persuade anyone of its 'truth'. It wouldn't be taken seriously and would have no means of regulating its own practice. Given this, it seems hardly possible to go on regarding texts as simply a convenient and contingent vehicle of communication. Consider, for example, the status and purpose of this book.

Reading Rogers' text 'otherwise' provided me with an experience of disconfirmation which made me review what I thought I knew. It led me to question my understanding of the authority of experience. It seemed to me that to privilege learning from experience over learning from texts was merely to reverse the 'traditional' binary opposition while still remaining trapped within it.

However, significantly, this disconfirmation and change in understanding did not come from my direct experience but from 'outside' it. Had I remained 'inside' my experience, I would not have had the interpretive resources, the Rogers' text, to disconfirm what my experience seemed to tell me about experience. I realized I had been so immersed that I could not see what I was immersed in. I needed something outside, something other, and for me this other was a written text. In engaging with Rogers' text, my pre-understandings were confronted, challenged and eventually changed. I reassessed my experience, I recognized it and my understanding assumed a different signification.

It seemed to me, therefore, that learning from experience is conditional on counterposing experience to something that is not-experience. Understanding experience requires a point outside experience, a confrontation with experience's other. Starting with experience is one thing, continuing and ending with it another. Moreover, whatever is not-experience, for example a written text, can function as this other and therefore need not be

178   *Robin Usher*

feared and rejected. That's just the influence of the humanistic discourse in which experiential learning is cast. But, as my experience showed, we are not its prisoners.

Making a difference

How, then, do we locate ourselves in an alternative discourse? First, I think we need a discourse where the experiencing subject is seen as situated rather than transcendental, subjectively relational rather than essential, and where sociality ceases to be the feared and rejected other, the source of the bad. This is not to reject the existence of oppression or self-oppression or of concrete limitations and constraints. But it is to recognize that we are social, situated beings with otherness within us, which no amount of 'conscientization' or 'getting in touch with one's authentic self' is going to eliminate.

It is precisely because the self is textually woven, precisely because we are characters in as well as the authors of the text, that we cannot escape otherness no matter how oppressively we may experience it at times. This is why the question of authority is so central and so troubling, as Rogers demonstrated so well without intending to do so.

Authority is cast as the mark of limitation which makes us dependent on others – on authority figures such as teachers and the 'authority' of the texts of formal knowledge. Yet 'authority' provides the necessary opposition or counterpoint which 'authorizes' the practice of experiential learning. Indeed, the discourse of experiential learning is founded on metaphors of authority. They are its common discursive currency, shaping the way experience is conceived and 'textualized'. Yet they are mirror-images of the founding metaphors of discourses of didactic teaching and learning as assimilation of formal bodies of knowledge.

An alternative discourse, therefore, should provide us with a way of looking anew at the troubling question of authority. For one thing, it would enable us to question the place of 'facilitation' as the preferred alternative to 'teaching'. In the discourse of experiential learning, teaching is rejected on the grounds that it distorts and constrains the process of becoming one's own authority independent of the authority of others.

I am not suggesting that teachers should be reinstated as the authority or that we should embrace didactic teaching. The problem with the notion of facilitation is that it capitalizes and reinforces the humanistic fear that whatever is 'outside' of experience will, by getting 'inside', exert a control which is always distorting and constraining and of which we may not even be fully aware. It proposes that I must teach myself from a source which is exclusively mine because then I don't need to fear that I will be controlled by others through their teaching. But as Richards (1989) points out, this is based on a 'fiction' of inner self-sufficiency, that I am in my very essence an originary, self-determining and self-sufficient 'I'. No-one can doubt either the reality or the power of this fiction. But I would argue that it is not one we should be seeking to perpetuate.

When we talk about experience in the everyday context of our lives, we tell a story about things that have happened to us, stories which often take an anecdotal form. In earlier writing, I came down quite hard on anecdotes (Usher, 1985) because I focused only on what anecdotes described, what in other words they purported to be about, and therefore completely missed other and more significant aspects. Telling stories is a way of communicating rather than merely describing experience and is therefore a means by which subjectivity is constructed. Moreover, a story is told in a communicative context, it is other-directed and it is the other(s)' response which confirms its 'meaning' and hence the subjectivity constructed.

I have many stories to tell and many ways to tell them. The response of the other is never clear and certain because the other, too, seeks confirmation. Subjectivity is therefore always shifting and uncertain, always in a process of continual re-formation, experience always open to reassessment and re-cognition.

Given this embeddedness in the stories that we tell, we formulate our learning from experience through a 'writing' where we are textually created and recreated. It follows therefore that the classroom needs to be a site of re-enactment where stories, rather than experience *per se*, can be communicated and where the emphasis is on neither the definitive meaning nor the definable outcomes of experience. Once it is, we are in the realm of experiential learning rather than learning from experience.

It follows also that reflexivity cannot be avoided. The communicative, intersubjective context of the classroom is not simply a neutral place for conveying the experiences of its participants most effectively or for methodically deriving learning outcomes. Rather it is a 'living' context that becomes part of the text of people's experience, and therefore a 'character' in the story. Above all, the classroom is a site of interaction, of others' responses and confirmations where meanings can be reassessed and learning redefined.

What this points to is that the words we use are neither coincidental nor incidental. We need to focus on them rather than beyond them to the 'reality' which the words are about. Language in its descriptive mode inclines us to look through words to the 'things' beyond words. But language in its performative mode creates rather than describes. Language, through the significations it makes 'present', is also imbued with power which can be both liberating and oppressive. The performativity and power of language implies that we should not look through but at words and the way they are put together in the stories people tell, stories of oppression and liberation in words of signification and significant words.

Perhaps, then, we should rethink the emphasis placed on the word 'learning'. It has a signification located in psychological discourse and by transfer, the discourse of experiential learning. In everyday contexts, 'learning' has a very different signification.

People don't see themselves as 'learners' in the way we facilitators under-stand the term. They don't 'naturally' see their fictional texts as exchange-able for 'learning outcomes'. That this is so is something which we regard as unfortunate, as a kind of false consciousness or a deficit in self-confidence which it's our job to remedy. But it is precisely this emphasis on 'learning' which opens the door to psychologism, method and individualism. Perhaps, therefore, what is most needed is that we should review our fictions, the kind of stories we are telling, and ask ourselves, whatever our intentions might be, whether our language is liberating or oppressive.

Postscript

In the text which has just unfolded, I have tried to say something about the textuality of experience. Everything that is written is informed by the understanding I have of my experience. But that understanding does not come from my experience alone. By writing, by telling my story of experi-ence, I have tried to show why that is. In so doing, as one always does when 'rewriting' one's learning, I have, once again, reconstructed my subjectivity. Indeed, readers may feel that they know a great deal about 'me' after having read this text. Perhaps, they will also have 're-read' themselves in the process.

In creating a text, I structured my 'message' through certain textual strategies and thus created a 'world'. This 'world' is a fiction and should be taken as such. Fictions present a truth but not the truth. I hope to persuade but in the end my meaning and its 'truth' are in the hands of readers of this text. What in the end makes a difference is to present as many truths of and about experience as possible.

References

Boud, D. and Griffin, V. (eds) (1987) *Appreciating Adults Learning: From the Learners' Perspective*. London: Kogan Page.
Boud, D., Keogh, R. and Walker, D. (eds) (1985) *Reflection: Turning Experience into Learning*. London: Kogan Page.
Foucault, M. (1972) *The Archaeology of Knowledge*. New York: Random House.
Gadamer, H.-G. (1975) *Truth and Method*. London: Sheed and Ward.
O'Reilly, D. (1989) On being an educational fantasy engineer: Incoherence, 'the individual', and independent study. In Weil, S.W. and McGill, I. (eds) *Making Sense of Experiential Learning*. Milton Keynes: Society for Research into Higher Education and Open University Press.
Richards, B. (1989) *Image of Freud*. London: Dent.
Rogers, C.R. (1967) *On Becoming a Person*. London: Constable.
Usher, R.S. (1985) Beyond the anecdotal: Adult learning and the use of experience. *Studies in the Education of Adults*, 17(1): 59–74.
Weil, S.W. and McGill, I. (eds) (1989) *Making Sense of Experiential Learning*. Milton Keynes: Society for Research into Higher Education and Open University Press.

Index

The Society for Research into Higher Education

The Society for Research into Higher Education exists to stimulate and co-ordinate research into all aspects of higher education. It aims to improve the quality of higher education through the encouragement of debate and publication on issues of policy, on the organization and management of higher education institutions, and on the curriculum and teaching methods.

The Society's income is derived from subscriptions, sales of its books and journals, conference fees and grants. It receives no subsidies, and is wholly independent. Its individual members include teachers, researchers, managers and students. Its corporate members are institutions of higher education, research institutes, professional, industrial and governmental bodies. Members are not only from the UK, but from elsewhere in Europe, from America, Canada and Australasia, and it regards its international work as amongst its most important activities.

Under the imprint *SRHE & Open University Press*, the Society is a specialist publisher of research, having some 45 titles in print. The Editorial Board of the Society's Imprint seeks authoritative research or study in the above fields. It offers competitive royalties, a highly recognizable format in both hardback and paperback and the world-wide reputation of the Open University Press.

The Society also publishes *Studies in Higher Education* (three times a year), which is mainly concerned with academic issues, *Higher Education Quarterly* (formerly *Universities Quarterly*), mainly concerned with policy issues, *Research into Higher Education Abstracts* (three times a year), and *SRHE News* (four times a year).

The Society holds a major annual conference in December, jointly with an institution of higher education. In 1992, it was 'Learning to Effect' with Nottingham Trent University. In 1993, the topic it was 'Governments and the Higher Education Curriculum: Evolving Partnerships' at the University of Sussex in Brighton, and in 1994, 'The Student Experience' at the University of York. Conferences in 1995 include, 'The Changing University?' at Heriot-Watt University in Edinburgh.

The Society's committees, study groups and branches are run by the members. The groups at present include:

Teacher Education Study Group
Continuing Education Group
Staff Development Group
Excellence in Teaching and Learning

Benefits to members

Individual

Individual members receive:

- *SRHE News*, the Society's publications list, conference details and other material included in mailings.
- Greatly reduced rates for *Studies in Higher Education* and *Higher Education Quarterly*.
- A 35% discount on all Open University Press & SRHE publications.
- Free copies of the Precedings – commissioned papers on the theme of the Annual Conference.
- Free copies of *Research into Higher Education Abstracts*.
- Reduced rates for conferences.
- Extensive contacts and scope for facilitating initiatives.
- Reduced reciprocal memberships.

Corporate

Corporate members receive:

- All benefits of individual members, plus
- Free copies of *Studies in Higher Education*.
- Unlimited copies of the Society's publications at reduced rates.
- Special rates for its members e.g. to the Annual Conference.

Membership details: SRHE, 3 Devonshire Street, London, W1N 2BA, UK. Tel: 0171 637 2766, Fax: 0171 637 2781
Catalogue: SRHE & Open University Press, Celtic Court, 22 Ballmoor, Buckingham MK18 1XW. Tel: (01280) 823388

MAKING SENSE OF EXPERIENTIAL LEARNING
DIVERSITY IN THEORY AND PRACTICE

Susan Warner Weil and Ian McGill (eds)

This book appraises the multiplicity of meanings and practices associated with experiential learning in an international context. It reflects the depth, breadth and complexity of current developments, and pushes at the boundaries of theory and practice.

The editors have identified four distinct 'villages' within the global village of experiential learning. One is clearly identified round the assessment and accreditation of prior experiential learning as a means of gaining access and recognition in relation to educational institutions, employment and professional bodies. A second is the place for those who centre their activities on changing the practice, structures and purposes of post-school education. Another can be identified amongst those who place learning from experience as the core of education for social change mainly outside educational institutions. Finally, there is a focus on the potential and practice of personal growth and development.

Contents

A framework for making sense of experiential learning – Meaning and practice in experiential learning – Some competing traditions in experiential learning – Learning from action – The principal meaning of dialogue for the construction and transformation of reality – Experiential learning – Learner autonomy – The autobiography as a motivational factor for students – On being an educational fantasy engineer – Generating integration and involvement in learning – Coming to know – Action learning – Our faculty goes experiential – Some critical issues related to assessment and accreditation of adults' prior experiential learning – Experiential learning and professional development – Reducing student attrition – Curriculum development for long-distance internships – Facilitating learning for adults through participation – Media, praxis and empowerment – Learning through the heart – Personal stances in learning – Continuing the dialogue – Index.

Contributors

Amina Barkatoolah, Avtar Brah, David Boud, Richard Bawden, Tom Bourner, Costas Criticos, Paul Frost, Dwight E. Giles Jr, Jane Henry, Susan Segal-Horn, Lucy Horwitz, Jane Hoy, Miriam Hutton, Annikki Järvinen, Phyllis Marie Jensen, K.J.B. Keregero, Mary K. St. John Nelson, Dave O'Reilly, Roger Packham, Shari L. Peterson, Marie Redwine, Roger Roberts, Phillida Salmon, Tara Serrao, Timothy Stanton, Danny Wildemeersch, Julie Wylde.

302pp   0 335 09713 8 (Paperback)   0 335 09549 6 (Hardback)

LEARNING TO EFFECT

Ronald Barnett (ed.)

This book discusses contemporary issues of curriculum change in higher education, and examines various ideas and initiatives concerned with making student learning more effective. It addresses curriculum purpose, curriculum delivery, and curriculum impact on the wider society. It considers the ways in which the higher education curriculum is changing in response to the wider society, how a higher quality of curriculum delivery might be achieved, and how the necessary institutional change might be effected. It covers, for instance, experimental learning, skills and training, competence and outcomes, assessment, student control over learning the quality of teaching and learning, curriculum theory, and the institutional context. More generally, it explores ways in which teaching approaches and the curriculum in higher education can be designed so as to have a demonstrably positive effect on the quality of student learning.

Contents
Introduction – Part 1: The institutional perspective – Institutional values and teaching quality – Reflection through action: peer tutoring as service learning – Promoting learning – Part 2: The professional perspective – An action-focus curriculum for the interpersonal professions – The law teachers' dilemma – Developing the knowledge base: a process perspective on professional education – Part 3: The course perspective – The humanities: from ivory tower to market place? – Experiential learning as learning to effect – Improving the quality of student learning through course design – Part 4: The national perspective – Credit accumulation and transfer and the student – Creating capability for change in higher education: the RSA initiative – Learning through enterprise: The Enterprise in Higher Education Initiative – Index.

Contributors
Graham Badley, Ronald Barnett, Gaie Davidson, Roger Ellis, Michael Eraut, Norman Evans, Malcolm Frazer, Graham Gibbs, Sinclair Goodlad, John Hughes, Elisabeth Lillie, Diana Tribe, A.J. Tribe, Susan Weil and Peter W.G. Wright.

240pp   0 335 15759 9 (Hardback)

THE TEXTS OF PAULO FREIRE

Paul V. Taylor

Paulo Freire can be numbered among the few, great educators this century. His classroom is the world of the oppressed: his subject is the literacy of liberation.

This volume provides a (re)introduction to Freire. The first part is a fresh, biographical sketch of his life, the context within which he worked and the texts which he has produced. The second part uncovers the genius of his eclecticism and discovers that, contrary to the myth, his revolutionary method is more a radical reinvention of classical pedagogy.

This sets the scene for a review and questioning of Freire's method and of his philosophy of contradiction. There is then a critical examination of his view of literacy through a close reading of the teaching material on which his successful method is based.

The concluding section attempts to reconstruct a practice of literacy, illustrating the importance of Freire's pedagogy of questioning for all those who are working in the field of literacy today.

Contents
Introduction: The textualizing and contextualizing of Freire – A biographical sketch – Backgrounds and borrowings: a review of selected sources and influences – Education and liberation: the means and ends of Dialogue and Conscientization – The 'Método Paulo Freire': generative words and generating literacy – Generating literacy: decoding Freire's ten learning situations – A reconstruction of literacy – Conclusion – Notes – Bibliographies – Index.

176pp   0 335 19019 7 (Paperback)   0 335 19020 0 (Hardback)